# SCANDAL IN THE PARISH

McGILL-QUEEN'S STUDIES IN THE HISTORY OF RELIGION
*Volumes in this series have been supported by the Jackman Foundation of Toronto.*

SERIES ONE   G.A. RAWLYK, EDITOR

**SERIES TWO  IN MEMORY OF GEORGE RAWLYK**

**DONALD HARMAN AKENSON, EDITOR**

# Scandal in the Parish

*Priests and Parishioners Behaving Badly in Eighteenth-Century France*

KAREN E. CARTER

McGill-Queen's University Press
Montreal & Kingston · London · Chicago

ISBN 978-0-7735-5660-7 (cloth)
ISBN 978-0-7735-5661-4 (paper)
ISBN 978-0-7735-5767-3 (EPDF)
ISBN 978-0-7735-5768-0 (EPUB)

Legal deposit second quarter 2019
Bibliothèque nationale du Québec

Printed in Canada on acid-free paper that is 100% ancient forest free
(100% post-consumer recycled), processed chlorine free

Funded by the     Financé par le
Government        gouvernement                                    Canada Council   Conseil des arts
of Canada         du Canada                                       for the Arts     du Canada

Publication of this book has been supported by a grant from the College
of Family, Home, and Social Sciences, and the Department of History at
Brigham Young University.

We acknowledge the support of the Canada Council for the Arts, which
last year invested $153 million to bring the arts to Canadians throughout
the country.

Nous remercions le Conseil des arts du Canada de son soutien. L'an
dernier, le Conseil a investi 153 millions de dollars pour mettre de l'art
dans la vie des Canadiennes et des Canadiens de tout le pays.

Library and Archives Canada Cataloguing in Publication

Title: Scandal in the parish : priests and parishioners behaving badly in
    eighteenth-century France / Karen E. Carter.
Names: Carter, Karen E., 1973– author.
Series: McGill-Queen's studies in the history of religion. Series two ; 84.
    Description: Series statement: McGill-Queen's studies in the history of religion.
    Series two ; 84 |
Includes bibliographical references and index.
Identifiers: Canadiana (print) 2019005266x | Canadiana (ebook) 20190052767
    | ISBN 9780773556607 (hardcover) | ISBN 9780773556614 (softcover)
    | ISBN 9780773557673 (EPDF) | ISBN 9780773557680 (EPUB)
Subjects: LCSH: Catholic Church—France—Clergy—History—18th century.
    | LCSH: Catholic Church—France—Clergy—Discipline—History—18th
    century. | LCSH: Rural clergy—France—History—18th century. | LCSH: Parishes
    —France—History—18th century. | LCSH: Scandals—France—History—18th
    century. | LCSH: Peasants—Religious life—France—History—18th century. |
    LCSH: France—Religious life and customs.
Classification: LCC BX1529 .C37 2019 | DDC 282.4409/033—dc23

This book was typeset by True to Type in 10.5/13 Sabon

# Contents

# Tables

# Acknowledgments

First and foremost, I am grateful to the many people who work, and who have worked, in the French archive system. Without the documents they have carefully preserved over the past several hundred years, books like mine would not be possible. The staff I have worked with personally have been helpful and curmudgeonly, just as archive staff should be. Although the research for this book took place primarily in the departmental archives of Doubs, in Besançon, and in the annex of the departmental archives of the Marne, in Reims, I visited archives in Agen, Beauvais, Clermont-Ferrand, Nancy, and Rouen during the research phase of this project. Even if what I found there did not make it into this book, I'm still grateful for assistance from the archivists and staff at those locations as well.

The College of Family, Home, and Social Sciences at Brigham Young University (BYU) in Provo has been generous in their support of my research. The college financed multiple research trips and gave me a semester off from teaching to write. I appreciate the opportunities the college and the university have provided. Funds from the Mary Lou Fulton Young Scholar Award, 2012–15, also helped to finance my research. A grant from the Office of Research and Creative Activities at BYU allowed one of my undergraduate students, Justine Carré, to travel back to her native Reims to do some follow-up research for me; I am grateful for her assistance and for her interest in the project.

Working with McGill-Queen's University Press (MQUP) has been a delight. The enthusiasm for the project demonstrated by my editor, Kyla Madden, is deeply appreciated. My profound thanks to the two anonymous readers for MQUP who made insightful comments on the manuscript and helped me pin down exactly what I wanted to say.

I'm also grateful to the anonymous scholars who read an article about this same topic that I submitted to a journal some time ago. Their comments made me realize that the material just did not work as an article and spurred me on to complete the book instead. Although I never finished the article, I incorporated many of their suggestions into the manuscript.

The first reader of the manuscript was my father, Dr Steven D. Carter. He has been reading my work since elementary school, and his comments are always instructive. A scholar of medieval Japanese poetry, he has published more books than I could ever hope to, and there's a little bit of him in this one too. Thanks, Dad. My colleague Chris Hodson read the complete manuscript and provided much useful advice. Amy Harris, another BYU colleague, may not have read much of this book (yet!) but we have discussed it *ad nauseam*, so she probably knows it just as well as if she had. I am supremely grateful to have such wonderful and supportive friends as these in my department.

Thanks as always to my family and friends, for countless small but encouraging demonstrations of support. Special mention goes to my mom, for being there no matter what, and to my former student Michèle Wilson, for voluntarily reading my first book, even though it was about catechisms instead of scandals.

# SCANDAL IN THE PARISH

# Introduction

On 20 April 1770, a fifty-year-old woman named Marie Jeanne Bellot, of the village of Mareuil-sur-Ay, appeared before a church court to provide information about her parish priest, or *curé*, Nicolas Hyacinthe Vernier. Among other things, she told the court that two of her children had attended Vernier's catechism classes at the presbytery when they were young, and she was scandalized by the fact that the curé seemed to spend more time telling stories and entertaining the children than he did instructing them. Sometimes, she said, he brought a chicken in a sack to class, and if the children approached the chicken and made it crow, he would "mark them with black" and tell them that the devil was coming for them.

When the officers of the court asked Vernier about this strange practice, he had a credible, if still bizarre, explanation. Vernier told his interrogators that sometime around 1760 he had made a small purchase – a special bookmark for the missal he used when saying the mass. The bookmark was decorated with several ribbons, and one day the curé noticed that a ribbon had been cut. Because the missal had been at the presbytery where he lived, Vernier guessed that the guilty party was one of the children of the village who had been in his home for catechism class. Wanting to know who had stolen the ribbon and damaged the bookmark, Vernier came up with a clever plan. First, he asked one of the children who lived nearby to go get a chicken from his house. Vernier took the chicken into a small room away from the children and put it in a cage covered with a cloth. Then he put a hat on top of the cage with some sort of blacking substance at the bottom of the hat. He left the cage, the chicken, and the hat in the room and covered the window so that it was completely dark. Returning to the children, he instructed them that they were to go into the room, one at a time, put a finger in the hat, and then touch that same finger to their forehead. When the child who had stolen the ribbon touched the hat, he told them, the chicken would crow and he would find out who was guilty. Vernier's plan was that the guilty child would believe that this chicken was actually some sort of truth teller, able to ascertain if the devil had in fact gotten a grip on his soul and led him to steal the ribbon. Not wanting to give the chicken the opportunity to crow and reveal his or her crime, the child would simply walk into the room, wait a few moments, and then return without touching the hat. The other children, certain of their innocence, would come out with black marks on their foreheads while the guilty one would be clean. This ruse worked exactly as he had planned, Vernier told the court, and he was able to punish the young thief appropriately.[1]

There was nothing sinister about what Vernier did – it was just a little unorthodox. Vernier clearly felt comfortable enough with his authority, and with his position in the parish, that he could choose any way he liked to try to enforce proper behaviour, at catechism class or otherwise. Then, as the story was passed along from the children to their parents, and from parent to parent through the village, it took on a life of its own, until one of those parents ended up testifying about a devil chicken in a sack. While this sort of odd conduct from a curé, who was the central religious figure in the parish and endowed with a certain spiritual power, could be considered scandalous, it was not the primary reason ten notable inhabitants of Mareuil-sur-Ay had decided to take Vernier to court. This incident tells us something about his personality, but not why his parishioners were so angry with him that several dozen of them willingly lined up, like Marie Jeanne Bellot, to give testimony against him.

In fact, this incident with the chicken was one of the most minor complaints about Vernier from his parishioners. Vernier had been curé of the parish of Mareuil-sur-Ay since 1747, and from that time until the beginning of the court case in 1770 he was accused of irregularities in the confessional, mistreatment of the poor and sick of the parish, inappropriate relationships with women, and a multitude of other grievous sins associated with his duties as the spiritual head of the parish. Altogether, Vernier was blamed for multiple scandals in his parish – scandal being a term both parishioners and clergy used as a sort of shorthand when talking about broken relationships and public disturbances of the peace. French curés who, like Vernier, did not get along with their parishioners created scandals. Sometimes, those scandals made it all the way to the courts. These scandals, and what they can tell us about rural parish life, curés and their parishioners, and the Catholic Reformation, are the subject of this book.

### An Alternative View of the Enlightenment, Religion, and the Eighteenth Century

It is nearly impossible to conceptualize the eighteenth century in France without grappling with both the Enlightenment and the Revolution of 1789. The eighteenth century is often characterized as a time of transition from the last stumbling steps of broken-beyond-repair political and economic systems to the first uncertain strides toward modernity. When religion is placed within this narrative, historians concentrate on upheaval and transformation as well, focusing on the buildup of anticlericalism leading to the burst of rapid dechristianization during the Revolution that gave way to the slow, but persistent, tide of secularization in nearly every aspect of society. Through all of this, so the story goes, *philosophes* railed against the clergy, the clergy preached against the lack of obedience, the politicians shouted about freedom from clerical tyranny, and the peasants – well, the peasants just did what they were told. Swept along by forces outside of their control, peasants first followed the laws of the church because they had few options to do otherwise, even if they did harbour some secret anticlerical attitudes; then when the Revolution came along they either embraced dechristianization or simply tolerated it, powerless to do much else.[2]

This book takes issue with the narrative presented above – or at least it invites us to complicate that narrative and recognize that while Enlightenment and Revolutionary debates were raging in Parisian salons, newspaper offices, and cafés, France was still primarily populated by rural peasants who continued to care about religion in profound ways. The secularization model often associated with the historiography of the eighteenth century and the Revolution of 1789 is much too simplistic, as it does not allow for the existence of multiple

and varied views of religion and religious practice within the same
time period.[3] For the rural people who appear in the following pages,
the Revolution had not yet happened, and they had no way of antic-
ipating it. Their behaviour, choices, values, and expectations cannot
be easily shoehorned into historians' narratives about revolutionary
roots or counter-revolutionary backlash. The people I have written
about were not ignorant peasants who accepted without thinking the
demands of their priests, nor were they revolutionaries-in-waiting,
somehow ready to destroy the power of the clergy by tearing down
churches and building monuments to the Supreme Being the minute
they got the chance. Anticlericalism, often assumed to be ubiquitous
in the Age of Enlightenment, did not mean the same thing to them
as it did to the *philosophes*. Peasants complained about their priests,
yes – but because they wanted better priests, not because they wanted
to get rid of the priesthood altogether.

My purpose for this book is to examine some aspects of what religion and parish life were like for the millions of rural Catholics who
still firmly believed in and practised the doctrines and tenets of their
church in the eighteenth century. Specifically, I study their relationship with the parish curé, who governed and influenced so much of
their religious lives in the public sphere. Rural Catholics ordered
their lives around the church's calendar, around the church's rituals
surrounding birth, marriage, and death, and, most importantly,
around the curé, who directed their access to these essential religious
activities. They were also the activities the laity engaged in the most
frequently, which meant that both lay men and women interacted
with their curés on a regular basis. Although the laity engaged in a
variety of religious practices, some of which were not under the
supervision of a priest, the rituals associated with parish services and
the sacraments were the most important of these. The sacraments
were seen as a gift of God's grace, and because that gift could only be
bestowed at the hands of the clergy, the relationship between curé
and parishioner was vital to parish life.

This relationship, however, is not an easy one to evaluate. Historians are at the mercy of their sources, and other than a few memoirs,
questionnaires, and the registers of births, marriages, and deaths that
curés were required to keep, parish priests produced little documentation. The laity themselves produced even less. Nevertheless, there is
one source that can provide valuable information about the priest–
parishioner relationship: court records. In the early modern period

the French church had a court system, known as the *officialité*, that had the power to prosecute priests for various spiritual and temporal infractions. These infractions included things like affairs with women, abuse of alcohol, and irregularities in tithe collection, but also improper performance of the mass, the sacraments, or other church services.[4] Often at the instigation of the parishioners themselves, the court collected witness testimony about the curé's performance, interrogated the curé, and made a decision as to his fate. I have used the records from three dozen of these cases, all found in the archdioceses of Reims and Besançon, to gain insight into the religious lives of both priest and parishioner in the eighteenth century.

I chose these two archdioceses simply because of the availability of *officialité* records. These sources do not lend themselves to quantification, both because of the nature of the material and because of the dizzying complexity of the early modern court system. I make no attempt to provide coverage of any particular region of France, nor do I imply that the experiences of the people involved in these cases were typical. Court records are valuable, nonetheless, for the human details they can provide about eighteenth-century religion in rural areas, even though we must be careful when making generalizations.

Court records have several advantages as historical sources. Most importantly, they provide the perspective of people whose voices often go unheard. Men and women, both literate and illiterate, gave their testimony and it was recorded by court scribes. This testimony was not entirely unfiltered, since scribes might either intentionally or unintentionally alter what they heard as they put it down on paper, and witnesses certainly framed their depositions according to prescribed norms.[5] Or, as we shall see, witnesses might have been influenced by their peers to say one thing and not another. Peasants certainly knew how to use the court system to their own advantage.[6] But without these records, even just these small indications of the views and experiences of the peasants who testified would be entirely lost.

Of course, historians read these records in ways never envisioned by those who produced them. Rather than trying to ascertain guilt or innocence, we are using the records to help us understand all kinds of things about everyday life.[7] Court testimony contains details about social networks, religious rituals, and interpersonal relationships that were rarely written about elsewhere. This is especially true when it comes to sacraments like confession and communion. No one kept records of what happened in the confessional, for that would violate the principle of confession itself. But court testimony contains glimpses into even this most private of spaces, as witnesses explained what they said and did when their priest ministered to them. Conflicts over the sacraments show up surprisingly often in *officialité* records, and by examining these conflicts we can better understand what the sacraments and other rituals meant to the people who participated in them.[8]

Using these sources, I believe I can make several important arguments that highlight an alternative view of the Enlightenment and the eighteenth century in France. The first argument is expressed in the focus on rural religion itself. Eighteenth-century religious practices in rural areas have often been overlooked, and material from court cases can give us a clearer picture of what those practices were and their critical importance to the cohesiveness of the parish. At the same time, religion mattered to rural people because they believed in the spiritual efficacy of these practices. Despite many historians' focus on secularization and dechristianization in the cities, in rural areas the regular rotation of mass, prayers, sacraments, and rituals framed everyday life and provided both meaning and comfort for Catholic believers. Although they were not blind followers of their faith – the existence of these court cases is certainly evidence of that – they did still believe in the overall necessity of the church and its clergy.

In making this argument, I do not mean to say that rural societies did not change over the course of the early modern period.[9] Village life was not static, and although it is not my purpose to illuminate all of the changes that occurred in rural societies it is clear that peasants were exposed to and even welcomed new ideas, including those of the Enlightenment.[10] The centrality of religion among rural peasants was not the result of stagnation, ignorance, or isolation. Instead, rural people chose to engage in religious practices and saw religion as a way to publicly express belief and devotion to God; it was a framework that their local societies were built upon. In this way, they had a great deal in common with their sixteenth- and seventeenth-century ancestors, even in the Age of the Enlightenment. Rituals may have been viewed or performed differently from one century to the next, but religion, in its various forms, was still fundamental to rural life during this period, just as it had been in the centuries immediately following the Protestant Reformation.[11]

Approximately four out of five French people lived in rural areas in the early modern period. A great deal of literature deals with the French peasantry, but it focuses primarily on agriculture and the economy. While religion is not completely ignored in these works, it could certainly use more attention.[12] There were about 32,000 parishes in France, ranging in size from a mere twenty-five to over 1,000 parishioners. People in small, rural parishes experienced their religion quite differently than those in large parishes; the simple fact that they constituted the majority means that their rural religious experience was much more typical than the urban experience, and it deserves more attention from historians.[13] In small- and medium-sized parishes, priests and parishioners interacted on a much more regular basis than their urban counterparts, and these interactions shaped religious beliefs and practices. The give-and-take involved in eighteenth-century religious activity is thus much more evident when we study rural parishes.

The second argument is about the nature of church and community in rural areas. Historians of medieval religion – centuries before the time period under study here – have often emphasized the communal nature of Christianity, showing that in many cases local ideas about religion, centred around practices undertaken by the parish or village community, superseded the official doctrines and practices of the church. Various religious activities, from the unorthodox (parish vows, miraculous shrines) to the orthodox (processions, missions, confraternities, the sacraments) cemented community ties and created a shared religious experience, while at the same time the already-existing village relationships gave meaning to the practices themselves.[14] Thus church and community went hand in hand – at least until the end of the seventeenth century. Then, as John Bossy argued,[15] the church became more focused on individual spirituality rather than the communal aspects of Catholic practice. Church and community, in this argument, became decoupled, and fundamentally transformed as a result. Andrew Barnes has even gone so far as to suggest that post-Tridentine parish priests, in the service of both orthodoxy and orthopraxy, were trained to ignore the real social needs of the community to such an extent that they lost their effectiveness in those communities. Without a cohesive religious community, secularization could proceed unfettered; Barnes notes that "the reform of the parochial clergy pushed the rural laity further away from the church."[16]

What I argue, however, is that the material from *officialité* cases demonstrates that a united, functioning religious community, cemented by a priest who performed the rituals associated with the sacraments, was still important to rural Catholics' understanding of society and religion in the eighteenth century.[17] If it had not been important, the parishioners would not have insisted on having curés who acted as the centre of that community. Nor would they have been distressed enough to take their curés to court and officially catalog their faults and infractions with the diocesan authorities. Testimony from parishioners demonstrates that the parish community was supposed to operate according to certain rules, and if those rules were broken, either by a parishioner or by the curé, it was seen as a scandal that had to be repaired; the laity's views of their individual spirituality as well as the spiritual health of the community were dependent upon this reparation. In essence, there could be no functioning community where a scandal existed. We will see, in later chapters, what exactly constituted a scandal and what that definition had to do with church and community.

At the same time that the sacraments were important for the unity of the parish, these rituals also became a space where disagreements between priest and parishioner played out.[18] If a curé did not perform the sacraments properly, he would be criticized for disrupting the community. Or, if a curé disrupted the community in some other way – perhaps through his affairs with women, or his financial disputes – those disruptions were often manifest through the sacraments. Parishioners did not just complain that their curé drank too much; they complained that when their curé drank too much he made errors during the mass, forgot the appropriate ceremonies during a baptism, or was unable to administer the last rites in a dignified manner. Arguments between village notables and curés over temporal affairs easily bled into religious life too, when sulking curés refused to work with churchwardens who disputed tithe payments or when a prominent *laboureur*[19] undertook a lawsuit against the curé and then discovered that his son was banned from first communion ceremonies. In one way or another, the cohesiveness of the parish community was tied to the performance of the sacraments and other church services, which acted as a barometer for the social and religious health of the community.

The third argument involves the Catholic Reformation. The Catholic Church's official response to the Protestant challenge came in the middle of the sixteenth century at the Council of Trent (1545–63). Over the course of these years, the bishops, cardinals, and other theologians who attended the meetings at Trent reaffirmed and clarified scores of Catholic doctrines, from transubstantiation to clerical celibacy to purgatory. At the same time, they agreed upon a long list of reforms that would need to be implemented in the decades that followed. Many of these reforms, often called Tridentine reforms, involved the behaviour of the parish clergy. Priests were expected to obtain more education and experience before they could become the curé of a parish, and once they did obtain a benefice their lives were to be full of study and prayer rather than farm tasks or other occupations suitable only for peasants. Curés and other priests had to give up their common-law wives, dress according to clerical standards, reside in their parishes, and maintain their churches properly. Bishops made hundreds of regulations about these things over the course of the sixteenth and seventeenth centuries.[20]

The spirit of the Catholic Reformation was alive and well in the eighteenth century. Many curés still had to be reminded of the now long-standing rules about clerical conduct, but much of the focus had shifted to the laity. The goal of reform-minded clergy, whether bishops or curés, was to create conformity to the rules and regulations of the church. Or, in more simple terms, to get the laity to behave. The clergy made significant progress throughout the early modern period, but there were limits to that progress; the evidence presented here highlights two essential reasons for those limits.[21] The first is that the laity pushed back when clergy interfered too heavily in their lives. Parishioners believed in their religion, but they also believed they were not obligated to follow their priests blindly. The second reason is that the church itself, in its policies and practices, limited the amount of change that could take place. Especially when it came to the sacraments of confession and communion, church regulations allowed a great deal of liberality and compassion and inadvertently favoured the laity over the curé. Religious life was thus the result of a process of conflict and compromise between clergy and laity.[22]

Finally, there is one argument that this book does not make. The material presented here cannot explain why religious institutions became so much less influential in the nineteenth century, nor can it demonstrate if this process of dechristianization was already underway in the eighteenth century before culminating in the French Revolution. From Marx on, historians have tried to find the roots of this transformation in the eighteenth century, blaming the problem on systemic failures within the church's hierarchy and institutions, as well as their failure to connect with the rank-and-file members of the church.[23] These answers seem to me unsatisfying. I have not yet found an explanation that convinces me that religious practice and religious debates were any less important in the eighteenth century than they had been in the sixteenth or seventeenth, and I am more likely to side with historians who view religion as an essential aspect of revolutionary culture.[24] More importantly, I believe that eighteenth-century religion deserves to be studied even if it does not necessarily help us to understand the Revolution. In her study of medieval English parishes, Katherine French argued that "medieval parishioners … were not waiting for the Reformation. The medieval parish was a dynamic and creative place in its own right."[25] I would argue that likewise, eighteenth-century French parishioners were not presciently waiting for the Revolution, and they deserve to be studied on their own terms.[26]

The book is organized in the following manner. First, it tells the story of Nicolas Hyacinthe Vernier, curé of Mareuil-sur-Ay in the diocese of Reims, who was called before the *officialité* court in 1770. Vernier's story is unique because there is so much documentation behind it (there are ninety-five witness statements, with over 600 pages of witness testimony), because of the nature of his scandals and because of the way the case turned out.[27] Vernier and his parish serve as the gateway for the discussion about rural religion and priest–parishioner relationships, and we will return to him again and again. His story provides the framework for the narrative of the book, and then subsequent chapters examine in more detail, using material from some three dozen additional cases, the various types of events, tensions, and difficulties that could take place involving curés and their parishioners. Both priests and the laity had their own agendas for what things should look like in the parish; sometimes those agendas overlapped and sometimes they did not. When they did not, scandal could easily be the result, and the ways that those scandals played out and were then repaired demonstrate why the parish as a community and the religious practices performed by that community were still central to eighteenth-century rural life.

Much of this book deals with obscure individuals, about whom we know little more than a few demographic details and a profession. They had no titles, little property, and little influence beyond their own family and village circles, yet their stories are still worth telling.[28] Although many of them were probably aware of the kinds of great events of their day that historians usually write about, they had little direct influence on those events and their activities could certainly be classified as squarely within that ambigious realm we call popular culture. The historiographical debate over the relationship between popular and elite culture has now fractured the term so deeply that it has become almost meaningless.[29] Popular culture should certainly be popular culture*s*, and there are multiple sites of overlap with elite culture – including, perhaps, the interactions between socially and economically superior curés and their rather more ordinary parishioners. The aspects of popular culture that I uncover here are primarily found in the ways that people interacted with each other, made most interesting because of the special dynamic between priest and parishioner. They are all part of the large tapestry that we refer to as popular culture. There was a system of shared meanings in these parishes – patterns of behaviour that repeated in their own unique iterations. These patterns demonstrate the centrality of religion in these parishes, even if religion was only one of many foci in the lives of rural peasants.

Although the moments of conflict described in this book were often not typical, nor representative of all rural parishes, they still give us insight into the inner workings of the community and the relationships of those who belonged to that community. Scandals make great stories – stories that historians can learn a great deal from. The stories I include in the pages that follow put a human face on the past, in ways that tax records or church decrees or confessional manuals cannot. There is no question that economic and social inequalities, along with conflicts over privilege, land, and trade, contributed to the conflict in Mareuil-sur-Ay and the other villages under examination here. What interests me, however, is not the aggregate causes of those conflicts but rather how they played out within the religious sphere and what they meant for individuals, their relationships, and their religious beliefs and practices. These court cases demonstrate that religious rituals were still one of the primary ways that all kinds of tensions could be displayed and either escalated or resolved; those tensions and conflicts are best examined on an individual basis. Man is a storytelling animal, and the men and women who appeared before the *officialité* court did their fair share of it. History should, in my view, be committed to re-telling those stories with the aim of a better understanding of human relationships and, in this case, religious beliefs.

I

# Priest, Behaving Badly

The curé has had difficulties with the parishioners for many years,
since the beginning of the time he was curé.[1]

Jean Poirot, *vigneron* of Mareuil-sur-Ay

The death of the priest Antoine Corbier must have come as somewhat of a shock to the parishioners of Mareuil-sur-Ay. After all, he had been their curé for forty-nine years, from 1698 to 1747. For the majority of the 500 or 600 residents of the parish, he was the only curé they had ever known. He had baptized their babies, ministered to them when they were sick, and buried their dead. They had poured out their guilt to him in the confessional (or perhaps he had dragged it out of them), and he had eased their consciences and assured them that despite their certainly numerous sins they were still valued members of Christ's flock. This was made powerfully apparent to them when he called them up each Easter Sunday to take communion with their fellow parishioners. Together, the people of the parish who presented themselves at the altar to receive the body of Christ made up an essential community, and Corbier was their earthly shepherd – the one who wrangled them all in and reminded them of their roles and responsibilities as part of that community.

In the mid-eighteenth century, at the time of Corbier's death, this particular community was a village in the Champagne region of France with a population of somewhere around 400 individuals old enough to take communion. Mareuil-sur-Ay was a medium-sized parish – much larger than its nearby neighbours Mutigny (fifty-four communicants in 1774) and Oiry (140 communicants) but considerably smaller than the nearby towns of Avenay (895 communicants), Ay (2,000 communicants), and Épernay (2,500 communicants), all within a six- or seven-mile radius.[2] Mareuil-sur-Ay was about twenty miles away, in different directions, from the two largest cities in the region: Reims and Châlons-sur-Marne (today, Châlons-en-Champagne). Situated on a branch of the Marne River, most of the population of Mareuil-sur-Ay either worked in the shipping business or in viticulture. By all accounts, there was nothing particularly interesting about Mareuil-sur-Ay as far as its social makeup, its community organization, or its religious activities. Any Protestants or Protestant-leaning individuals had been rooted out long ago; as in most French parishes in the eighteenth century, the sense of community held by the inhabitants was created out of their shared participation in Catholic rituals and sacraments, presided over by the curé.

There is no evidence to suggest that during the years of Corbier's tenure as curé the people of Mareuil-sur-Ay were unhappy with the religious life of their parish or with Corbier himself in any significant way. Certainly, there would have been disputes from time to time – perhaps some parishioners complained that the curé said the mass a little too early or a little too late, and surely a farmer or two had tried to get away with paying less than he owed in tithes. Maybe Corbier suffered from some of the most common shortcomings reported about curés in seventeenth- and eighteenth-century France: card playing (and gambling), hunting, and a tendency to indulge in a little too much wine.[3] If the parishioners had any major reason to complain to authorities outside of the parish about Corbier, there is no record of it. And since the village named a street after him – there is still a Rue Corbier in Mareuil-sur-Ay today – chances are he was fondly remembered as a respected curé. But after Corbier's death, any hope of continued peace and tranquility in the parish seems to have vanished with the arrival of the new curé, Nicolas Hyacinthe Vernier. No Rue Vernier exists in Mareuil-sur-Ay, for this new curé was, to put it mildly, difficult.

Perhaps it is a bit sad that we cannot focus on the apparently functional relationship between Corbier and his parishioners, because it was probably more representative of the majority religious experience in eighteenth-century France. But happy relationships between parishioners and their curé did not produce much documentation. Vernier's scandals, on the other hand, created a long paper trail. Vernier was the curé who angered his parishioners not just because he said the mass at inconvenient times, but because he failed to say the mass at all. He was suspected of inappropriate relationships with servants, schoolmistresses, and a female cousin. His behaviour ranged from odd (dressing up his dog like a jester) to violent (beating a beggar who asked for alms) to criminal (spiriting away a pregnant servant in the middle of the night). Vernier was the source of the scandal in the parish, so it is Vernier that we study. In the process, we learn what life in a parish was supposed to be like and how it could all go horribly, or sometimes just amusingly, wrong. From a close and careful reading of the materials produced during the Vernier case, we learn what parishioners expected from their curés, how they related to each other, and how the parish functioned.

Like most curés, Vernier was an outsider to the parish to which he was assigned in 1747. But unlike most priests in the diocese of Reims, 88 per cent of whom had been ordained in the diocese, he was from the diocese of Verdun, just to the east of Reims.[4] He had studied in Paris as well, receiving a bachelor's degree in theology from the University of Paris sometime in the mid-1740s. We do not know what sort of training he received other than that theology degree, or whether he attended a seminary for any period of time (although it is likely that he had).[5] It is possible that he served as an assistant priest (*vicaire*) or as a chapel priest after receiving his degree, since many curés at the time did,[6] but it is clear that his first official position as a curé was in Mareuil-sur-Ay, when he was age twenty-eight.[7] From then on, and for the next twenty-three years until the *officialité* case against him began, Vernier was responsible for the spiritual well-being of the parishioners of Mareuil-sur-Ay. And those years were rocky ones for seemingly everyone in the village, as far as their religious lives were concerned.

So rocky, in fact, that by 1770 tensions that had been building for decades exploded into a legal battle that lasted for three years. The inhabitants of Mareuil-sur-Ay were so fed up with their curé that they took him to court. The first step in that process came early that year when ten village notables from six influential families presented their grievances to the authorities. The ten plaintiffs in the case, listed in the initial complaint as "former churchwardens and inhabitants of the parish of Mareuil-sur-Ay," argued that Vernier was derelict in his duties as curé. These ten village notables were among the wealthiest and most influential men in the village; they worked in the shipping business, owned significant property, ran vineyards, and held public positions like notary and *procureur fiscal*.[8] They were not just a handful of outliers, complaining about a few foibles or perceived slights. They presented a lengthy list of wrongdoings, and any one of them, if proved, might be grounds for serious reprimand, if not permanent removal.

The court followed up on this complaint by opening a case and asking for witness testimony in a process called an *information*. Ninety-five people, from Mareuil-sur-Ay and from neighbouring parishes, gave their testimony over several weeks in the spring of 1770. The *information* resulted in a fat stack of 600 double-sided pages, each one containing vivid descriptions of Vernier's scandalous activities. These documents provide ample evidence of everything that had gone wrong in Mareuil-sur-Ay under Vernier's care. Among other things, Vernier was accused of failing to instruct his parishioners, refusing to visit and administer to the sick, and denying absolution to his parishioners when it would benefit him politically or financially. Dozens of people claimed that he mistreated his servants and anyone else who worked for him, chronically underpaying them or refusing to pay them at all. His violent temper, his questionable relationships with certain women, and his failure to perform parish services properly were all well documented in these pages. And it all seems to have started from the very moment that Vernier arrived in the parish in 1747.

### The First Argument: Vernier Fires the Vicaire

The first sign of trouble between the villagers of Mareuil-sur-Ay and their new curé centred around the issue of an assistant priest, or vicaire.[9] Most English speakers are probably familiar with the terms for parish clergy used in the English church, where the parish priest was called a vicar, and his assistant was a curate. In France, however, the terms were swapped – the head of the parish was the *curé*, and the assistant was the *vicaire*.[10] Vicaires were essential to rural parishes in the eighteenth century. Not only did he help with parish services, say masses, and hear confessions, the vicaire could administer the sacraments when the curé was absent, ill, or otherwise unable to administer them himself. The presence of a vicaire in a parish was critical to the spiritual and psychological well-being of rural residents. In towns, if a newborn infant needed immediate baptism or a sick person needed the last rites and the curé was unavailable, running a few streets over to find a preacher, a member of a religious order, or just an itinerant priest was usually easy to do. But in rural villages messengers might have to travel for miles to find another priest – unless there was a vicaire. So, most rural people needed and wanted to have vicaires in their parishes.[11]

But vicaires could also cause some tensions for a curé. As the only official clergymen in the parish, the two men would have to work closely together, and if for some reason they did not get along, religious services and the administration of the sacraments might be disrupted. When Vernier arrived in Mareuil-sur-Aÿ there was already a vicaire in the parish who had been serving under Corbier; his name was Philippe La Planche, and, according to court documents, the parish had been happy with his services and his character. But La Planche only stayed for a few weeks after Vernier's arrival: by 10 December 1747, a new vicaire had arrived.[12] The plaintiffs claimed that Vernier had dismissed La Planche, not because he was failing at his duties or for any other legitimate reason, but simply because the curé was worried that his vicaire would discover his scandalous behaviour and report him to the authorities. He presumably wanted a vicaire who was less scrupulous – or perhaps no vicaire at all.[13] Certainly, it would have been hard for Vernier to hide his various affairs and indiscretions from a vicaire, and it is suspicious that La Planche left so soon after Corbier's death. The diocesan authorities apparently had no problem with La Planche, since they made him a curé over his own parish soon after he left Mareuil-sur-Aÿ – a position he was still holding in 1770 when the case began. The truth seems to be that there was some reason that Vernier and the vicaire could not work together and that the authorities saw this transfer – or promotion, rather – as a viable solution to the problem.

Vernier's difficulties with La Planche may also have stemmed from a financial issue. One of the other major tensions surrounding the placement of vicaires in rural parishes is that someone had to pay for their living expenses and lodging. Most of the time, that someone was the curé, and the expense could easily become problematic. Church archives are full of disputes between curés and their parishioners over who should pay for a vicaire. Usually, the people went to the bishop or to local courts to demonstrate that it was the curé's responsibility to provide a living for a vicaire. Sometimes, the laity won, and the curé was ordered to pay for a vicaire. Other times, the parish itself had to pay, or else a compromise was reached and the parish and the curé shared the expenses. But generally speaking (with some exceptions, of course) parishes wanted vicaires, and curés did not.[14] Perhaps Vernier simply had not wanted to pay for a vicaire out of his own pocket.

In 1683, a previous curé of Mareuil-sur-Ay reported to a diocesan visitor that the income from his benefice was about 900 *livres* a year, and that from that income he paid a vicaire 250 *livres*.[15] In 1718, curé Corbier reported that he also paid 250 *livres* for the support of a vicaire, and the parish registers indicate that throughout his tenure Corbier did indeed make use of various assistants. But when Vernier arrived, his trouble with Mareuil-sur-Ay's vicaire suggests that he believed his predecessors had paid for a vicaire to help them with their duties voluntarily, rather than because they had been required to by previous agreements or orders. The parish disagreed, and a conflict ensued. It came to a head in either 1750 or 1751, and twenty years later the villagers brought it up again in the 1770 proceedings. Three witnesses testified about one particular incident involved with this early dispute (although none of them were sure of the exact date or year the event took place).[16] A number of inhabitants had made a complaint, which they had signed and sent to the courts. The bailliage court of Épernay had sent a notary to attend a village assembly and report on the issue. Village assemblies were usually held directly after the mass on Sundays,[17] and at that mass before the assembly, the witnesses testified, Vernier had gone to the pulpit and told his parishioners that he would personally bring to ruin any of them who did not take his side on the vicaire issue. Shaking with anger, he had threatened them that he would send the case to *parlement*[18] and that they would lose all of their goods, right down to the straw from their beds. Paul Nicolas Blondeau, a cooper of Mareuil-sur-Ay, indicated that this so-called sermon lasted about half an hour; he also complained that the curé had not bothered to preach the word of God at all.[19] Vernier had lost this particular battle, despite his threats; he employed a vicaire regularly for the remainder of his time in Mareuil-sur-Ay and reported in a diocesan questionnaire that he paid the vicaire's salary of 250 *livres* per year out of his own pocket. No matter who won or lost in this dispute, however, the incident shows that Vernier and his parishioners had difficulty getting along right from the very start.

## Scandal in the Parish

This dispute over the vicaire was just the first in a long line of troubles between Vernier and his parishioners. According to the 1770 complaint, "Vernier's excesses, of all types, from 1747 to the present, have brought trouble to families, alarmed all consciences, and revolted the virtuous people who have been witnesses to the disorders of their pastor."[20] The plaintiffs indicated that their first official complaint about Vernier had been submitted to the archbishop in 1750 and that more had followed.[21] In 1753, they had received a promise that Vernier would be moved to another parish, but the diocese had not followed through. They had continued to complain (patiently, they insisted, since they only wanted to calm the storm and restore public order), until 1770, when the case was finally brought to the courts. That spring, witnesses lined up to tell all they knew about the excesses and scandals that had plagued them for so many years. The parishioners who testified about Vernier's questionable character, his meager capabilities, his shortcomings, his offences, and the scandals that he had caused painted a picture of a curé who had failed them in the most fundamental ways. He had betrayed their trust and caused them to lose confidence in their curé, and the fabric of the community had thus been torn apart.[22] In short, they accused Vernier of causing a scandal in the parish; the only way that scandal could be repaired, according to his parishioners, was his removal from the parish.

French parishioners did not use the term scandal lightly. A scandal, in terms of Catholic doctrine, was an infraction that would lead to sin in others. It was thus an extension of an individual sin to the larger community. In the three dozen cases that I have studied, witnesses referred only to certain categories of events, described below, as scandalous. These categories had one thing in common: the infraction was public and well-known, and thus might damage others' faith or cause them to sin. Part of the scandal was that everyone was talking about it – the discussion and rumour surrounding the event might be as bad as the event itself.[23] When witnesses described a scandalous event or action to the court, they often noted that there was a great deal of murmuring about it in the parish, making it easy to imagine gossipy conversations in streets and courtyards, at the cabarets, or in the cemetery after the mass.

For example, when Jean Baptiste Le Grand, curé of Semide (Reims) was accused of fathering a child with a servant his parishioners were scandalized when the servant, after giving birth to her illegitimate child elsewhere, returned several times to the presbytery to visit the curé. This caused murmurs and scandals, reported witnesses; the accusations against the curé were bad enough, but the subsequent visits reopened old wounds and reminded everyone of the public nature of the scandal. According to one witness, because of these vis-its people refused to confess with the curé or go to the mass, which caused a "great disturbance" in the parish.[24] In another case, curé Charles Berteche of Branscourt (Reims) was accused of drunkenness; not only did the entire parish know that he was a drunk, but people in other communities had been witness to his scandalous conduct as well. The court heard from one witness that he had been travelling through a village a few miles from Branscourt during Holy Week and had noticed a man in ecclesiastical dress stumbling through the streets. He had asked the locals about it and had been told that it was just the curé of Branscourt, whom "everyone knows is a drunk."[25] It was bad enough if everyone in the parish knew about it, but when news of a scandal travelled outside of the community it compound-ed the scandal significantly. The parishioners of Branscourt were ashamed of the reputation their curé had and did not hesitate to describe that reputation to the court in hopes of replacing their drunk curé with a sober one and repairing the damage done to the public image of their community.

The two cases described above also highlight two of the categories of scandal that parishioners were likely to complain about: affairs with women and drunkenness. A third category was violence – curés who physically injured their parishioners or their servants, or both. These three categories make up the bulk of the complaints to the *offi-cialité*, but there is also a lot of overlap between these three categories and the fourth: failure to perform sacraments or church services prop-erly. Often, parishioners complained that their curé's affairs, drunk-enness, or violence kept him from his duties as a pastor, increasing the sense of scandal. In many cases, a curé's misbehaviour had gone on for years, but only when his activities got in the way of the sacraments or took away from the sacred nature of church services did the peo-ple complain. Of course, there were complaints in this category that were not connected to drunkenness or affairs at all. For instance, curés were accused of failing to say the mass when it was required or of irregularities when they did say the mass. This included failure to treat the host with the respect it deserved – for example, one curé, Antoine Michel, was accused of taking the tabernacle (a sacred vessel used to hold the consecrated hosts) home to his house and storing it in a cabinet for a time because he did not want to bother taking it back to the church.[26] Irregularities with the sacraments were pointed out as well; curés who refused to give people communion or who allowed parishioners to die without the last rites were criticized regularly. Again, all of these were events that were public, in the sense that either the curé had committed some infraction in full view of the parish itself, often in the church or in the village streets, or the infraction was known to multiple people in the parish.

The final category of scandal highlights the public aspect of the term as well: failure to keep peace in the community. Keeping the peace was one of the basic duties of a curé, and if he did not work to make sure that everyone got along there were generally significant complaints. Some curés themselves caused discord in the parish by using the pulpit to insult their parishioners. It was a curé's prerogative to admonish his parishioners in general, through sermons, but the laity overwhelmingly believed that any corrections made to specific individuals should be taken care of in private or in the confessional. If a curé named names, so to speak, during a sermon or during any discourse from the pulpit, he was essentially encouraging discord among his parishioners and thus causing a scandal.

Now we return to Vernier's case, and the specific scandals that he was involved in. The remainder of this chapter will provide details from the witness testimony collected in 1770 that explain why Vernier was such a controversial figure in Mareuil-sur-Ay. Remarkably, these witness depositions show that Vernier caused scandals that fall into every one of the above categories, with the notable exception of drunkenness. Just one witness indicated that Vernier had a bit of wine after the mass on Sundays that made him sleepy, but other than that Vernier seems to have been a completely responsible drinker. Drunkenness was thus not the cause of Vernier's problems, but he struggled mightily with just about everything else and piled scandal on top of scandal in his twenty years as curé of Mareuil-sur-Ay. The most common complaint struck at the heart of what it meant to be a curé: parish services.

### Parish Services

Vernier's failure to perform parish services according to his parishioners' standards is an overwhelming theme that runs throughout the witness testimony. Parishioners reported that the required mass was said each Sunday and each feast day, but more often than not it was the vicaire who performed it rather than Vernier. The vicaire at the time of the case, Jean Louis Harlin, testified that indeed he was the

one who said mass on Sundays, especially during the winter.[27] Parishioners also complained that Vernier never celebrated masses on working
days. Furthermore, the timing of parish services was all wrong. In parishes throughout France, Sunday mass was usually said sometime between
seven and ten in the morning depending on the time of year and local
circumstances. According to the Reims *rituel*, or diocesan handbook, in
the summer mass was supposed to be at eight and in the winter at
nine.[28] The church bells were rung about a half hour before the curé was
ready to start so that everyone had enough time to get to the church.
After the service, the parishioners then returned to their homes for the
midday meal, and they came back to the church at around two in the
afternoon for evening prayers, or vespers.[29] In rural areas travel on foot
from the countryside to the church might take a significant amount of
time, and parishioners did not want to arrive early and then have to wait
around for mass to start. Nor did they want to hear the bells announcing the start of services rung any earlier than they expected, making
them late or causing them to miss the service altogether.

A priest who failed to begin mass or vespers at the prescribed times
could easily draw the ire of his parishioners, who had their own plans
for how they wanted to spend their holy days. Twenty-four people
indicated in their testimony that during Vernier's tenure as curé there
were no set hours for services. Sometimes he rang the bell for vespers
at two in the afternoon, sometimes two-thirty, and sometimes three –
even as late as four or five. *Vigneron* Rémy Poncelet testified that during the winter vespers was sometimes so late that it was dark by the
time they left the church. Dame Marie Magdelaine Calixte Cazin, a
widow in the prominent Salmon family, stated that often it was so
dark they had to bring candles to read the prayers. One might easily
assume that the reason for the lack of consistency in start times was
sheer laziness, but one parishioner, river-worker François Durand,
opined that this was more than just laziness or ineptitude on
Vernier's part: he believed that the curé held services at different
times solely out of contempt for his parishioners.[30] A few witnesses
claimed that the true reason why vespers was often late was because
Vernier liked to take a nap after his noon meal and would not allow
anyone to wake him. The vicaire provided some corroboration for
this – he testified that the curé did usually nap after lunch but indicated that if Vernier failed to awaken on time he conducted vespers
himself so that the parish would not be deprived of the service.[31]

Besides the timing of the mass and vespers, the people of Mareuil-sur-Ay had one more major complaint about the way Vernier conducted parish services – his failure to provide appropriate instructions for them. We should remember that at the time there was more to the mass than just the prayers and singing that preceded the miracle of transubstantiation and the approach of communicants to the now-holy elements of the Eucharist. Ever since the upheaval caused by the Reformation, Catholic Church leaders had emphasized the necessity of instruction at the parish level. Priests were required to make sure that their parishioners knew and understood the doctrines of the Catholic Church. The church insisted that this be done in two ways. The first was through regular catechism classes, which will be discussed later, and the second was through instruction at the mass. By the time the Catholic Reformation was winding down in the eighteenth century, the laity absolutely expected a sermon to be preached at the mass. They also expected that relevant texts from either the missal or the *rituel* would be read to them during the mass. This instruction, known as *prône*, was seen as a standard part of the mass, and thus the curé's responsibility. The Reims *rituel* contained a section more than ten pages long on *prône*, and Vernier definitely would have been aware of this requirement in his ministry.[32]

As far as this instruction is concerned, Vernier was evidently failing miserably. Of the seventy-nine witnesses who were living or had lived in Mareuil-sur-Ay, forty-nine of them specifically complained that the curé failed to give any sort of sermon or instruction at the mass. Even the vicaire, Harlin, who in his testimony seemed reluctant to complain too vehemently about the curé,[33] testified that in the five years he had been serving in Mareuil-sur-Ay, Vernier had not personally done any pastoral instructions for his parishioners at mass on Sundays or feast days. He himself had read from the *rituel* about a dozen times in that five-year period, Harlin said.[34] Considering that there were fifty-two Sundays in a year and a few dozen feast days of obligation as well,[35] a dozen readings from the *rituel* hardly seems sufficient. Harlin also testified that in September 1768 one of the diocesan officials from Reims visited the parish for confirmation services and had reprimanded Vernier about his failure to instruct his parishioners during the mass. Harlin indicated that since that time Vernier had instructed him to read from the *rituel* during the mass at least three or four times. But it is hard to believe that this would have satisfied the parishioners or made up for all of the scandals Vernier had caused in this respect – infractions one might call scandals of omission that were witnessed in the church, during the mass and other services.

One of the most memorable church scandals during Vernier's years as curé happened on Ascension Day in 1763. According to long-standing parish practice, this particular feast day was celebrated with a procession from Mareuil-sur-Ay to Avenay, a small town about two miles to the north. The entire parish would have gathered at the church and solemnly walked together, singing or saying prayers, until they reached the abbey church in Avenay where they attended the mass. After the mass, everyone was supposed to walk back to Mareuil-sur-Ay together to reinforce the solemnity of the occasion. But there was a market or fair in Avenay that day, and a good number of the Mareuil-sur-Ay residents stayed behind to mingle with people from nearby parishes and participate in the festivities. Certainly, the cabarets would have been busy that day, as well as any other establishment that served food and drink.

Among those who lingered in Avenay for a time were seven young adults of Mareuil-sur-Ay, and they got into a bit of trouble by cutting through the fields and trampling on the grain on their way home. According to the twenty-two witnesses who discussed the events of Ascension Day 1763, however, the real scandal began not with the activities of the youths but at vespers that evening. Contrary to his usual custom (he usually had the vicaire conduct vespers), Vernier suddenly rose to the pulpit to preach. But he gave no sermon – instead, he began to *apostropher*, or scold sharply, his parishioners. He pointed out the seven young adults and described their crimes in front of the whole parish. He started with Françoise Patron, the twenty-three-year-old daughter of *laboureur* Pierre Patron. Catherine Adam, a carpenter's wife, was one of many witnesses who gave an account of the day, and since she was sitting behind Françoise in the church she seems to have maintained a rather detailed memory of what occurred.[36] According to Adam, Vernier shouted at Françoise to go and get her father so that he could tell him exactly what she had been up to that day. At that moment Pierre Patron happened to enter the church and Vernier began to chastise this unfortunate father openly, from the pulpit, asking him if he was going to be able to pay for the damages that his daughter had caused in the fields. Without waiting for a reply, Vernier told everyone in the church that he knew for a fact that the *laboureur* would not be able to cover the costs.

Next, Vernier began to upbraid Valentine Guimbert and Étienne Labbaye for traipsing through the fields together as well. Having built up a good head of steam, Vernier then shouted that he had seen "that big head" belonging to Antoine Henry, accompanied by Marie Jeanne La Marle, climbing on the walls above the courtyard belonging to Michel Cartier. If God had abandoned them, Vernier lamented, they would have fallen into the courtyard and from that height probably killed themselves. The mention of this incident seems to have reminded Vernier that he had something to say to Michel Cartier's son, Michel Antoine, too: he accused the young man of being seen "constantly" in the fields with the daughter of Jean Baptiste Visse, Geneviève.

This so-called sermon, ostensibly given as part of the vespers service, caused a great scandal in the parish. Witnesses reported that everyone was murmuring in the church, causing a great commotion; some people got up and left immediately after Vernier's speech, and soon everyone in the village was talking about what had happened. None of the youths involved testified in the *information*, but one woman, Marie Jeanne Jacquot (Visse), Geneviève Visse's mother, did, and she was furious at what had happened. [37] She went to see Vernier immediately after the services (other witnesses testified that they had seen her do so) to complain about the wrong he had done to her and her daughter in dishonouring her publicly. She also accused the curé of lying about what had happened, because she insisted her daughter had been with her all day. Jacquot threatened to take the matter to court until Vernier promised that he would retract what he had said the next Sunday from the pulpit. He never did, though, Jacquot lamented in her testimony; she did not bother to start a court case either. The event itself was not forgotten, however; parishioners held onto that memory until they finally had their chance to be heard in court, seven years later.

Other events that took place during Mareuil-sur-Ay's church services also reveal the tension between Vernier and his parishioners during his time as curé. Some were seemingly small events, but they had larger repercussions. One such event involved the *pain bénit*. In France the custom of distributing the *pain bénit* during the mass was still fairly common in the eighteenth century. This particular ritual probably evolved because most people took communion very infrequently, as they were required by church law to do so only once a year. In place of communion, the priest blessed a loaf (or loaves) of bread that was passed around to all in attendance as a symbol of the unity of the body of Christ in the parish.[38] Like many church rituals, this one became both an honour and an obligation in that the community provided the bread. Wealthy families usually rotated the responsibility and thus shared both the expense and the gratitude of the congregation and the church. But one year, sometime around 1760, Vernier seems to have slighted one of the most prominent families of the parish by refusing to receive and bless the bread that they offered during the mass. The head of the family in question was Jean Baptiste Salmon, who would later become one of the plaintiffs in the case.

When asked about this event in his interrogation, Vernier gave a long justification for why he had not accepted Salmon's offering. He explained that at the time workers doing repairs had put up scaffolding over the main altar, so all masses had to be done at one of the chapels. This caused considerable confusion during the ceremonies, and on the day in question Vernier said that he just forgot to bless the bread. He had not meant to ignore the offering, he insisted – he simply had not seen Salmon's servant bring it to the table. It is difficult to know who was telling the truth about this incident; it could have been an oversight, as Vernier suggested, or it could have been his way of publicly insulting one of the most prominent men in the parish. This event seems to have escaped the attention of most of the other parishioners, as only one person brought it up in their testimony,[39] yet it was important enough to the court officials that they asked Vernier about it, and he did have a carefully rehearsed and perfectly logical explanation.[40] But another slight to another prominent family caused an even greater scandal.

This event also revolved around a feast day – the Feast of Corpus Christi, or Fête-Dieu. As its name suggests, this feast celebrated the Body of Christ, or the Eucharist. The procession associated with this feast was often one of the more elaborate of the church year, since the goal was to carry the Holy Eucharist throughout the streets of the town or village. The power of the Eucharist would thus be spread to every corner of the village through this procession. And, because of the solemnity of the feast, sumptuous materials were required to properly display the Body of Christ. The Eucharist itself was placed inside a special vessel carried by the priest. In Mareuil-sur-Ay, the priest and the vessel were covered by a canopy, carried by four of the principal male inhabitants of the parish. In 1759, one of these village notables and a future plaintiff in the case, Jean Baptiste Billecart, was the warden of the confraternity of the Holy Sacrament. This was a popular confraternity in the seventeenth and eighteenth centuries; its members professed a special devotion to the Eucharist, and Fête-Dieu was one of their most important holy days. Confraternities were often governed by wardens, who regulated the list of members and accounted for donations and expenses.[41] Billecart had obtained from a local noblewoman a donation of a large piece of fine fabric to be used to make a new canopy for the Fête-Dieu procession. As warden, Billecart himself furnished additional fabric and paid for the construction of the new canopy; from 1759 on it was proudly carried by four prominent members of the confraternity during the procession.

In 1767 Vernier once again threw a wrench into the works by upsetting this long-standing tradition. As dictated by custom, the special canopy was made ready the night before, and at the appropriate time in the ceremony the four chosen men came forward carrying it, at which point the curé should have placed himself under the canopy while holding the Eucharist and then begun the procession. But on this particular day, Vernier stopped the four men carrying the canopy and asked them to leave. Witnesses described Vernier as trembling with anger and abrupt in his manner when he insisted that the men withdraw. After some confusion, they did walk away, and a smaller canopy was carried by two altar boys instead of the four notable parishioners. This event caused a great scandal in the church, and those in attendance were appalled by the fact that Vernier had been holding the Eucharist in his hands when he used such harsh words against the four men. They described women weeping, too afraid to raise their eyes from the floor. Claude Eloy Mayeux, one of the altar boys that Vernier asked to carry the smaller canopy, even made a special point in his testimony to explain that he had not wanted to participate but felt unable to deny the curé's request.[42] Thus even this young boy understood the ramifications of Vernier's actions and had not wanted to be a part of it at all.

Vernier's very public difficulties with the Billecart family continued the next year. In September 1768 the parish was preparing for a visit from a bishop who was going to give confirmation to any children and young adults who had not yet received the sacrament. Since confirmation could only be administered by a bishop, and bishops did not often travel to rural parishes, this event was a significant one and the villagers wanted to put their best foot forward. As part of the preparation for the visit, Marie Jeanne Joffrin, the wife of churchwarden Jean Baptiste Billecart and the daughter of Jean Joffrin (both men were plaintiffs in the case), went to the church to arrange the altar – decorate it, set out new candles, and change the linens. Several parishioners testified that this was the normal practice and that the churchwarden's wife was always the one in charge of decorating the altar. But Vernier seemed to have other ideas. When he came to the church and saw what she was doing, he began arguing with her right in the middle of the church. He told her that the decoration of the altar was none of her business. She tried to tell him that he was wrong and that she was just doing what she had been charged to do. He grabbed her by the arm and dragged her down the three steps that descended from the altar; the argument was loud enough that everyone in the church got to their feet to see what was happening. Marie Jeanne Jacquot (widow Thierry) even told the court that some people were standing on the benches to get a better view of the scuffle.[43] Once again, the curé was responsible for a public scandal.

Another common source of conflict between Vernier and his parishioners was catechism class, which was an extension of Sunday services. One of the curé's responsibilities was to prepare the children and young adults in his parish to take their first communion, and this meant teaching them church doctrine (i.e., the catechism). Ever since the Protestant Reformation, the catechism as a pedagogical tool had been growing in popularity with both Protestants and Catholics, and by the end of the eighteenth century it was ubiquitous in France. Learning the catechism meant memorizing it, so that when the priest asked a prescribed question, children could repeat the correct answer using exactly the same words and phrases found in the text. Children learned catechism in schools, including the village schools run by lay schoolmasters (Mareuil-sur-Ay regularly employed a schoolmaster throughout the eighteenth century), and from the parish clergy.[44]

Curés and vicaires were instructed to hold catechism classes in the church on Sundays and feast days, but Vernier also taught catechism at his home, in the presbytery. Three different parishioners who had attended Vernier's classes testified that he mistreated the children during catechism, kicking them or hitting them with a stick. Marie Thomas claimed that he made fun of children with physical abnormalities, which mortified them and made others laugh.[45] Louis Lombart told the court that one of the teenaged girls in the class was reprimanded by the curé for missing catechism the previous Sunday; he accused her of spending time with one of the male servants working in the village instead. This made everyone laugh, and other students made fun of her as a result. Lombart also said that whenever a student could not recite the assigned catechism text correctly, he dragged them by the hair around the church, kicked them, hit them with his fists, and made them kneel under the crucifix during vespers with their arms outstretched.[46]

*Vigneron* Jean Thomas Poncelet was one of these delinquent students. He told the court that one day he was five minutes late to catechism class because he had come directly from working in the fields. He claimed that as soon as he heard the church bell ringing he immediately left his work to get to the church on time, but by the time he arrived class had already begun. Vernier made him kneel under the crucifix in the church until his strength failed him; he had to continue the punishment later by kneeling under the cross again during parish services on another day.[47] Vernier was also reluctant to give the boy permission to receive confirmation from a visiting bishop. His mother, Scholastique Duval, had to send him to another parish to be confirmed with the children there instead. Duval also testified about the poor treatment her other son had received from Vernier during his religious education. The boy was preparing for first communion by memorizing some texts from the gospels, as Vernier had insisted he do. He had a copy of the gospels that he was using to complete the task, but one day Vernier grabbed it out of his hands and would not return it. Duval begged for it back, but in response, the curé threw it into the fire and refused to reimburse her for the value of the book or give her another.[48]

Other than these incidents, most of the complaints about Vernier's instructions were not that he was too strict with the children, but just the opposite: many parishioners believed that in most cases he had failed to teach the children adequately, and he often left them alone to get into trouble. Parishioners indicated that sometimes the curé would force the children to wait in the street outside the presbytery, boys and girls mixed together, before announcing that there would not be enough time for class that day. This was problematic not only because the children could easily get in trouble while they were waiting and idle but also because it caused the loss of valuable work hours. Most children preparing for first communion would have been at least twelve years old, and their labour was valuable to their families. Many parents counted on the income that their children brought in, so wasting time waiting for the curé was more than just an inconvenience. By not holding class according to a regular schedule, Vernier showed he had no sensitivity for the needs of his parishioners.

Furthermore, when Vernier did hold class, he sometimes seemed to be more interested in entertaining the children than in teaching them. Eleven witnesses complained of ribald and inappropriate talk, instigated by the curé, during catechism class. Others noted that Vernier had a dog that he would dress up like a jester, to get the children to laugh. He asked the children suggestive questions as a way of entertaining them as well. He might ask a boy how old he was, and when the boy responded he would exclaim, "You should have at least two children by now!" or, "You should be a grandfather by now!" A lot of this teasing apparently had a sexual component. Marguerite Coinon claimed that once the curé had taken her aside and asked "if your father kisses your mother well."[49] He made fun of one child's name, Cochet, associating it with *coq* and asking the children if "the cock mounts the hen."[50] Christine Berthe Durand described one instance when he gave them all pieces of a tart, distributing the pieces himself and placing them into the mouths of the children as he would the Eucharist; she quoted him as saying, "Open your mouth, you have a tongue like *une pelle à four*," which translates literally as "oven shovel."[51] No wonder that one of Marie Jeanne Bellot's children came home from catechism class one day and said, "Oh, mother, the curé really made us laugh today!"[52]

## The Sacraments

If Vernier was not using the time during catechism class to teach children religious doctrine, then parents might worry that their children would not be instructed enough to take first communion. For that was the main purpose of catechism class: it was the prerequisite to the sacraments that parishioners participated in as adults. Of the seven sacraments in the Catholic liturgy, curés were regularly required to perform five: baptism, penance (confession), the Eucharist (communion), marriage, and extreme unction (the last rites). The other two, confirmation and holy orders, could only be administered by a bishop. Needless to say, the worst thing that could happen to a Catholic was to be excommunicated, because that meant being excluded from all of the sacraments and thus disqualification from salvation in the afterlife. So if a curé did not perform the sacraments properly, people might feel just as though they had been excommunicated. They would fear for their well-being in this life and for their salvation in the next. It should not be a surprise, at this point, to discover that Vernier created that kind of fear in his parishioners, by failing to administer these sacraments in the way that they expected.

The importance of baptism at the time cannot be overstated. In the Catholic tradition, baptism was necessary to remove original sin and it was the gateway to the Lord's grace and all other sacraments, for which it was a prerequisite.[53] It was also the only way to become a Christian and a member of God's church. Church doctrine dictated that no one could possibly obtain eternal life without the sacrament[54] and that if an infant died without baptism, its soul was effectively condemned to hell for eternity. This helps explain why if neither the curé nor the vicaire was available to perform this sacrament, worried parents would be very upset with their curé. For example, in October 1753 Scholastique Duval, the wife of *vigneron* Rémy Poncelet, gave birth to twins. Because both infants were in danger of dying, a message was sent to the presbytery to ask Vernier to come and administer baptism. Neither he nor his vicaire were anywhere to be found. Poncelet then began a search for any other available priest who could administer the sacrament to his children. He went on foot to Avenay, Mutigny, and Ay (each a distance of several miles) but found no priest who was able and willing to travel to Mareuil-sur-Ay to baptize the infants. Finally, he found an Augustinian from Reims who agreed to make the trip. He and Poncelet returned to Mareuil-sur-Ay but found that one of the twins had already died with only temporary baptism; the Augustinian baptized the other, a boy named after his father, on 15 October 1753. The baby died three days later.[55]

This sort of infraction was unforgiveable in the eyes of the parish. Yes, temporary baptism had been administered, but everyone believed that the rite really needed to be performed by a priest to be legitimate. Furthermore, there were other infractions that Vernier committed involving the baptism of healthy infants. One of the most important, and therefore most contested, aspects of the baptismal ceremony involved the godparents. An infant presented for baptism would be accompanied by two individuals, a man and a woman, who were supposed to assist the parents in the moral and spiritual education of the child as it grew up. In August 1749, two children of innkeeper Jean Blondeau, Jean Jacques (age sixteen) and Marie Anne (age fourteen), were presented as godparents for the infant daughter of *vigneron* Philippe Genest. Witnesses told the court that Vernier refused to accept them – in fact, after an argument he took the two youths by the arms and forcibly threw them out of the church. The curé then found a boy and a girl (described by a witness as ruffians) who were playing in the streets around the church and brought them in to serve as godparents instead.[56] The parish register shows that indeed Jean Jacques and Marie Anne Blondeau had initially been entered into the record as godparents, but their names were crossed out and two others substituted.[57]

A similar incident happened again in Mareuil-sur-Ay less than a year later, involving one of the most prominent families in the parish. On 5 February 1750, *laboureur* Paul Billecart brought his infant son to the church for baptism, accompanied by family members, the midwife, the intended godparents, and various other residents of Mareuil-sur-Ay. Billecart and his wife had chosen their niece and nephew, the infant's cousins, to serve as godparents. Nicolas Billecart, the godfather, was at the time fourteen years old and the son of Paul Billecart's brother Pierre. Nicolas would also be one of the plaintiffs in the case against Vernier, twenty years later. Louise Joffrin, the godmother, was the seventeen-year-old daughter of Jean Joffrin, another future plaintiff, and the niece of Paul Billecart's wife. Thus all of these people were closely related, and they would later be instrumental in the case against Vernier. Indeed, perhaps this was the very event that started the animosity that would then grow and fester for the next twenty years. For on this occasion, Vernier once again expressed his qualms about the designated godparents. He began asking the two youths questions from the catechism. The godparents took offence at this, saying to Vernier that they had come to baptize an infant, not to be tested on their catechism, which so angered Vernier that he refused to proceed any further with the baptism ceremony. Paul Billecart testified that he took the baby and left the church, and the entire party went to Ay to have the child baptized; however, according to the complaint submitted by the plaintiffs, because of the long trip to Ay in the winter the infant became sick and died soon after, leading to further resentment toward the curé.[58]

Besides baptism, by far the most frequent sacraments any curé would administer were confession and communion. Although they were separate sacraments, the two were nearly always tied together because confession was required before admittance to the altar for communion could be granted. Additionally, the church required all Catholic adults to confess and then take communion with their curé each year, during the two-week period of Easter, or risk excommunication. This requirement, known in the documents most often as simply *paques*, the French word for Easter, easily became rather complicated whenever a curé had more than a few dozen parishioners. Curés, following diocesan rules, often permitted their parishioners to confess with other priests and gave them a document stating that permission, called a *billet*. Once the parishioner had confessed with the appropriate confessor, he or she could then return to their own parish and participate in the communion ceremony.

But again Vernier seems not to have followed the usual patterns of practice. For unlike most curés, he seemed to have no interest in allowing his parishioners to confess with other priests. Witnesses testified that Vernier often refused to issue *billets* for no good reason. One of the curé's servants, Pierre Philippot, testified that during the nearly six years he worked for Vernier many people would come to visit the curé to ask for permission and be turned away multiple times before he would finally give in. Philippot was usually the one that Vernier sent to deliver the *billets*, so he knew exactly how many were given out. Furthermore, Vernier usually wrote in Latin, so that the parishioners would be unable to read whatever he wrote. This caused a great deal of consternation – it seems many people worried that Vernier was giving the confessor a list of their sins and shortcomings, creating shame and embarrassment. Their fears seemed to be well founded; Philippot told the court about one *billet* that the curé issued to a widow of the parish, testifying that he had overheard Vernier boasting to his friends that he doubted very much if she had been able to use it for confession.[59]

Vernier played a similar game with Denis Pierre, a cooper of Mareuil-sur-Ay. Pierre testified that he had received a *billet* in Latin from Vernier and then had gone to the curés of four nearby parishes looking for a priest who would hear his confession. After reading what Vernier had written, none of them wanted to serve as his confessor. Finally he went to Châlons-sur-Marne where he found a member of a religious order who read the *billet* and "groaned" but wrote a letter for Pierre to take to some of his colleagues in Ay explaining that they should ignore Vernier's *billet* and hear Pierre's confession.[60] But this only took Pierre right back to Vernier, because the clergy in Ay still would not let Pierre confess with them before Vernier gave them specific permission. After going to Vernier three more times and begging for permission to confess elsewhere, the curé finally gave in.

Vernier apparently did not want to let anyone besides either himself or his vicaire administer to his parishioners in the confessional and tried everything he could to keep them from seeking out confessors elsewhere. Despite his best efforts, some parishioners did slip through the cracks and manage to take communion without confessing to the curé. After all, with around four hundred communicants in the parish, even a priest as vigilant as Vernier could not be expected to keep track of everyone. But if Vernier found out that someone had managed to confess with another priest and still take communion in Mareuil-sur-Ay, he made sure that the individual knew they had committed a sin. Catherine Adam testified that sometime around 1760 Vernier said from the pulpit that one of his parishioners had done his Easter communion without first getting permission to confess with another priest.[61] Vernier did not say who the individual was but publicly declared his communion sacrilegious. Another time, Vernier went to the pulpit on Holy Thursday and declared that one of his parishioners had taken communion at the mass in Mareuil-sur-Ay that day, without first receiving permission to confess elsewhere. Once again, he publicly declared this communion to be sacrilegious. This caused a great deal of murmuring, especially since only one person had taken communion that morning – the surgeon Desiré Cuiret – so that everyone believed they knew whom Vernier was talking about. Nicolle Billecart, widow of a merchant, also testified that she had once taken communion in Mareuil-sur-Ay on a holy day and then been surprised to find the curé's servant knocking on her door after the service, summoning her to the presbytery. When she arrived, the curé greeted her with the words, "*Voila*, a nice sacrilegious communion you did there." He told her that her confession and communion were damning because she had confessed with someone else.[62] In at least one incident, Vernier went as far as publicly denying communion to an individual because he had confessed elsewhere, even though he had permission. Three parishioners testified that carpenter Louis Bellot (who had since died and was thus unable to give his own testimony) presented himself at the holy table during the Easter season in 1755 but the curé just passed him by without giving him communion. Several parishioners declared that they had witnessed this public refusal and insisted that they knew for a fact that Bellot had obtained a *billet* and thus should have been able to take communion with a clear conscience.

It appears that Vernier's problems in this regard extended beyond his own parish. He even had the audacity to disagree with other curés and religious officials about the issue of Easter confession. Rémy Bouvette, curé of the nearby parish of Fontaine-sur-Ay, testified that in 1764 future plaintiff Nicolas Billecart had confessed and taken communion in his parish. Bouvette told the court that he had agreed to do this only because Billecart had received express permission from one of the vicars-general of the archdiocese of Reims.[63] The letter of permission had not explained why Billecart was doing his Easter duty outside of his own parish, but Bouvette felt he should obey the orders of the diocesan official and he gave communion to Billecart. Some time later, Bouvette was travelling and stopped in Mareuil-sur-Ay to see his colleague. During the visit, Vernier expressed his unhappiness about what Bouvette had done for Nicolas Billecart. Bouvette told him about the letter of permission he had received, but Vernier tried to argue that the vicars-general did not have the authority to grant such permission. Bouvette was indignant, and he told Vernier that if they did not have the authority to do this, then who else would?[64]

Vernier's refusal to give *billets* for confession became problematic enough that some members of the parish decided they should take the curé to court for this reason alone, sometime around 1765. Étienne Claude Dupuis, a royal court official (*huissier royal*) testified that in that year five or six inhabitants of Mareuil-sur-Ay asked him to require Vernier to either hear their confessions or give them *billets*. Dupuis went to the curé, who simply responded that he had his reasons for refusing to hear their confessions and give them absolution. Dupuis never followed through with the case because, he said, certain people told him that they had been counselled by their families to stop the proceedings.[65] This close call did not change Vernier's attitude. The curé of Mutigny, Jacques Moury, testified that he had regularly confessed at least fifty inhabitants of Mareuil-sur-Ay over a nine- or ten-year period. Since his parish was small, he had the time to hear confessions from people in nearby parishes, including Mareuil-sur-Ay and Avenay. Then, in 1768, a diocesan official had requested a meeting with him and informed him that he no longer had the power to confess anyone from outside his own parish. Moury explained that he had been surprised by this since it had never been a problem before, and he had asked if it was because the curé of either Avenay or Mareuil-sur-Ay had complained. Cagily, the official had responded that the curé of Avenay was not the one who had asked for the change but then had refused to say anything more. Moury could only conclude that Vernier did not want him to confess any of the inhabitants of Mareuil-sur-Ay.[66]

So it appears that Vernier was working hard to force his parishioners to confess with him and him alone, while they were working just as hard to confess with other priests. And they had good reason to do so, for those who did confess with Vernier did not have many good experiences to report. Confession was always difficult, as anyone who has ever had to admit wrongdoing is easily aware. But confessing one's sins was also supposed to be therapeutic – the act of confessing was seen as good for the soul. In this sense the priest was not just supposed to listen to the list of sins and then mete out punishment; it was expected that he would give encouragement to the sinner, listen to their woes, and try to offer suggestions for how to change their ways. Curés had to walk a fine line between judge and healer, and Vernier seemed to stay firmly on the side of the former.[67]

For one thing, he treated anyone who sold wine in the village – legally, as *cabaretiers* (tavern-keepers) or otherwise – as the worst type of sinner and often refused to give them absolution unless they promised to give up their business. He also forbade his vicaires from absolving wine-sellers too. For example, in 1767 Marie Hardy, wife of a *cabaretier*, did her Easter confession with the vicaire, and after hearing her confession he told her to return in a week for absolution. When she did, he told her that he could not absolve her because the curé had instructed him not to allow any of the *cabaretiers* to take communion unless they gave up selling wine. Hardy told him that she had already bought the wine and paid for it and that this business was necessary for the subsistence of her family. The vicaire told her that it did not matter – she could do whatever she liked with the wine, but per the curé's instructions he was unable to absolve her. So she left without receiving absolution. She told the court that since then she had not done her Easter communion even though she had tried every year.[68]

In another incident that began in 1764, butcher's wife Marie Madeleine Cognon found herself unable to do her *paques* because she sold wine in the cabaret. After three years, she asked for a *billet* from the curé so that she could confess elsewhere but he only shouted at her, threatened to beat her, and called her *salope* – a common vulgar term meaning slut. He then threw her out of the presbytery and continued to insult her, telling her that if her house was in a field and she was inside the house he would set fire to it and that it would be better for her to steal in the streets than to sell wine. About three months later her daughter, Jeanne Louise Patron, went to confess with the curé and took the opportunity to beg him to give her mother a *billet*, explaining that she had frequent stomach attacks that threatened her life and wanted to be able to receive the sacraments in case she came close to death. Vernier responded by saying that if Cognon died, instead of giving her a church burial he would bury her in a ditch, condemning her soul to hell for eternity.[69] Vernier then refused absolution to Patron herself and tried to get her to move out of her parents' house. He said that he would find her a good job – presumably as a servant – if she left, but she refused this offer. So Vernier told her that she obviously had little care for her salvation.

In a similar instance, Marie Reine Thierry testified that until 1764 or 1765 she had always confessed with the curé, but then she stopped going to him when he refused to absolve her unless her widowed mother, Marie Jeanne Jacquot, stopped selling wine in the cabaret. He sent her to the vicaire and she confessed with him for about two years without any problems, until the curé's heart hardened even more. At Easter she was giving her confession to the vicaire when he suddenly left and went to the curé's confessional a few feet away for a whispered conversation. When he returned, the vicaire told her that he could not absolve her. Not only did Vernier give Thierry a hard time in the confessional, he also refused to admit her siblings for first communion; her mother was forced to send them outside of the parish to learn their catechism and take their first communion.[70]

Vernier denied absolution to other parishioners for reasons besides selling wine – although those reasons were not always explicit. Elizabeth Trouson was told by the curé that she could not be absolved unless she agreed to move out of her parents' home. Trouson testified that she had gone to the curé for confession sometime in either 1759 or 1760, when she would have been about sixteen or seventeen, and the curé tried to convince her to move away from home and find a job as a servant. She declined to follow his advice, and she claimed that she went back more than twenty times to try to get absolution. But he always refused, so she could not do her *paques* that year. After that, she went to the vicaire, with whom she had more success. Trouson offered no explanation for why Vernier wanted her to leave her parents' home, though – her father appears in records as a *vigneron* and there is no indication that either he or his wife sold wine. Another time Vernier refused to allow the daughter of Charles Méa to take communion because he claimed that she was no longer his parishioner. The girl was learning the seamstress trade in Ay and only came home on weekends. Vernier sought her out in the church and told her that if she approached the altar he would refuse her. The complaint indicates that he did this just to cause her parents pain.[71]

Vernier seemed to want to cause the parents of Marie Margueritte Salmon pain as well. When she was about sixteen or seventeen, the curé asked if she would agree to do a collection for the Confraternity of the Virgin. One teenage girl was chosen each year for this responsibility, and Salmon said that she would do it as long as she got her parents' permission first. When her parents refused to give her permission, Vernier told Salmon that he would not give her absolution, nor would he allow any of her eleven brothers and sisters to be admitted for first communion when they came of age. She tried to explain that she had no choice as she could not disobey her parents, but the curé refused to change his mind; the next day she went to the curé of Mutigny for confession, and her father had to send two of his children to neighbouring towns to learn their catechism and take their first communion.[72]

Vernier also tried to use the confessional for financial gain. François Durand, river worker, testified that one year during his Easter confession Vernier told him that if he wanted to receive absolution he would need to return with a plate of fish.[73] This request seems fairly innocuous, but it was certainly against the rules. On a more serious note, several parishioners also reported that during tithe disputes they were suddenly barred from confession with either Vernier or the vicaires. Like many in his position, Vernier probably used the court system, violence and intimidation, and village politics to try to maximize the tithes that he received, but he apparently used the confessional to do this as well. Anyone involved in tithe disputes, even if through no fault of their own, might be prevented from receiving absolution in the confessional until they agreed to Vernier's terms. Those who did not give in to his demands found themselves unable to do their *paques*, sometimes for several years in a row.

How many other times did Vernier deny absolution to his parishioners, for reasons that were unfair, callous, or contrary to established church doctrine and practice? How many people suffered spiritually because of Vernier's practices but did not speak up? In a *memoire* published by the plaintiffs in August 1770, Vernier's use of the confessional was described in the following way: "A crowd of witnesses have told the court about all of the times that they have resisted the unjust and tyrannical will of the curé Vernier in the Tribunal of Penance, and they were refused absolution. About how they could not obtain *billets* of permission to present themselves to other priests, and if they approached the vicaire, he only consulted with the curé to find out if he should grant or refuse them absolution – that even in the church the curé had the audacity to go to the vicaire and defend him from granting absolution … How many parishioners have found themselves deprived for a long time of their Easter Communion!"[74] At this point it should be obvious that Vernier's conduct as a confessor was at best confusing and at worst arbitrary and cruel. In some cases, he did everything he could to make sure that his parishioners could only confess with him, but at the same time he seems to have purposely driven others away, giving them *billets* to confess with other priests while refusing those same *billets* to others. Whatever his motivations were in individual cases – greed, vindictiveness, petty pride, or sheer meanness – we can be sure that he was always looking for some advantage, some sort of edge that reminded his parishioners that his power and authority were real and far-reaching.

Parishioners who wished to confess their sins and receive communion when they were sick and the last rites when they were dying also found Vernier difficult to work with. Twenty-six individuals testified about Vernier's lack of care for the sick and the dying. Some of them simply stated that it was well-known in the parish that Vernier refused to visit the sick and sent his vicaire instead. But many others gave detailed examples of the pain that Vernier had caused them by refusing to visit and provide sacraments for them during illnesses, or for their sick and dying relatives. Their testimony outlines thirteen such incidents over the course of twenty-two years. There were probably many others, but these were the ones people remembered and told the court about. Some seem to indicate that Vernier was too lazy to do his duty – as was the case with the sister of *vigneron* Charles Mayeux, who died without the sacraments because Vernier complained about going too often and asked, "Is it necessary to parade God through the streets every day?"[75] Other incidents demonstrate the existing tensions between Vernier and his parishioners. Paul

Billecart testified that his daughter had been dangerously ill, and the curé was her regular confessor. Vernier was asked at least twenty times to come and see her, as she was very anxious to confess and receive the sacraments before she died. The vicaire came instead, and he told Billecart that Vernier had refused to come because he was afraid of finding in Billecart's house "faces that did not please him."[76]

Carpenter's wife Catherine Adam testified about the treatment her dying father, Rémy Adam, had received in 1748. She explained that when her father became very ill she sent for Vernier to administer to him and give him the last rites. When Vernier arrived, he told the family that Rémy was not sick enough to warrant the last rites. He also said that he would not bring the Eucharist because the sick man was being kept in a room that was too small. Catherine told Vernier that he was too sick to move, but Vernier continued to refuse to administer the sacraments. Finally, the family threatened to bring in a sergeant who would force Vernier to follow their wishes and the curé capitulated. Rémy Adam died on 29 December, and the parish register indicates that he had confessed and received the sacraments before expiring.[77]

The family of the baker Claude Thierry also testified of the poor treatment they had received during his illness and at the time of his death. Thierry's wife and daughter called for Vernier to administer to Thierry many times. Vernier was Thierry's regular confessor, and he wanted to give his last confession to the curé himself and not the vicaire. After the family sent the curé many messages asking him to come to their home, Vernier did finally hear Thierry's confession on what turned out to be the day before he died. Thierry's son Gérard, who was living in Épernay at the time but had returned to Mareuil-sur-Ay because of his father's illness, testified that he was shocked at the things Vernier said at his father's bedside when administering the sacraments. Instead of trying to calm his conscience, the curé told the dying man that he was "miserable," and that God would punish him for selling wine at the cabaret. Then, after hearing Thierry's confession, the curé left and the vicaire administered the last rites. It was the vicaire who did the burial too, despite the family's wish for the curé to do it himself. They also complained that it took three days after Thierry's death for the burial to be done. This may have been a bit of an exaggeration – the parish register indicates that Thierry was buried on 13 October 1761, just two days after he died.[78] But in any case, it is clear that the family found Vernier to be unresponsive and negligent in his duty.

Several incidents involving the last sacraments happened in 1764. In May, a widow named Claudette Prunet was ill, as was her daughter, Scholastique Duval. They called for Vernier to administer to them and give the last rights to Claudette, who seemed in danger of dying. Vernier refused to come, saying that he feared what he would be exposed to by entering their home, listing bad air, scurvy, and cancer as possibilities. He sent his vicaire in his place. Duval recovered and later gave testimony about this event, but Prunet died as a result of her illness.

At the same time, another woman in the parish, Jeanne Hennequin, was seriously ill and bedridden. Hennequin was the wife of Christophe Robert, *procureur fiscal* and future plaintiff. Vernier refused to visit her during her illness as well. The initial complaint submitted to the court about Vernier indicates that the curé was asked more than fifty times to administer to her. Before her illness she had always confessed with Vernier, and therefore she wanted to do her last confession with him and no one else. But despite her requests, he sent only his vicaire. She died in July, apparently having received no visit from the curé.[79]

Vernier's refusal to properly care for the sick and the dying was obviously one of the parishioners' major complaints. Fear of dying without sacraments was a strong motivator, and even if Vernier had done nothing else wrong these incidents may have been enough for a court case on their own, or certainly some form of censure from the diocesan administration. But Vernier committed many additional serious infractions in his relationships with his parishioners. Even if his behaviour was not specifically related to parish services or the sacraments, the incidents were still upsetting to the people. In the eighteenth century, the religious and social lives of the village were intimately tied together, and a curé who could not get along with his parishioners outside of the church was just as problematic as one who failed in his functions inside the church.

## Upsetting the Peace of the Parish

Late one evening in July 1765 Pierre Gérard had already retired to his bed when there was a knock on his door. It was one of Vernier's servants, Pierre Philippot, who told the *laboureur* and *syndic* that the curé wanted to see him.[80] Gérard told Philippot that he would go and see him the next morning, but the servant said Vernier was leaving

Mareuil-sur-Ay for personal business the next day and that it was an urgent matter: the curé had received information concerning the community and had to speak with Gérard immediately about it. So, Gérard reluctantly went to the presbytery. It turned out there was no urgent matter – Vernier wanted to discuss the meeting that the community had recently held about tithe collection in the parish. As *syndic*, Gérard would need to finalize, with his signature on an official document, the agreement that the curé and the parish had worked out, and Vernier had the document drawn up and waiting for him.

Instead of just signing what the curé put in front of him, Gérard carefully read through the document and found that it misrepresented what had actually transpired at the parish assembly; this document favoured the curé rather than the community. When Gérard pointed this out, the curé told him that he hoped that Gérard would sign it anyway, since they were friends. Vernier told him that there was nothing to worry about and then hinted that he might refuse to perform parish services if Gérard did not sign. When the *syndic* continued to hesitate, the curé got angry and told him that he would ruin him sooner or later, just as soon as he had an opportunity. Gérard then tried to leave but the servant Philippot took him by the neck and pushed him into the kitchen, telling him that he had to sign the document. There was also a large dog in the room, giving Gérard additional cause for concern. Vernier promised that the community would never know that he had signed the document, so Gérard finally gave in and was allowed to return home unharmed by dog or servant. A few days later, he was horrified to find out, however, that everyone in the community was talking about the fact that he had signed the curé's document.[81]

This incident shows just how dishonest and manipulative Vernier could be. He brought the *syndic* to his home at night, under false pretenses, when there would be few witnesses and no one Gérard could turn to for help. He first tried to get Gérard to sign the document without even explaining what it was. Then he used flattery, followed by threats, both verbal and physical, to get what he wanted. The entire episode was carefully calculated, and Vernier ended up succeeding in every aspect – he got whatever it was he wanted as far as the agreement over the tithes was concerned, and he had damaged the reputation of the village's *syndic* with the rest of the community.

Vernier was also accused of having a violent temper. Denis Pierre described one incident that happened sometime around 1754 or

1755. He explained to the court that at about ten o'clock one night as he was getting ready to go to bed, he heard his dog barking and whining outside. When he went to investigate, he found that someone had been beating his dog so severely that it had lost an eye. Pierre looked around and saw someone walking away down the street; he caught up with the assailant and grabbed him by the collar. He was surprised to find that it was Vernier. Pierre reported that he told his curé, "If you were my equal we would decide this quickly," implying that if he were anyone else but a member of the clergy then he would have taken his revenge through violence, right there in the street. Pierre might have been unable to restrain himself from hitting the curé if his wife had not appeared at that moment and placed herself between the two angry men. She convinced her husband to let the affair drop.[82]

Vernier was also notorious for refusing to pay for services provided. *Vigneron* Pierre Lemaitre testified that he had worked in Vernier's vines for a time in 1762 and was still owed seven *livres* in wages. Catherine Adam told the court that her husband, a carpenter, had worked for Vernier in 1760 and was owed nine or ten *livres*; ten years later they were still trying to get him to pay but he always made an excuse and they had yet to see a *sou*. Leonard Noel, a mason, testified that he had worked for the curé many times and was owed sixty *livres*. He brought a case against Vernier to the court in Épernay to try to force him to pay but the case became too expensive for Noel, a father of nine children, to pursue. He ended up dropping his complaint and just accepted the loss of his money.[83]

One of Vernier's female servants, Nicolle De L'Epine, also testified that she had received poor treatment from her employer. She worked for him for about fourteen months, although she said that she had wanted to leave once her original contract year was up because Vernier had hit her and mistreated her. But he made her stay for an extra two months and then subtracted a sum of eighteen *livres* from her wages for dishes that he claimed she had broken, although she insisted they had been broken before she arrived. De L'Epine ended her testimony by saying that the curé was a hard and difficult man and that he had treated her like a harlot. A male servant, Simon Charlemagne, also described his employer as a hard man. Charlemagne's wife, living in another village, was expecting a baby at one point while he was working for Vernier, and the curé had promised him that he would be able to go and be with her during her confinement. Vernier allowed him to leave when the time came, but when

Charlemagne's wife experienced difficulties he asked for three more days off; because of this, Vernier docked his pay by nine *livres* – three times the amount that he would have earned in those three days.[84]

Vernier's most unhappy servant (among the males anyway; as we shall see, the female servants had more to complain about than perhaps anyone else in the entire village) was Claude Descottes, who worked for the curé from April to August of 1765. At the time, Descottes would have been only seventeen or eighteen, and he was a newcomer to the parish. Vernier told the young man to harvest a certain piece of land. But the field contained only a small amount of grain, and the rest was grass that the curé had abandoned. Its only value would have been for animal feed. At least, that's what Descottes thought, until Vernier told him to wait until dark and then cut the grass and bring it back to the curé's property. Simon Charlemagne, Vernier's other servant at the time, told Descottes that he should not cut the grass because the curé was going to tell everyone that the grass had been stolen by "certain people." So Descottes disobeyed his master and left the grass alone.

The next day Descottes and the other workers went to work in the fields as usual, and when they returned for lunch the curé gave Descottes bread and water while everyone else got wine and cheese with their bread. The curé told him that this is what he would get until he obeyed. Upset, Descottes demanded his wages, intending to leave the curé's service. The curé went to say mass but when he returned he searched Descottes out and was about to beat him with a stick when Vernier's sister (and housekeeper) prevented him from doing so. Then Vernier ordered Descottes to go back to work, and Descottes complied because, he testified, he was afraid of what the curé would do to him if he did not. That evening when he came back for the evening meal, the curé told him that he had worked so hard that he should go straight to bed without supper; rest was more important than food. Three days later Descottes finally left and went to his brother's in a nearby village. Still hopeful of collecting his wages, he returned to the presbytery the next day, but when he asked for his money the curé hit him three times with a stick and would have continued if Vernier's sister had not once again intervened. Descottes had no choice but to gather his things and leave without his wages. Descottes ended his testimony by saying that it had been five years and the curé still had not paid him.[85]

Marie Nicolle Baudier also testified that the curé had refused to pay for services her husband had provided, in this case, work in his vines. But she emphasized in her testimony that it was the "bad faith" on the part of the curé that disturbed her more than anything else. She explained that there had been a dispute over what her husband, Claude Mayeux, was to be paid because the original contract had been lost in a fire. Baudier appealed to Vernier's position as curé and told him that even if the record was lost, his conscience was not, and he should make good on the agreement. Baudier and Mayeux continued to work for two more years for the curé, and he owed them twelve *livres*. During that time Baudier went for confession with the curé, and because of their disagreement over wages, Vernier refused to give her absolution. Seeing the bad faith on the part of the curé, she decided not to go to him for confession after that, but when she sent her daughter to get a *billet* for her, he refused that as well.[86]

Not surprisingly, Vernier also argued with the churchwardens over money. Any property owned by the parish, in the form of lands, endowments, or buildings, was known as the *fabrique*, and each parish chose at least one or two churchwardens to administer the income generated by the property. Curés obviously had a vested interest in the administration of the *fabrique*, and conflicts could easily occur.[87] For example, Charles Mayeux served as churchwarden for Mareuil-sur-Ay in 1755, and when he was doing the accounts at the end of the year he realized that the curé had not yet paid thirty-five *livres* in rent for a piece of land belonging to the *fabrique* that he had leased. As churchwarden Mayeux had to use thirty-five *livres* of his own money to balance the accounts, and ever since then, he and his wife had been trying unsuccessfully to collect the debt from Vernier. Just a week before giving testimony, Mayeux's wife asked Vernier about the debt once again, and he told her that he had not had time to reconcile his accounts (apparently he needed longer than fifteen years) but once he had done so, and was certain that he owed the money, he would pay.[88]

*Affairs with Women*

The final difficulty with Vernier, according to his parishioners, was that he had failed to keep his vow of celibacy by engaging in affairs with several women. One of these was a female cousin who lived with him in the presbytery. Few French curés actually lived alone – in fact, they often maintained rather large households, including other clergy (vicaires or visiting priests and monks), relatives, and servants, both male and female. Vernier seems to have regularly employed a number of live-in servants of both sexes who performed agricultural labour as well as the usual household tasks of cooking and cleaning. Until the end of 1764, Vernier's sister Reine lived with him, governing the household and providing help and company for her brother. But Reine died a few days before Christmas that year, so sometime around Easter in 1765 two other women arrived to take charge of Vernier's household – another sister, and a so-called cousin.

A so-called cousin, because the people of the parish did not believe that she was his cousin at all and found the familiarity of their relationship troubling. Most of the testimony in this matter comes from Vernier's servants, who were obviously in a position to witness much that went on in the household. First of all, they noted that the cousin's bedroom was right next to Vernier's bedroom. For awhile, Pierre Philippot testified, the cousin and the sister had shared a room on the floor above the curé's room, but then for unknown reasons the cousin had moved downstairs. Even more disturbingly, the cousin's new room was just a small chamber at the back of Vernier's room. It had no other entrance into a hallway or to any other room in the house; to get to her bed, the cousin had to pass through Vernier's bedroom. This struck the servants as odd, and the parishioners did not like it much either.[89]

Servant Simon Charlemagne testified that he had been an eyewitness to the "familiarities" that the curé had with his cousin. He said that Vernier treated her like a lover or a mistress, putting his hand on her bosom and kissing her. Claude Descottes told the court that he had seen the pair walking in the garden together many times and that they sat together for meals. He also said that she and Vernier had kissed each other in his presence and in front of Charlemagne as well. This behaviour was also upsetting to Vernier's sister; Charlemagne said that at times the sister was so disturbed that she had to get up and leave the room. Descottes described Vernier's sister as a wise and moderate woman but lamented that she had been relegated to second-class status by the arrival of the cousin. Philippot said that the sister actually spoke to him about this, complaining that her brother had lavished all of his affection on the cousin and had none left for her.[90] Parishioner François Durand gave secondhand testimony about the curé and his cousin; he said that he had run into one of Vernier's former servants in Paris on one occasion, and she had told him that she had actually caught the pair in the act. Instead of appearing ashamed, or trying to hide what had happened, the cousin had simply showed the servant a gold watch and said that the curé had given it to her as a present, for the "game" that they played. She told the servant that if she wanted to play the same game, she could expect the same kind of reward.[91]

If these witnesses were telling the truth, then it seems that Vernier had found at least one woman who was willing to engage in a sexual relationship with him. Unfortunately, he also harassed and assaulted other women – his female servants – and they were, as far as we can tell, unwilling participants. Marie Jeanne Bellot and her husband, Denis Pierre, the curé's neighbours, observed some of these misdeeds. Pierre told the court that Vernier treated his servants badly, with regard to "morals and chastity." Bellot gave more graphic descriptions of things that she had seen and heard; for example, one afternoon she was doing a collection for the church and went to the presbytery to speak with Vernier. While there, she looked into a room and saw a woman lying on a bed, while the curé was walking around the room. Another time Bellot saw a young girl leaning on Vernier's bed, her face close to Vernier's face, and her hands "who knows where." Bellot also told the court that one day she encountered one of the curé's servants exiting the presbytery with a bundle of clothes under her arm, indicating that she was leaving for good. Bellot was surprised, since she knew this particular servant had only been in service there for about a month. When asked, the woman told Bellot that when she had been married she had not had any children, but now that she was a widow she certainly did not want to make any bastards with the curé. Bellot's daughter, Antoinette Elizabeth Pierre, was also a frequent witness to the curé's indiscretions; she testified that once she overheard an argument between the curé and his sister, Reine. During the argument Reine told her brother that if she was able to get along fine without a man, then he could very well get along without a woman. Evidently, she was wrong on this point.[92]

Marguerite Thérèse Lamarle testified that the curé had tried to seduce her when she was his servant, saying that he had put his hands on her "in lust." But, she told the court, she was an honest girl and had always preserved her virtue, despite these assaults. Claudette Gérard gave secondhand testimony about another servant, age seventeen or eighteen, who had suffered through a similar experience; the curé had instructed her to warm his bed with a warming pan but then when he got in the bed he tried to make her touch him inappropriately. Marie Thomas, a servant of Pierre Trubert, testified that she had heard from another servant of Vernier's that one night Vernier had come to her room completely naked. She was horribly afraid but managed to escape to another room and she left the curé's service the next day. *Vigneron* Rémy Poncelet testified that Vernier had once hired him to drive one of his servants to Châlons-sur-Marne where she was going to look for another position. On the drive, the woman complained about the way that Vernier had treated her, saying that he had wanted her to come into his room at night when he was in bed. Poncelet said that the woman had wanted to tell him more details, but that he had no desire to hear anything else and asked her to stop talking about it for the remainder of the drive.[93]

Bellot and Pierre also testified about Vernier's treatment of another servant. They told the court that her name was Marie and that she was from a nearby village. One day they saw Vernier chasing Marie through his yard; she was screaming, and he had a stick in his hands. She tried to hide under a piece of farm equipment, but he succeeded in dragging her out by her legs and began beating her. Later, Marie sought out both Pierre and Bellot and told them that Vernier had beat her because she had tried to refuse his sexual advances. She implied that Vernier had raped her – although she did not say so directly. Either that, or neither Pierre nor Bellot wanted to speak openly to the court about such an upsetting matter. Their description of what Marie told them leaves little to the imagination, however. She said that Vernier came into her room and threw her violently onto the floor. He put a handkerchief in her mouth to stop her from screaming. "You are a stupid fool," he said; "It's fine for anyone to do this, priests used to be married; there is nothing bad in it, and I know better than you." Despite her protests, she was not able to get away, and "he did what he wanted."[94]

As troubling as this story is, it did not get much attention during the court case. Instead, the court and the witnesses went into great detail trying to figure out exactly what had happened to another servant, Marie Madeleine Appert. Appert, the daughter of Jean Appert and Marie Gougelet of Athis, came to work as a servant for Vernier in 1762, when she was twenty-six years old. At some point the curé's other servants began noticing that the curé and Appert were closer than they

should have been. Pierre Philippot said that once on a Sunday afternoon he went looking for the curé and found him in his bedroom,
asleep in his chair, with Appert resting her head in his lap. Appert gave
him a silent signal that he should leave, so he did. Simon Charlemagne
testified that he saw the two laughing together in the curé's garden
and that the curé "handled her breast the way a husband would."
Another time he was going up the stairs and had a view through a window into the curé's room and saw the pair kissing beside the bed.
Charlemagne said he was so surprised that he just kept walking, not
wanting to be a witness to any more of their caresses.[95]

Charlemagne also gave details about a bit of bed-swapping that was
taking place in the presbytery while Appert was in service there. He
said that the curé assigned him to sleep in three different rooms at different points in time during his employment. Once, according to the
curé's orders, he slept for three nights in Appert's bed, not knowing
where she slept or even what bed would be available for her. One of
those nights he had a toothache that kept him from sleeping, and
since his room was right next to the curé's he could hear the curé and
Appert laughing and chatting together. Charlemagne also said that
around this time Appert fell ill, and the curé did everything he could
to help her, bringing her soup and wine, even though there were others in the house who could have done it.

Appert's mother was also suspicious of her daughter's conduct,
according to secondhand testimony (Gougelet did not testify in the
1770 *information*). Marie Madeleine Fournier, a servant for the Salmon
family, told the court that during a conversation that took place in
Gougelet's home the widow had told her that she knew that Vernier
"lived badly" with her daughter. Gougelet said that she had spent the
night at the presbytery once, and in the morning she had noticed that
there was a cord running between Appert's room and the curé's room,
which would open and close the door. Marie Jeanne Jacquot (Jacquot)
testified that Gougelet had been even clearer with her suspicions in
their conversations, indicating that during her visits to the presbytery
she had actually seen Vernier in bed with her daughter.[96]

Finally, the inevitable happened. Appert became pregnant – or at
least that is what the witnesses believed. Charlemagne said that at the
end of March 1765 he started noticing that Appert had a look about
her that women get when they are expecting. Others in the village
began noticing Appert's condition as well: Marie Nicolle Baudier testified that she saw the girl getting water in the curé's garden and

could see that her belly was growing. Baudier estimated that she must have been at least four or five months pregnant.[97] The plaintiffs noted in their complaint that in mid-May 1765 Appert had been to Athis to visit her mother, and many people that she saw during her visit believed that she was pregnant.[98]

But perhaps the most damning testimony came from a surgeon from Avenay, Nicolas Fortemps.[99] Fortemps was regularly called in by Vernier to look after his servants when they were sick (in fact, Fortemps complained during his testimony that Vernier owed him forty *écus* for treatments and medicines), and he had been asked to treat Appert as well. He said that when he first examined her he thought she had a menstrual problem, but over time he began to realize that she was pregnant. She had never said to him that she suspected a pregnancy, and they never spoke of it, but he continued to treat her as though she were. He also testified that the girl told him that Vernier mistreated her often and violently, and he saw that she had sustained bruises as a result of this abuse.

Fortemps seems to have told other inhabitants of Mareuil-sur-Ay that Appert was pregnant, and the rumours spread throughout the region. The gossip only got worse when suddenly Appert disappeared. Vernier's servant Claude Descottes described how it happened in his testimony. He claimed that two or three weeks before Pentecost both he and Appert were sick. Vernier sent for Fortemps, who bled Descottes but not Appert. Descottes thought this was unusual, and he believed that it was because she was pregnant. Then two days before Pentecost Appert did not come out of her room for meals according to her usual habit. She was, however, seen crying in different parts of the house, and she came to the kitchen for food at odd hours. On the day of Pentecost, she did not attend the mass. But she did have some lunch, and that was when she told Descottes that she was very unhappy and miserable. Then she disappeared again. After the curé returned from services, he asked Descottes if he had seen her, and the servant told Vernier that she had eaten some bread and had had some wine before hiding again. The curé told him to call her, but still she did not appear. The next day the curé gave Descottes a letter to take to the vicaire of a neighbouring parish to ask about getting another servant, and when he came back in the evening he learned that Appert was gone.[100] The rumour in the parish was that Vernier had gotten a man named Le Clerc, one of the servants of the curé of Chouilly, to take Appert away in the middle of the night, and that she had ended up in a hospital in Paris where she died some time later.

With this final, damning evidence – that Vernier had broken his vow of celibacy, impregnated a servant, and sent her off to Paris – the plaintiffs in the case believed that they had shown that their curé was deficient in nearly every possible way. He failed to say the mass. He misused his power in the confessional. He insulted the sick and the dying instead of comforting them. He was violent and treated servants, children, the poor, and the elderly with contempt instead of Christian charity. He failed to pay his bills, was dishonest in nearly every type of financial affair he was involved in, and corrupted his servants. Surely the villagers must have been confident that the ecclesiastical administrators of the diocese and the *officialité* would recognize that Vernier was unfit to maintain his position and give the people of Mareuil-sur-Ay a new curé whom they could trust and respect.

But they did not. At the end of the case, despite the 600 pages of testimony against him, Nicolas Hyacinthe Vernier was reinstated as curé of Mareuil-sur-Ay.

# Parishioners, Also Behaving Badly

The majority of the parish would be easy to govern if it weren't for a dozen bad subjects who recognize no authority, and destroy by their pernicious advice and examples all the good that a pastor might do.[1]

Nicolas Hyacinthe Vernier, curé of Mareuil-sur-Ay

Since Nicolas Hyacinthe Vernier was not removed as curé of Mareuil-sur-Ay in 1772 when his case was completed, and since he was still serving as curé in 1774, when he made the above statement, the story told in chapter 1 now seems incomplete. The remainder of the book will probe more deeply into the relationship between Vernier and his parishioners and attempt to explain why the diocesan administration did not remove him from his position after his long and very public trial. Since the court interrogated Vernier at length after they heard depositions from the villagers, we get his side of the story as well. It turns out that he was able to provide some reasonable excuses for his actions as well as demonstrate to the court that his parishioners were far from innocent themselves. Parishioners sometimes behaved as badly as curés did; the realities of Catholicism in rural parishes were shaped by both clergy and laity in that respect. It is tempting to see the story as being about a faithless curé and his parishioners' attempt to remove him from his position, but in fact it is about expectations for religious life on the part of both the clergy and the laity and how those expectations were met or unmet. It should not surprise us that conflict could be the result of attempts to realize differing visions for religious practice in rural parishes, and those conflicts reveal a great deal about what religion meant in the eighteenth century.

*Vernier Gets to Have His Say*

In his interrogation, Vernier provided a number of excuses for his failure to say the mass, which was, according to his parishioners, a major
breach in their relationship and in the fulfillment of his duties. The
priest's most important job was, after all, to celebrate the mass for his
parishioners. The mass could only be performed by an ordained
priest, although he did require the help of deacons, subdeacons, altar
boys, or, especially in rural parishes, schoolmasters, if no other clergy
could be found. If he was sick or absent, then he had to find someone
else to say the mass in his place: a vicaire, a member of a religious
order, or another curé. Other masses might be performed throughout
the week, but no matter what, the mass had to be celebrated each Sunday and each feast day.

   On the whole, curés were not really required to do that much in
terms of masses: they had to perform just one or two per week,
depending on the number of feast days. They might do more – a lot
more, in fact – but they were often paid extra for these services. If
parishioners wanted more than one mass said on Sundays, or if they
wanted masses said on working days, then in some cases they had to
pay the priest for those masses. Many people also wanted masses said
for their souls after they died, and these had to be paid for too, usually through legacies left in their wills. But every Sunday and every feast
day, the curé was required as part of his benefice to perform one mass
in his church, no matter what. That meant that rural Catholics took
the official Sunday and feast day masses very seriously. These were the
services they had a right to, as Christians and as tithe payers. The laity
knew this, and they wanted their curés to perform these masses properly and according to long-established local traditions. Villagers also
knew that if they told the authorities that there had been no mass in
their parish on a Sunday or a feast day, it would get their attention. In
their testimonies the people of Mareuil-sur-Ay claimed, as we saw in
chapter 1, that their curé was not following either tradition or diocesan rules by holding the mass and vespers at odd hours or by failing
to say the mass at all.

   Vernier, however, repeatedly insisted that he had always fulfilled his
duties and functions as a curé – as much as his health allowed.[2] He
explained to the court that he regularly suffered from illnesses as a

result of a weak chest and that he had to have the vicaire say his masses for him as a result. Cold weather aggravated his chest condition, he stated, and if he spoke for too long in cold air then he would start coughing up blood. Colds and fevers sometimes left him unable to leave his bed in the winter, but these illnesses did not automatically make him derelict in his duties, he insisted; if he could not say mass or preach, he always made sure that another priest or the vicaire filled in for him. Ordinarily, he noted, the main mass was at nine and vespers was at three but for some time the clock in the village had not been working properly, so this may have led to errors in the timing of services. He further explained that he sometimes altered the prescribed starting times for services not to cause irritation but rather because he was trying to accommodate the needs of his parishioners. He had also, on some occasions, changed the times for mass and especially vespers because he had had other duties to perform, like administering the sacraments to a sick person or hearing confessions. Certainly the court would have to agree, he insisted, that he could not leave a parishioner in the middle of a confession just because vespers was supposed to begin. Another common accommodation he made was to hold off ringing the bell for vespers until five during harvest time, to give people more daylight to work in their fields. Again, he insisted, he was simply trying to accommodate the needs of the people despite the fact that they rarely seemed willing to offer him the same accommodation.

As far as instructions at worship services were concerned, he testified that he read from the *rituel* as much as he could at vespers, but not at mass because of his weak chest and his tendency to cough up blood. The vicaire did the readings for him, he said, and he indicated that they were therefore done just as frequently as in his colleagues' parishes in the region. With regard to sermons, he admitted that he rarely preached because an illness he had suffered as a student in Paris had caused a lingering impairment in his memory that made memorizing sermons impossible. During Advent and Lent he brought in preachers on Sundays and feast days, either vicaires or other priests, to make up for what he could not do himself.

The plaintiffs, as might be expected, refused to accept this excuse – in the *memoire* they had printed after the first *information*, they noted that in general Vernier was "very vigorous." When he did perform the mass he had a good, loud voice; they argued that his complaint about a weak chest was thus only another one of his lies.[3] If we give Vernier

the benefit of the doubt, however, and if his condition was only aggravated at certain times and under specific circumstances, this would
explain the inconsistencies in his preaching habits. It is also possible
that if witnesses were biased against Vernier, they might have underreported the amount of instruction being done in the parish, since
they knew that the ecclesiastical leaders might be willing to listen to
their complaints on this issue more than others.

Vernier's excuses about the timing for services are not unusual either;
the hours for services were irregular everywhere. By the eighteenth century most parishes probably had their own clocks, so there was no
excuse on that front for not starting mass at regular hours.[4] However,
curés might have their own reasons for altering the prescribed times.
Just like Vernier, Nicolas Hourblin (curé of the parish of Muizon, diocese of Reims) was accused of changing the time of the mass according
to his own whims, and Hourblin gave the same response to this accusation: he said that he only changed the hour when his parishioners
asked him to, usually during harvest time.[5] Out of the three dozen cases
examined here, twenty-one involved some accusation of irregularities at
mass or other church services. If every priest whose parishioners complained about late masses had lost his job, there would have been few
curés left. Some curés gave excuses for missing or late masses that
would hardly be considered legitimate: Jean François Coyer, for example, told his parishioners that there would be no mass in his annex,
Sécheval (Reims), one Sunday because there was a furniture sale taking
place in a nearby village and he wanted to go to that instead.[6] Compared with this excuse, Vernier's insistence that his health was to blame
for his absences seems much more acceptable.

When it came to the administration of the sacraments, Vernier continued to argue that he had always done his duty as best he could. Cit-
ing his poor health, he explained that there had been times when he
had been forced to rely on his vicaires or other priests to perform the
sacraments if he was indisposed.[7] This is what he maintained had
happened during the last illness of Jean Salmon, just a few months
before the beginning of the court case. The Salmon family and the
plaintiffs in the case cited Vernier's refusal to visit Salmon and hear
his confession during his last illness as one of their major complaints.
Vernier insisted that he himself had been sick at the time, but that
besides that he had never been Salmon's regular confessor, and no
one had ever asked him to visit. Once Vernier learned "from the pub-

lic" that Salmon was sick, he sent the vicaire to see him on three different occasions to find out if he needed the sacraments, but the vicaire was always told that his services were not required. Vernier noted that both a doctor and a surgeon had been to visit Salmon, who had reported to the vicaire that the illness was not a dangerous one. Then, about two months after the vicaire's first visit, Salmon suddenly and unexpectedly lost consciousness. The family asked the vicaire to come, and he did, but since Salmon was unconscious the vicaire could only give him the last rites without confession or communion. He died about an hour later. Vernier insisted that he had instructed his vicaire to let him know if Salmon asked for him, and that he was willing to administer the sacraments despite his own poor health. But, he told the court, neither the family nor Salmon himself had ever asked for him.[8]

Vernier repeatedly proclaimed his innocence when it came to his treatment of other sick and dying parishioners as well. His most common justification was that many of the people who complained about his failure to visit them had not actually been his penitents. Early modern Catholics often visited just one confessor, rather than confessing with any priest who was available; they might choose the curé as their primary confessor, or a vicaire, or some other priest in the area, depending on their personal preferences. So when Vernier insisted that some of his parishioners had always confessed with the vicaire or another priest, he could easily have been telling the truth. This was his response to questioning about Jeanne Hennequin, the wife of plaintiff Christophe Robert. Her relatives insisted that the curé had been her confessor, but Vernier said that Hennequin had not been his penitent for a long time; instead, she had been confessing with the vicaire, who had gone to see her regularly during the course of her illness. He gave a similar excuse in the cases of Claudette Prunet and her daughter Scholastique Duval, who had also complained that the curé had refused to hear their confessions when they were ill.[9]

In another instance, Vernier claimed that the family of the sick person should have been looking at their own treatment of their so-called loved one instead of complaining about their curé. When he visited Catherine Adam's father, he said, he told the family that it would be better for the sick man (both in terms of his health and for the dignity of the sacraments) if they moved him to a larger and more decent room. He said he had found Rémy Adam lodged in a tiny, uncomfortable, and unhealthy closet and had only been concerned for the man's welfare.[10] Other problems with the sacraments had arisen because of circumstances beyond his control, Vernier insisted. For example, he claimed that it was not his fault at all that Rémy Poncelet had been forced to search several villages for a priest to baptize his infant sons. Vernier explained that he had gone to Reims to meet with the vicars-general about getting a new vicaire, since the previous one had accepted a position elsewhere, and when he returned he found out about the twins' birth. He regretted his "forced absence" but still felt that he was in no way responsible for the fact that one of the babies had only received temporary baptism from the midwife before he died. He noted that he buried the child with the appropriate ceremonies the next day.[11]

But these issues were only the tip of the iceberg when it came to Vernier's administration of the sacraments. Could he really argue that all of the parishioners who complained that he tried to deny them absolution for inappropriate reasons were lying? As were all of those who told the court that he used the confessional for personal gain? In some cases, it is possible that yes, his parishioners were lying – or perhaps exaggerating. We must allow for this possibility, simply because of the nature of confessional practice itself. What went on in the confessional was supposed to be entirely private. The seal of the confessional was taken seriously by everyone, both clergy and laity. The clergy knew that if they violated the seal of the confessional and revealed the sins of their penitents then no one would ever be willing to confess.[12] As much as priests might have wanted to report the misdeeds that they heard in the confessional to the authorities or even just to other people in the parish, they could not. Any information learned in the confessional was strictly off limits.

In fact, in the cases examined here, only one priest was accused of violating the seal of the confessional. A man named Grivel from a village close to Ruffey (Besançon), where Gabriel Mottet was curé, told the court that he had put up some boundary markers on his property that were later mysteriously removed. Mottet came to him and said that he knew who was responsible. Grivel asked him how he knew who it was, and the curé said that "he knew it from the place that is the most secret," giving Grivel every reason to believe that he had learned it from the confessional.[13] No other witnesses, in any other case, made similar claims about their curés. Violations of the confessional seal were, it seems, uncommon; the laity did not complain about it, and the diocesan administrators did not feel they even had to ask about it.

When parishioners told the court what had happened when they confessed with Vernier, they could easily lie or exaggerate and there would be no way to prove they were being dishonest. At the same time, when Vernier was interrogated about infractions that his parishioners claimed he had made within that private and holy space, he also had a ready-made and entirely believable excuse that was difficult for anyone to effectively contradict: he simply denied that those infractions had ever taken place. He told the court that he had never tried to use his powers as a confessor inappropriately. He insisted that he had never asked any questions within the tribunal of penitence except for those that were relevant to the exercise of his ministry. He said that he had never denied anyone absolution because they sold wine – although he admitted that he might have urged wine-sellers to consider the disorders that they caused in the parish because of their business.

Vernier insisted that he had not influenced his vicaires to deny absolution to anyone in the parish either – in fact he claimed he had never forbidden his vicaires anything that had to do with the exercise of their ministry. He may have warned them of some of the problems of his parishioners so that appropriate actions might be taken, but he had never told them to categorically refuse anyone absolution for any reason whatsoever. He was adamant that there was no truth to Marie Margueritte Salmon's story that he had denied her and her siblings absolution and first communion because she had not been willing to do a collection for a confraternity. Court officials asked about it twice, and each time he responded that the accusation was completely without foundation. And he certainly had not asked François Durand for a plate of fish in exchange for absolution, he said, further insisting that he had never asked for anything as a payment for his duties in the confessional.[14]

Vernier also told the court that he had not tried to deny other priests the opportunity to hear the confessions of his parishioners. There had been some difficulties at times with some of the missionary priests who had tried to restrain his rights in the confessional, but he had never forbidden them from hearing confessions altogether. He did indicate that because there were only two confessionals in the church it was not always possible for other priests to hear confessions in Mareuil-sur-Ay, since he and his vicaire both occupied the space.

But he had never purposely tried to deny them access to the confessionals at times when they were not being used.[15] He also insisted that he gave *billets* freely to his parishioners when they requested them, and that they always conformed to the rules of the diocese. The only time he remembered denying anyone a *billet* was once when one of the Billecarts came to ask for one on Holy Thursday right before an evening sermon for which the parish was already assembled. He told Billecart that he would have to wait until after the service, but Billecart never came back. Vernier claimed that he had never used damaging language in the *billets* (and asked the court to produce one of these *billets* if they wanted to prove that they existed) and suggested that if people were refused by other priests it was because of their sins and not because of what he had written. The vicaire's testimony corroborated this – Jean Louis Harlin said that indeed the curé wrote *billets* in Latin, but he had read several himself and none of them contained anything injurious or derisory.[16]

Marie Magdelaine Calixte Cazin, the widow of the merchant Louis Salmon, testified in the *information* that once on a Holy Thursday Vernier had told the entire parish that someone had done a sacrilegious communion at the mass earlier that morning. Cazin indicated that everyone knew Vernier had been referring to the surgeon, Desiré Cuiret. Vernier had a reasonable response to this serious accusation, however. He admitted that once, as was his right, he had indeed gone to the pulpit to tell his parishioners that one among them had caused a great scandal by taking communion without having completed a proper confession. But, he said, it would have been impossible for anyone to know whom he was talking about. First of all, he insisted, there was no early mass in Mareuil-sur-Ay on Holy Thursday. It had simply never been a part of their regular services. Furthermore, even if there had been an early mass, there would have been more than just one person who took communion: elderly people, pregnant women, or people with weak stomachs would have attended that mass. So, when he condemned the sacrilegious person from the pulpit, he had been talking about someone who had taken communion at the main mass, along with many other communicants. Since he had given his condemnation anonymously, he felt he was justified in his actions.[17]

Vernier also insisted that if he had denied absolution to some of his parishioners, it was with good reason, but he could not give that reason to the court because of the sanctity of the confessional. For example, *vigneron* Helain Coinon complained that the curé tried to exact a

payment of twenty-four *sous* from him because he had not participated in Ash Wednesday services, and then when he could not pay he
was denied absolution and Easter communion for two years. Vernier,
when asked about this, said that he felt he was within his rights to
keep silent on the issue and should not be asked to explain what goes
on in the tribunal of penitence. If Coinon had not done his Easter
communion for two years, it was because he had not been in a state
to do it, he argued. Similarly, Pierre Blondeau testified that the curé
had sent him away without absolution seven different times because
he would not admit that he was responsible for the pregnancy of a
girl in the village. As a result of this, he was unable to do his *paques*
for four years. Vernier again responded that he was not at liberty to
say what went on in the confessional but that he had never gone
against the rules prescribed by the diocese about church discipline.[18]

Vernier thus portrayed himself as a conscientious priest who was
striving to fulfill his functions as best he could despite his struggles
with poor health and a general difficulty with public speaking. Problems might occur, but they did in all parishes with a busy curé. If he
was unable to perform some required aspect of his ministry, then he
got another priest to replace him. He (and his vicaire) admitted that
he sometimes conformed only to the letter of the law and that it was
unlikely he would do more than what he was paid for, but he would
not admit to dereliction in his prescribed duties. As to the other
infractions cited in the *information* and then investigated by the court,
Vernier claimed they had simply not happened. He was, he insisted,
the victim of the worst kind of slander – his parishioners had banded
together to drag his name through the mud and damage his reputation in the community. He had found sinners in his parish, and when
he tried to bring them to repentance they rebelled against him and
instigated the court case. Instead of changing their ways, as God and
the church dictated, they were trying to change their curé.

## A Conspiracy of Enemies

At this point, some background on the composition of rural villages
may help us in our examination of Vernier's claims of conspiracy and
scandal. Who exactly were these "enemies," who seemed to hate their
curé so much? In the eighteenth century there was no typical village
in France, or even in the region of Champagne, where Mareuil-sur-Ay
was located, but we can sketch some general characteristics of rural

communities that might help us answer this question. Somewhere between half and three-quarters of the rural populations across France were primarily involved in agriculture.[19] At the bottom of the social scale were people who worked only for wages and had no land, either owned or leased. Slightly better off were those who were able to secure a small plot of land through a lease; they farmed this land and probably worked for other farmers for wages as well. In Mareuil-sur-Ay, most of the agricultural land was devoted to vines, and the term *vigneron* would have included wage-workers and leaseholders. The *laboureurs* were their betters, both economically and socially. They leased (or in a few cases owned) the largest tracts of land and had the necessary animals and equipment to work it. The landowner was known as the *seigneur*, and he leased the land to farmers of all sorts. The *seigneur* might have been a nobleman or a member of the bourgeois classes, but the title also came with legal and judicial rights over peasants. Religious orders served as *seigneurs* as well. A village like Mareuil-sur-Ay would also have had a number of artisans and tradesmen, like masons, shoemakers, carpenters, and coopers. Many of the *laboureurs* would have employed servants, so they were always present in the village as well. Further up the social ladder, moving into elite status, were merchants, lawyers, government officials, and surgeons. Almost no one did just one thing for a living – agricultural workers might be involved with the textile industry and do piecework at home during the off season, while artisans might still engage in farm work or in more than one trade. *Laboureurs* were also merchants in some cases, and men of all sorts of professions might own land even if they did not work it themselves.[20]

Social status in the village was not determined entirely by profession; it was just one of a whole host of categories that contributed to one's social standing in the community. As I have examined elsewhere, schoolmasters often held an important social position within their villages, for example, and even considered themselves on par with the *laboureurs* although their income was certainly much lower.[21] As we will see below, family and marital ties were also significant in determining social status, as were the ties created by various institutions and activities, such as residence in hamlets or neighbourhoods, membership in religious, professional, or trade organizations, godparent relationships, or simple sociability. A congenial evening at the cabaret with a stranger might lead to a long-lasting personal relationship, or a wage labourer might create a significant social tie with the farmer he worked for, even though he was clearly inferior economically.

At the same time, there were also plenty of opportunities for rifts and enmities to open up between members of the same community – again, regardless of economic standing. A village like Mareuil-sur-Ay would have experienced constantly shifting loyalties between families and individuals over time, and the curé might have ended up right in the middle of them. Some of the rifts might have lasted for lifetimes, while others fizzled out within a few weeks. Because of these complex and shifting loyalties, it would be much too simplistic to argue that all of Vernier's parishioners were his enemies, all of the time, but some of them surely were. Some of Vernier's enemies may have become enemies not because of anything that had happened to them personally but simply because of their ties, socioeconomic or other-wise, with other members of the parish who did have significant problems with their curé.[22] The reasons why certain people lined up against Vernier are actually less interesting to me than the fact that all kinds of grievances, whether social, economic, political, or religious, ended up playing out within the religious sphere. This demonstrates the centrality of religion in these parishes as a community function. Whatever role religion played in people's personal lives (about which we can know very little) it still played an important public function, and disagreements over just about anything could easily be displayed in sites normally reserved for religion.[23]

The ninety-five witnesses who gave depositions to the court repre-sent a good cross section of Mareuil-sur-Ay's adults, even if the demo-graphics by themselves do not give us any clues as to why these indi-viduals might have been Vernier's enemies. Fifty-one were men and forty-four were women.[24] The youngest witness was age sixteen, and the oldest was eighty-two; the average age of all witnesses was forty-two. Thirty were living outside of Mareuil-sur-Ay at the time of the case, but fourteen of these had once been residents of Mareuil-sur-Ay or servants for Vernier. Others had been involved in various activities with Vernier, either as surgeons or as farmers who worked for him. Occupations, listed in table 2.1, were given for ninety-one of the wit-nesses. Thirty (33 per cent) were *vignerons* (or the wives/widows of *vignerons*) and represent the largest category by far. The second largest category was made up of servants – there were eleven of those. Seven individuals listed their occupation as *tonnelier*, or coop-er, which is expected in a wine-making region like Mareuil-sur-Ay. A

Table 2.1   Occupations of the ninety-five witnesses in the Vernier case (1770)

| Occupation* | No. of witnesses |
| --- | --- |
| *Vigneron* | 30 |
| Servant | 11 |
| *Laboureur* | 9 |
| Cooper | 7 |
| Bargeman | 5 |
| Clergyman | 3 |
| Schoolmaster | 3 |
| Surgeon | 3 |
| Baker | 3 |
| Carpenter | 2 |
| Cobbler | 2 |
| Merchant | 2 |
| Dame | 2 |
| Mason | 1 |
| Butcher | 1 |
| Gardener | 1 |
| Locksmith | 1 |
| Military officer | 1 |
| Vinegar maker | 1 |
| Shepherd | 1 |
| Tailor | 1 |
| Innkeeper | 1 |
| Court official (*huissier royal*) | 1 |
| Unknown | 3 |

*Occupation of the witness, or the witness's husband or father

handful of other artisans testified as well, but at the top of the social hierarchy were two women listed simply as "dame," two merchants, a military officer, three clergymen (including the vicaire of Mareuil-sur-Ay and two curés from nearby parishes), and nine *laboureurs*. Witnesses thus represented every social category of the village – even a shepherd (*berger*). Some of them, perhaps even many of them, were Vernier's enemies.

As might be expected, curés commonly blamed their problems on a conspiracy of enemies when they appeared before the *officialité* court. Nicolas Dumontier, curé of Roupy (Noyon), told the court that he and all the previous curés of the village had been mistreated by the parishioners, because they were trying to "shake off the yoke" of any curé who tried to get them to reform. He insinuated, in a letter he wrote to the court, that this was the reason there was even a case in the first place – the people just wanted a curé who was more lenient with the church's rules.[25] As part of Dumontier's trial, the court conducted what was called a confrontation, during which witnesses and the curé had the chance to react to the other's testimony; this allowed Dumontier to give the court reasons why he believed specific witnesses should not be considered reliable:

- Pierre Billard testified against him out of enmity because of a previous lawsuit; he was also guilty of sleeping in church instead of praying.
- Louis Hennocque stays out late, once stabbed someone with a knife, and has no respect for the clergy or holy places.
- Charles Doitre has not done his Easter duty and refused to pay the tithe.
- Louis Cristophe blasphemed during an argument at the church.
- Marie Anne Landa wore a mask during carnival. She also goes to the cabaret on Sundays and feast days with young men, and he has had to reproach her and her parents about this many times. She lacks respect for holy things and for priests.
- Jeanne Martin had a child six months before her first marriage. Then, she had another child six months before her second marriage. She hardly ever attends mass or vespers.
- Eloy Deshumbles tried to keep 150 *livres* from the *fabrique* during his time as churchwarden; if the curé had not asked for a revision of the accounts he would have gotten away with it.[26]

Dumontier insisted multiple times that all of these people had poor character and only testified against him because of their spirit of animosity and vengeance. Presumably the court believed him; Dumontier was allowed to keep his parish after a brief stay of six weeks in the seminary.[27]

Another curé who tried to blame his problems on a conspiracy of enemies was Nicolas Hourblin of Muizon (Reims). He was accused of drinking in the cabarets, using obscene words, and committing acts of violence against his parishioners. Because of his drinking and his tendency to waste time playing games on feast days and Sundays, he neglected his duties. A long list of witnesses gave their testimony about Hourblin's infractions, but then Hourblin in turn gave a long list of the problems with those witnesses. In the confrontation, Hourblin named three people in the parish who were his greatest enemies. Then as he was confronted with each witness, he explained how that witness was connected to one or more of those individuals. He claimed that he was the victim of a conspiracy, and that his so-called wrongdoings were all invented or exaggerated.[28] Unlike in the Dumontier case, the court did not side with Hourblin; he was permanently removed from his parish and sentenced to six months in the diocesan seminary before he could be considered for another position elsewhere.[29] Similarly, Jean François Person, curé of Buzancy (Reims), also told the court that three parishioners had formed a cabal against him and slandered him. Person insisted that the parish was divided into two groups – those who supported him, and those who supported his enemies. One of these enemies, a former churchwarden, had publicly threatened the inhabitants of the community who were on the curé's side and kept them from testifying in his favour.[30] The court did not believe Person's excuses and sided with the parish; Person had to give up his position and was forbidden from possessing any other benefice charged with the care of souls in the diocese.[31]

These two curés were not able to successfully prove the existence of a conspiracy against them and lost their positions as a result. But there is also evidence to suggest that parishioners could – and did – purposely slander their curés. Perhaps these curés, as well as Vernier, were not making everything up. One especially interesting case from the diocese of Besançon demonstrates this. On 17 December 1744, Luc Vuillemin was interrogated by the *officialité*. Vuillemin was a *vigneron*, age thirty-five, and a resident of the village of Lods. The village did not have the status of parish; it was an annex served by the curé of Mouthier, Antoine Bullet.[32] Unfortunately, the people of Lods did not get along with Bullet, and some of the villagers, Vuillemin included, went so far as to physically assault their curé in the sacristy on one occasion. Here is Vuillemin's testimony about the event, as recorded by the court:

1 Asked if 16 August 1743, feast of Saint Théodule patron of Lod, after vespers which was celebrated in the chapel of Lod by Bullet, the people, animated by Nicolas Regnaud priest, surrounded the curé and elbowed him from all sides, and said to him that he did not know his catechism, or how many gods there

were, and that he would be better as a swineherd than a curé;
asked if he [Vuillemin] was among those surrounding the curé.

Responded that he doesn't know what happened after vespers because he wasn't there, he was at table with friends who
came to see him.

2 Asked if on 20 March last he attended the mass in the chapel of
Lod celebrated by the curé, and if the curé told the parishioners
that he was taking away the key to the tabernacle in order to
engage them to satisfy their Easter duty in the mother church
of Mouthier.

Responded that he did not attend this mass.

3 Asked if after this mass those who attended, and many other
people, assembled in front of the chapel to deliberate about the
ways to keep the curé from taking away the key, and if he was
part of this assembly.

Responded that if there was an assembly, he does not know
about it, and he was not part of it.

4 Asked if it was resolved at the assembly that they should not
allow the curé to take away the key to the tabernacle, and keep
him in the sacristy until the night, and if he [Vuillemin] said
that they should break his arms, or nail his hands to a board, or
go and ask him during the night to attend to a sick person, and
then wait for him on the road to kill him and bury him under
a rock if he refused to give up the key.

Responded that he did not hear any of this spoken.

5 Asked if then the curé was locked up in the sacristy by many
individuals, about ten or twelve, and if he [Vuillemin] put his
hand on the mouth of the curé to keep him from shouting, and
if he tried to put his hand in the curé's pocket to get the key,
and if he tore the curé's soutane.

Responded that he was not in any way involved and perpetrated no violence against the curé.

6 Asked if the curé, having been liberated, was followed through
the streets by many people who shouted all sorts of injurious
things at him.

Responded that he knows nothing.[33]

This is one of twelve very similar interrogations, all of residents of
Lods. All contain comparable denials and excuses – each man (all
twelve who were interrogated were men) said that he either had

attended mass and then gone straight home, taking no part in any assaults on the curé, or had not attended mass at all. Several said they were home in bed the whole time. Their responses were, like Vuillemin's, short, simple denials.[34] Unfortunately for these twelve men, there were eighteen other witnesses who described the attack on Bullet in detail, providing the narrative that the court used in the interrogations. These witnesses listed, again and again, the names of those who perpetrated the violence against the curé, including that of Vuillemin.[35]

It is clear to anyone who reads the documents of the case that these twelve men were lying. What happened to Bullet was a huge scandal: the entire village, and the surrounding villages, knew about it, and they knew exactly who was responsible for the attack. Yet the perpetrators insisted that they had not been involved. Not only that, they claimed they had not even heard about what had happened, an absolutely unbelievable assertion. It's not every day that a curé ends up locked in the sacristy, so everyone within a fifteen-mile radius of Lods and Mouthier would have heard something about this. They were lying, and everyone, including the court, knew it.

Why does this matter? Because if these men, faced with incontrovertible proof of their wrongdoing, still lied to the court, then we must also assume that other people – perhaps the inhabitants of Mareuil-sur-Ay – lied to the court too. What is at work here may be a political dynamic that goes beyond individual accusations and offences. If Vuillemin and his comrades could lie about something so grievous as assaulting a curé and plotting his death, it would have been easy for François Durand to lie to the court and say that Vernier had asked him for a plate of fish in exchange for absolution. After all, no one knew what passed between priest and parishioner in the confessional, so Durand would have known that it was simply his word against the curé's.

This incident also demonstrates that villagers might conspire together to get their curé into trouble for their own partisan reasons. The men of Lods probably agreed in advance of their interrogations that they would all lie and claim that they had not been at mass on the day that Bullet was attacked – some parishioners probably worked together in a variety of situations to try to get rid of curés they did not like. In another case, against Jean François Coyer, curé of Les Mazures and its annexes Sécheval and Anchamps (Reims), parishioners persuaded the curé to go shooting with them one day.[36] Coyer told the court that he did not usually use firearms (as this was against the rules) but since his parishioners insisted he had agreed to go out with them in a spirit of congeniality. His gun was not in a good state because of lack of use, so someone lent him one of theirs. He was testing it out and shot at a large rock. Immediately, a cry went up that the curé had shot someone – a young girl who had been passing by. Coyer thought this was a trap and took two men with him as witnesses to find out what had happened. They caught up with the girl, who was entirely uninjured. Crumbling under the curé's questions, she admitted that she had been stopped by a woman of the parish who had convinced her to lie and say that she had been shot. Initially, she agreed to the deception, but then because of her "honest nature," she told the curé, she could not continue with the lie.

This incident shows us that these parishioners, upset with their curé for a variety of reasons, tried to create a situation that would make him look bad and perhaps force his superiors to take action against him. First they lured him into breaking the rules by going shooting, and then they contrived to create a tragic accident that would certainly have brought in the authorities. However clumsy their attempt (even if the girl had stuck with her story it would have been difficult to prove that she had been shot by the curé without being able to show the authorities an actual wound), they had still conspired against Coyer. Perhaps some of the parishioners in Mareuil-sur-Aÿ had done the same thing.

This, it seems, was Vernier's main defence in the case brought by his parishioners against him. He argued repeatedly that some of his parishioners – his enemies, as he called them – were involved in a vast conspiracy to try to oust him from his benefice. These enemies included the ten plaintiffs in the case – the village notables and former churchwardens of the parish (see table 2.2). He told the court that he was nothing more than a priest trying to do his best with some difficult subjects. In fact, he said, his parishioners were so selfish and dishonest that they saw his attempts to help them and make them better Christians as attacks against them, and they twisted the meaning of his actions far from his actual intent. As for some of the worst accusations against him, either he insisted that the witnesses were lying or he provided alternate explanations for events that were often quite convincing. He steadfastly maintained his innocence

Table 2.2   The ten plaintiffs in the Vernier case (1770)

| Name | Occupation |
| --- | --- |
| Jean Baptiste Billecart | *Négociant* (merchant) |
| Nicolas Billecart | *Bourgeois* |
| Pierre Billecart | *Marchand voiturier par eau* (merchant) |
| Jean Joffrin | *Notaire & contrôleur des traittes* (notary) |
| Pierre Marlot | *Marchand commissionnaire de vin* (merchant) |
| Christophe Robert | Former *procureur fiscal* |
| Nicolas Christophe Robert | *Bourgeois* |
| Pierre François Robert | *Bourgeois* |
| Jean François Salmon | *Officier chez le Roi* (royal officer) |
| Pierre Trubert | None listed |

throughout his testimony, portraying himself as a conscientious curé who was never negligent in his duties.

At the same time, it would have been hard for the court to ignore the sheer volume of testimony about Vernier's bad behaviour. Even considering the legitimate justifications that Vernier gave, he still had to fall back on some version of "No, I didn't do that, my enemies are slandering me," again and again during his interrogation. Would the court really have believed that Vernier was the victim of a vast conspiracy? When we examine the testimony more closely, however, some of the witnesses' stories seem a bit dubious. For example, cooper Denis Pierre gave detailed testimony about an incident from Vernier's first years as curé, when the community ended up paying for work to be done on the schoolmistresses' house. They had removed a staircase and put bars over a window to prevent Vernier (their immediate neighbour) from gaining entry to the house. But Pierre was the only one to mention this. Why did no one else remember the fact that the curé had been sneaking into the schoolmistresses' house through a window? It is possible that the alterations to the house were made for a reason entirely unrelated to Vernier, and Pierre falsely laid the blame on his curé just to make him look bad.

Some of Pierre's other evidence seems questionable as well. He testified that one year a miller was renting a loft from the curé, in which he stored grain. The loft was bordered by the cemetery and by another building, also belonging to the curé. The miller came to Pierre and reported that the loft had been broken into, through the door that adjoined the curé's property. Pierre then sought out the curé's female servant and accused her of stealing the miller's grain. She put the blame back on the curé, saying that he had ordered her to break into the loft and transfer some of the miller's grain into the curé's stores. This certainly could have been a lie on the part of the servant. Pierre also testified that Vernier owed the miller sixty *livres* and the miller had a receipt that proved it. But that receipt suddenly disappeared, right about the time that the miller's wife died and the curé came to help sort out the property. The miller told Pierre that Vernier had taken all of his papers as part of this process, and the receipt had never been returned.[37]

All of this seems possible, but it is also easy to see how the court might not trust what Denis Pierre had to say since he was the only witness to these events. Vernier, of course, denied all of this, and no one else testified that the curé ever stole anything outright from them – he may have been less than honest when it came to tithe collection or paying wages, but Pierre's accusations here seem to go quite a bit beyond that. With events like this, it all came down to whether the court believed Pierre or Vernier. Given the outcome of the case, it seems they believed Vernier. In fact, they threw out Pierre's testimony altogether, along with his wife's, and the testimony of sixteen other witnesses (see table 2.3).[38]

French judges and court officials could reject testimony for a variety of reasons. Witnesses who had close family ties to or even close friendships with either party in the case, or who were known as enemies, could be rejected. Even witnesses who had suspect morals might be excluded.[39] In this case, the court gave several more specific reasons why they rejected the testimony of these witnesses. In some instances, the court believed that the testimony itself did not hold up under scrutiny. They also rejected much of the testimony provided by servants, both those who worked for Vernier and those who worked for the plaintiffs. It was not uncommon for unhappy servants to complain about their masters in the hopes of ruining their reputations; perhaps the court felt the testimonies of servants like Charlemagne and Gérard were nothing more than sour grapes.[40] Some witnesses were rejected, unsurprisingly, because of their close familial relationships with the plaintiffs. Marie Jeanne Bellot, for example, was the niece of the plaintiff Jean Joffrin, and that may have led to the rejection of both her testimony and that of her husband. Similarly, François Durand was the brother-in-law of another plaintiff, Nicolas

Table 2.3  Rejected witnesses in the Vernier case (1770)

| Witness | Occupation | Relationship(s) |
| --- | --- | --- |
| Madeleine Billecart | Wife of a *vigneron* | Unknown |
| Jean Réné Blaudinne de Marassé | Military officer | Unknown |
| Paul Nicolas Blondeau | Cooper | Nephew of Pierre Billecart; cousin of Nicolas Billecart |
| Pierre Blondeau | *Laboureur* | Nephew of Pierre Billecart; cousin of Nicolas Billecart |
| Marie Magdelaine Calixte Cazin | Widow of Louis Salmon, merchant | Aunt of Jean François Salmon |
| Simon Charlemagne | *Vigneron* | Former servant for Vernier |
| Claude Descottes | Servant | Former servant for Vernier |
| Étienne Claude Dupuis | *Huissier royal* | Unknown |
| François Durand and his wife, Margueritte Coinon | Bargeman | Brother-in-law of Nicolas Christophe Robert |
| Nicolas Fortemps | Surgeon | Unknown |
| Claudette Gerard | Servant | Servant for Nicolas Christophe Robert |
| Marguerite Thérèse Lamarle | Servant | Former servant for Vernier |
| Nicolle De L'Epine | *Vigneron* | Former servant for Vernier |
| Louis Lombart | Unknown, but son of the intendant of the seigneur of Mareuil | Unknown |
| Denis Pierre and his wife Marie Jeanne Bellot | Cooper | Niece of Jean Joffrin |
| Rémy Poncelet | *Vigneron* | Unknown |

Christophe Robert, and both his and his wife's testimonies were excluded. Although the reasons varied, the effect was the same: the court decided to disregard the testimonies of eighteen witnesses, thus reducing the weight of the evidence against Vernier. All of this shows that right beneath the surface of the documents were social realities that people at the time would have recognized but might be obscure to modern readers. The court's rejection of certain testimonies reflects their attempt to compensate for a myriad of complex issues and get at the truth.

For the most part, many of the accusations against Vernier still stood despite the loss of this testimony. Many of the rejected witnesses had not provided any information that was wholly unique. For example, in her lengthy testimony, Marie Magdelaine Calixte Cazin (the widow Salmon) discussed Vernier's failure to provide instruction at mass, the fact that the main mass was not said at regular times, difficulties in getting permission to confess with other priests, and the incident when Vernier first arrived in the parish and dismissed the vicaire. Plenty of other witnesses testified about the same things, so the loss of Cazin's testimony was not particularly damaging to the plaintiffs' case. She was the only one to report that Vernier had accused a surgeon of a sacrilegious communion, but this incident was not as crucial as many of the other accusations.

More damaging, however, was the loss of the testimony of the servants and the curé's neighbours, Denis Pierre and Marie Jeanne Bellot. Without their accounts, we know very little about what happened behind the walls of the presbytery. It was this testimony that provided most of the evidence in the Appert affair and about the other cases involving the abuse of women. The surgeon's testimony was the most damning when it came to Appert's pregnancy, but it seems the court did not believe him and rejected his testimony too. The accounts of former servants Margueritte Jacquot and Pierre Philippot, who were not excluded, still make it seem like there was something going on between Vernier and Appert, but they presumably did not provide enough evidence on their own to justify Vernier's removal from his position. Without the testimony of the neighbours and the servants, the case against Vernier starts to look less and less damning. He might have been a difficult priest when it came to confession, catechism, and tithes, but he may not have been a rapist or even a womanizer.

Furthermore, Vernier's accusations of slander and conspiracy seem less far-fetched if we take a closer look at the family relationships of the plaintiffs and the witnesses. Mareuil-sur-Ay was a small village, and certainly many of the witnesses were related to each other and to the plaintiffs. It would have been nearly impossible to find ninety-five people who knew what was happening in the parish but who were not related in some way, however distantly. Yet the close family relationships of many of the individuals involved are somewhat suspect. For example, all but one (Pierre Marlot) of the ten plaintiffs in the case were related in some way. Jean Baptiste Billecart was Jean Joffrin's son-in-law, for example. Jean Baptiste was also the first cousin of Pierre Billecart. Pierre's wife was Marie Jeanne Salmon, and Jean François Salmon was her first cousin. Pierre's nephew Nicolas Billecart was also one of the plaintiffs, and one of his nieces was married to Nicolas Christophe Robert. The Robert family was one of the major clusters of plaintiffs – Christophe Robert and his two sons, Nicolas Christophe and Pierre François, along with Pierre François's father-in-law, Pierre Trubert. The plaintiffs thus represented three overlapping extended families – the Roberts, the Billecarts, and the Salmons – a kind of alliance that could easily be seen as a conspiracy of enemies.

It turns out that many of the witnesses were part of these same extended families as well. If we use the record of births, marriages, and deaths kept in the parish and take the Billecart family tree back several generations, for example, we find that sixteen of the witnesses and plaintiffs all descended from, or had married descendants of, Pierre Billecart and Anne Regnault. The couple married in 1675, and four of their six surviving children went on to have large families; it was members of these families that provided a significant amount of testimony in the case against Vernier. Similarly, Jean Salmon and Madeleine Lefevre, who married in 1657, had three sons, Pierre, Guillaume, and Jean. Each of these sons married sisters: Marguerite, Nicolle, and Anne Pierre. Each of these families became something of a dynasty in Mareuil-sur-Ay. The three families split off over the generations into nine branches, and at least one representative of those nine branches was either a witness or a plaintiff in the case.[41]

The witnesses can be grouped into six clusters when we consider their familial and marital relationships, as seen in table 2.4. Each of these clusters contains witnesses who were related to each other, by blood or by marriage. Of the seventy-nine Mareuil-sur-Ay witnesses who testified, forty-eight fit into one or more clusters. All of these witnesses had close family relationships with other witnesses and

Table 2.4  Familial and marital clusters among witnesses in the Vernier case (1770)

| Billecart cluster | Durand cluster | Jacquot cluster | Joffrin cluster | Mayeux cluster | Salmon cluster | No cluster |
|---|---|---|---|---|---|---|
| Jean Baptiste Billecart | Madeleine Billecart | Jeanne Duval | Joseph Baudoin | Marie Nicolle Baudier | Joseph Baudoin | Catherine Adam |
| Nicolle Billecart | Paul Nicolas Blondeau | Scholastique Duval | Marie Jeanne Bellot | Claude Eloy Mayeux | Marie Magdelaine Calixte Cazin | Madeleine Bouda |
| Paul Billecart | Nicolas Boulanger | Marguerite Jacquot | Paul Billecart | Jean Charles Mayeux | Pierre Gérard | Étienne Chaillot |
| Jean Blondeau | Helain Coinon | Marie Jeanne Jacquot (Jacquot) | François Durand | Jean Louis Mayeux | Marie Hardy | Marie Madeleine Cognon |
| Jean Jacques Blondeau | Marguerite Coinon | Marie Jeanne Jacquot (Thierry) | Claude Folliat | Marie Anne Pierre | Jeanne Robert | Étienne Dufrene |
| Paul Nicolas Blondeau | Marguerite Colin | Marie Louise Jacquot | Marie Hardy | | Marie Margueritte Salmon | Marie Anne Gougelet |
| Pierre Blondeau | Christine Berthe Durand | Marie Nicolle Jacquot | Antoinette Elizabeth Pierre | | | Marie Agnes Jacquot |
| Christine Berthe Durand | Catherine Hebert | Rémy Jacquot | Claude Denis Nicolas Pierre | | | Marie Jeanne Jacquot (Visse) |
| François Durand | | Jean Lamarle | Denis Pierre | | | Pierre Labbaye |
| Marie Louise Jacquot | | Jacques Michaut | | | | Jeanne Lemaitre |
| Marie Nicolle Jacquot | | Marguerite Michaut | | | | Pierre Lemaitre |
| | | Jeanne Moret | | | | Jean Malton |
| | | Jean Thomas Poncelet | | | | Leonard Noel |
| | | Rémy Poncelet | | | | Jeanne Louise Patron |
| | | Marie Anne Robert | | | | Marie Anne Françoise Piquot |
| | | Gérard Thierry | | | | Jean Poirot |
| | | Marie Reine Thierry | | | | Elizabeth Trouson |

often with the plaintiffs as well. Even though the witnesses came from a variety of socioeconomic backgrounds, these family relationships may have affected their loyalties and tainted any interactions with Vernier as well as their testimony. Furthermore, members of the Billecart, Salmon, and Joffrin families served as godparents for a significant portion of the parish, creating additional religious relationships that are not always obvious.

The seventeen people who did not fit into any of the six clusters were not necessarily friends of Vernier's, either. Catherine Adam provided a great deal of detailed testimony against him, for example, and she does not seem to have had any close family, marital, or religious ties with the major families of the parish. The butcher's wife, Marie Madeleine Cognon, and her daughter Jeanne Louise Patron appeared to be among Vernier's enemies as well, even though Cognon was a newcomer to the parish.[42] None of the witnesses outside the six clusters had anything overwhelmingly damaging to say about Vernier, however. In fact, it is surprising that at least two of the individuals in this category had very little to say, given their position in the village: the schoolmasters. Simon Abel Reboult, a former schoolmaster, was not questioned in the initial *information* but gave his deposition a few months later. He explained to the court that he had not been able to answer the call for witnesses earlier because he no longer lived in Mareuil-sur-Aÿ and his hemorrhoids kept him from travelling. But then when he did finally arrive all he said was that he remembered Vernier had had a dog that was dressed up like a jester and that the child of Paul Billecart was baptized in Aÿ instead of in Mareuil-sur-Aÿ, and that he did not remember how much Vernier charged children who were doing their first communion.[43]

Similarly, Étienne Chaillot did not complain about Vernier despite the fact that he had been Mareuil-sur-Aÿ's schoolmaster for ten years. He testified that it was rare for the curé to preach from the pulpit but that he regularly said the main Sunday mass unless he was sick or out of town. He also mentioned the three main public scandals that had taken place in the parish – the Ascension Day sermon, the Fête-Dieu procession, and the argument between Marie Jeanne Joffrin and Vernier that had taken place in the church before a bishop's visit. These were all well-documented in the *information*, so Chaillot's testimony adds little unique material.[44] This testimony – or rather lack of testimony – from both the schoolmasters is highly significant. In rural parishes, schoolmasters worked closely with curés and vicaires

and helped to provide religious services for the people of the community. They often trained the altar boys, conducted evening
prayers, took care of the church and its ornaments, and acted as cho-
risters during the mass and other services.[45] We do not know exactly
what services Chaillot performed in Mareuil-sur-Ay, but it is likely
that he would have been more intimately acquainted with Vernier
and his habits than any other layperson in the parish. Chaillot and
Reboult should have been able to speak freely in their testimony
since they had each moved away before the case began and had no
vested interest in protecting Vernier. The fact that they did not corroborate the stories of many of the other parishioners is telling and
makes Vernier's accusations of slander and conspiracy seem more
and more believable.

If we examine the evidence thus far, even taking into account not
just what *is* there but what is *not* there, it seems that Vernier probably
did not perform services and sacraments in the way that his parishioners expected, and he was perpetually in a state of conflict with
them as a result of that as well as his tendency to treat people, including his servants and other workers, poorly. But the accusations of sexual assault, willful neglect, and gross misconduct have been called
into question. Perhaps at this point it is important to take a step back
and look at the parish priest in the early modern period, to see if general trends can help us decide whether we should believe Vernier or
the parishioners who testified against him. Were parish priests fulfilling their duties faithfully in the eighteenth century? Or were problematic priests more common than conscientious ones?

### Reform and the Eighteenth-Century Curé

Two hundred years before this period, when the Protestant Reformation was in full swing, many reformers spoke out about the sad state
of parish clergy throughout Europe. Curés and other clergy were criticized for their lack of education, intelligence, and ability, their negligence in performing their duties, their common-law wives, and their
lack of respect for the priestly office. During the Catholic Reformation, begun also in the sixteenth century but continuing into the seventeenth and eighteenth centuries, parish priests were thus an obvious target for reformers.[46] Bishops opened seminaries so that curés
could receive training and education before being placed in a parish
with care of souls.[47] More and more priests had a university education

as well, especially in dioceses that contained universities within their boundaries, like Reims. In 1774, 39.3 per cent of the curés serving in the diocese of Reims had at least some university education, and 93.3 per cent of those had received a degree of some kind.[48] Bishops also held regular synods once or twice a year, where curés could receive correction and instruction; many bishops conducted visitations of the parishes under their jurisdiction as well and used those visits to check up on the conduct and morals of the curés.[49] It took years for many of these reforms to be implemented and then bear fruit, but by the eighteenth century real progress had been made.

French curés actually had a fairly positive public image at the end of the early modern period and were represented in some of the literature of the time as a stock character: *le bon curé*.[50] Curés were viewed as the enlightened rulers of their parishioners, guiding them not only in their religious duties but in every other aspect of their lives as well. They were supposed to give advice and direction on agriculture, medicine, law, and education. They helped the poor, even sacrificing their own comforts to do so. Overall, they were portrayed as the best of all good citizens in the village – the ultimate example of someone who would always put the good of the community above his own needs and desires.[51]

There were still some common problems among the parish clergy: alcoholism, worldliness, gambling, and hunting, for example. But education, better surveillance, and cultural change had greatly lessened the incidences of common-law wives, outright ignorance in matters of doctrine or policy, and serious moral lapses. Thus perhaps Vernier, accused of violence, sexual incontinence, and problems with the sacraments, was an aberration – a holdover from the era of lackluster and negligent curés. The *officialité* records alert us to these aberrations, and although cases from just two dioceses are not enough to detect a pattern, it should remind us that curés with significant moral failings did still exist in the eighteenth century. At the same time, however, it is also possible that the villagers, knowing the types of violations church authorities paid the most attention to, purposely set out to slander their curé when they wanted to get rid of him. Vernier might not have been an aberration, but instead the victim of badly behaved parishioners.

Why would these parishioners want to get rid of their curé? If he was as blameless as he said he was, what reason would they have for asking the court to investigate him? More in-depth answers to this question will be provided in later chapters, but it is important to examine another possibility. Perhaps historians are correct to point out that curés were better behaved in the eighteenth century than they had been in previous centuries. But just because their behaviour had improved did not mean that curés automatically got along better with their parishioners. In fact, they may have gotten along worse, with significant consequences. It is possible that the tensions between Vernier and his parishioners were the result of deep-seated and widespread resentments created by the Catholic Reformation itself.

In his research on the relationship between the clergy and the laity in the city of Lyon, Philip Hoffman argued that one of the effects of the Catholic Reformation was the creation of a certain social and intellectual distance between the parish priest and his parishioners. Priests had better education and identified more with the urban elites than they did with the vast majority of the laity. When introducing reforms to institutions like confraternities, reforming priests transformed them from communal, unifying associations into more elitist organizations that emphasized personal spirituality at the expense of the community as a whole. The lower classes also resented any attempts by parish priests to separate the sacred from the profane – one of the major reforms advocated by clergy at all levels. As a result, according to this argument, a significant rift opened up between curés and the majority of their parishioners. This increased austerity, elitism, and the lack of shared values between priest and parishioner is then noted as a factor in the loss of influence of the church in the modern period.[52]

Hoffman's argument is limited by the fact that his evidence comes from urban parishes, where cultural and intellectual differences between curés and their lower class parishioners may have been more pronounced.[53] But it is also possible that increased education, along with increased ties to elite culture, did create a disconnect between the cultural and social worlds of rural curés and their parishioners as well.[54] Since it seems many, if not most, of the priests working in rural parishes actually came from urban areas and from comparatively wealthy families, this disconnect may have been significant. Before taking orders, future priests had to provide proof of an income of around 100 *livres* a year that would sustain them until they were given a benefice.[55] This meant priests were almost always from the upper levels of the socioeconomic scale.[56] This may not be the primary reason for the church's decline in status, but it could certainly have created tension in rural parishes – tensions that are, in fact, often visible in court cases.

For example, in 1754 Jean François Aubriot de Boncourt was brought before the *officialité* and accused of a variety of misdeeds against his parishioners, the villagers of Sorbon. In the *information*, they testified that their curé had engaged in multiple inappropriate relationships with women (and fathered a child with one of them), failed to bring the sacraments to the sick and dying, failed to say the required Sunday mass two different times, and used violence against his parishioners on several occasions. The court decided to sentence the curé to a week's retreat at a Dominican convent and then moved him to a different parish in the diocese.[57] The curé who took over for him in Sorbon, Robert Carez, apparently got along much better with the villagers. He was still their curé in 1774, twenty years later, and when asked about their character in a questionnaire he described them as fundamentally good, charitable, of good faith, and uncomplaining. There were some who worked on Sundays unnecessarily, but otherwise there were no blasphemers, rascals, vagabonds, smugglers, thieves, or concubines, he said.[58] Even though Aubriot de Boncourt's sentence was fairly light, it still seems as though he had been the one responsible for the problems in Sorbon.

His interrogation and confrontation provide more insight as to why that might have been the case. Given a chance to speak, Aubriot de Boncourt used every opportunity to emphasize his intellectual, religious, and social superiority in comparison to his parishioners. When confronted with his parishioner Claude Fay, he told the court that once when they were together on the road to Rethel, Fay had said such horrible things to him that he did not want to repeat them and force the scribe to dirty the paper with the words.[59] Similarly, two other men related an incident involving the curé and a stream that they needed to cross. They told the court that the curé pointed out several girls working in the fields nearby and suggested that the men just get one of those girls to ferry them across. There were apparently sexual overtones to this request, and when asked about it Aubriot de Boncourt responded that those words were "too crude and unrefined to have come out of his mouth."[60] Similarly, when asked if he had used crude language, and "offensive and injurious words," he responded that he had better manners than to say such things, and that only "coarse peasants" are familiar with those sorts of terms. The curé also blamed his parishioners' poverty and lack of sophistication for their poor behaviour.[61] When asked about hitting one of his tenants with a cane, Aubriot de Boncourt denied it and added that he only allowed the man's lease to continue out of charity, despite the fact that the tenant had insulted him and created "a thousand arguments."[62] The curé thus portrayed himself as the magnanimous landowner, thwarted by backward peasants.

Aubriot de Boncourt also stated outright that the court needed to respect his position of authority. He seemed to believe the whole procedure was completely unnecessary simply because of his status as a curé and a member of the clergy. In one incident he was accused of chasing a boy out of the church and kicking him. The boy's father then confronted the curé, who slapped him. The curé testified that the reason he had chased the boy from the church was because he had climbed the bell tower, urinated off the top of it, and then rung the bell, even though it was not yet time for vespers. The curé added that the boy's actions, as well as the father's, merited a lot more than a slap if justice was to be given to curés who were just trying to do their duty.[63] The final question in the interrogation demonstrates Aubriot de Boncourt's attitude perfectly. The court asked if he knew that these irregularities and accusations had caused his parishioners to lose confidence in him. He responded, "If people did not listen so avidly to the slanderous charges made by peasants, and if the spiritual court was better on their guard against the jurations of the parishioners, the curés would be better managed, and they would put an end to the spirit of revolt always in foment among the inferior."[64]

Another example, this time from a curé's own writings, also demonstrates the social distance that might exist between priest and parishioner. Sometime around 1700, a curé of the parish of Sennely, diocese of Orléans, wrote an account of his main concerns as curé. Christophe Sauvageon described his parishioners in great detail, and his descriptions give us some hints about his position in the parish. It is clear that he thought of himself as superior to his parishioners in nearly every way. Even if he did give a positive report of some of their good qualities, he appears rather condescending. For example, he said that his parishioners had a great deal of respect for all priests – except for the priest of their own parish. They believed the mendicant priests to be "saints," he said, and gave them alms liberally, while refusing to grant him the money he needed to equip the parish with nice ornaments and furnishings.[65] He saw himself as set apart from his parishioners, and in a paternalistic role. As one analyst of Sauvageon's account, Gérard Bouchard, argued, he was always an outsider to his parish, wanting his parishioners to behave differently but always being forced to compromise.[66]

Sauvageon did have a lot of good things to say about his parishioners. He noted that they had great zeal for the rituals of their religion – the divine office, the candles and the bells, and the processions. They were very charitable toward the poor, he said, and it was unheard of for a *laboureur* to turn away a poor person passing through the village without offering them food and a place to sleep. He happily remarked that the parishioners even spoke to these beggars civilly and gave them clothes if they needed them.[67] However, the list of vices Sauvageon provided was much longer than the list of positive qualities; he declared that his parishioners were prideful, envious, ungovernable, enemies of correction, infinitely cowardly, lazy, perfidious, liars, murmurers, slanderers, malicious, without honour, great drunks, and thieves; he said that both men and women were shameless, having little care for the future, and were little persuaded of the judgments of God. Further indicating a sense of distance between him and his parishioners, he claimed that they were all "sworn enemies" of their masters and their superiors and that they meditated eternally on the ways to do bad things to them. "All superiority is odious to them," he concluded.[68]

A questionnaire filled out by curés in the diocese of Reims in 1774 sheds additional light on what curés thought about their parishioners. The archbishop and his administrators sent out a lengthy questionnaire to all the parish priests in that year, hoping to find out about the state of the diocese. They asked many questions about property, income, and church buildings and ornaments, but they also asked the curés to indicate what the character of their parishioners was, as well as their good qualities and their vices. Curés and vicaires responded to the questionnaire in large numbers, describing the character of the people in several hundred parishes and annexes. Sometimes the parish and its annex(es) were lumped together and sometimes they were dealt with separately, but in all there were responses from 500 curés and vicaires. Do these responses show overt animosity between curés and parishioners as a result of social or economic inequalities?

The most common response about the character of the people was that they were a mix of good and bad: this was noted by just over 100 respondents. Often curés cited scripture, demonstrating the way that they felt about their parishioners; the curé of Avaux-le-Chateau, for example, wrote, "Although I can say nothing against my parishioners I can assure you that there is no wheat without tares."[69] Another curé said that his parishioners were "mixed merchandise."[70] But overall, curés seemed to think that their parishioners were fairly good, even if there were some bad apples in the mix. In addition to the 163 who said that their parishioners were either good or some mixture of mostly good, fifty said that there was no major vice in the parish. A significantly higher number of priests noted that their parishioners attended mass and approached the sacraments (forty-six and thirty-three, respectively) than those who said that they neglected these services (eight and fourteen, respectively) (see table 2.5).

Many curés also willingly named their parishioners' good qualities (see table 2.6). Sixty-nine said that they were hardworking, compared with only six who said they were lazy. Forty-eight noted that the people in their village were charitable toward the poor, especially when tragedy struck. Other good qualities included honesty, piety, respect for the curé, and a willingness to listen to the word of God. Sixty-four curés further indicated that their parishioners were docile or easy to govern. For example, the curé of Rumigny said that his people were both good and bad, but that there were "many who are docile to the voice of their pastor."[71] The curé of Saint-Juvin had even more good things to say about his parishioners: "Following the example of Saint Juvin, the inhabitants are hardworking and well-managed. For the most part, they keep up the exercise of religion, and engage in the exercises enough; there are very good people. They are docile enough and do not resist their curé at all; the original inhabitants of the place especially. They are charitable enough; they give some old poor people enough to survive, without them even having to ask."[72]

As for negative qualities, the list of often-repeated vices is much longer and more varied (see table 2.6). Parishioners were accused of being too attached to material things, swearing (although only one complained of blasphemy), envy, pride, and avarice. One curé just said that his parishioners' vices were all of the seven capital sins.[73] The most frequently listed negative quality was self-interest: parishioners cared more about their own personal interests than the good of the community as a whole. As one curé put it, the people of La Neuville-en-Tourne-à-Fuy were afflicted with a "love of themselves" and a "negligence for the public good."[74] This often led to lawsuits, mentioned

Table 2.5   Parish priests' assessments of the character and religious activity of their parishioners, in response to a questionnaire distributed in the diocese of Reims in 1774

| Positive assessment | No. of responses* | Negative assessment | No. of responses* |
| --- | --- | --- | --- |
| Good character | 30 | Bad character | 1 |
| Most are good, or good enough | 30 | | |
| Some good and some bad | 103 | | |
| No major vice, scandal, or disorder | 50 | | |
| Character is not bad | 5 | | |
| Regularly attend mass and other services | 46 | Neglect the mass and other services | 8 |
| Regularly approach the sacraments | 33 | Neglect the sacraments | 14 |

*Out of a sample of 500

Table 2.6 Parish priests' assessments of the positive and negative characteristics of their parishioners, in response to a questionnaire distributed in the diocese of Reims in 1774

| Positive assessment | No. of responses* | Negative assessment | No. of responses* |
|---|---|---|---|
| Hardworking (*laborieux*) | 69 | Self-interested | 62 |
| Docile, easy to govern | 64 | Maliciousness (*medisance*) | 39 |
| Pious, have the essential sentiments of religion | 50 | Drunkenness | 30 |
| Charitable | 48 | Inflexible, not easy to govern, insubordinate | 25 |
| Peaceful | 36 | Litigious (*processif*) | 20 |
| Honest | 31 | Work on Sundays/Feast days | 20 |
| Respectful toward the curé | 12 | Slanderous (*calomnie*) | 18 |
| Lively (*vif*) | 9 | Too attached to material things | 18 |
| Not litigious | 8 | Ignorant, uneducated | 16 |
| Willing to listen to the word of God | 6 | Swearing | 15 |
| Attend instructions/Are well instructed | 6 | Lack of religion, piety | 15 |
| Unified | 6 | Division | 15 |
| Polite | 5 | Unsophisticated (*grossier*) | 14 |
| | | Envy | 11 |
| | | Untrustworthy | 11 |
| | | Pride | 11 |
| | | Theft | 9 |
| | | Dishonest, deceitful | 9 |
| | | Hatred among each other | 8 |
| | | Stubborn | 8 |
| | | Vindictive | 7 |
| | | Lazy | 6 |
| | | Avarice | 6 |
| | | Anger | 6 |
| | | Vengeance | 5 |
| | | Enmity | 5 |

*Out of a sample of 500. Only characteristics mentioned by at least five curés have been included by twenty curés, as well as division and enmity. As might be expected, curés also complained about problems at cabarets, drunkenness, working on feast days and Sundays, and theft. It is interesting to note that the second-most mentioned negative characteristic was *medisance*, or maliciousness. *Medisance* and *calomnie*, or slander, were often mentioned together, and curés thus portrayed the laity as often being involved in cabals against their fellow parishioners or their curés. The curé of Louvergny even indicated that these vices were simply part of the peasant character: "There are some honest people, but others are subject to the ordinary vices of the countryside, which are *medisance*, *calomnie*, and a lack of loyalty."[75] It is not hard to imagine that *medisance* in general could easily translate to slander of curés. The curé of Draize indicated as much when he noted that "all of my predecessors were slandered; it is known what they did to me. I am now tranquil enough and I pardon them."[76]

Some of the curés' responses do indicate a certain amount of division between priest and parishioner, however. For one thing, thirty-seven curés refused to answer the question. These were not curés who simply left the space on the questionnaire blank, but curés who told their superiors that they would not answer, at least not on paper. Some said that they did not want to put into writing the negative qualities of their parishioners. One said that he could not reveal their vices because he was their confessor,[77] and others indicated that a pastor should not say negative things about his flock. Several wrote in Latin, probably hoping to keep their parishioners from knowing what their curé thought of them. Some wrote that they had not been in their parish long enough to know the character of their parishioners. This may have been true in some cases, but it was also a way of making a statement about the difficulty of the question; the curé of Launois gave this excuse but he had been in his parish for fifteen years.[78] A few indicated that they could not respond because of hostilities in their parish. The curé of Buzancy wrote, "The affairs which have happened in Buzancy, and their present bad will against me, exempt me from saying anything more."[79]

One other answer to the questionnaire reveals something important about the relationship between priest and parishioner. One of the reforms undertaken by the church during the Catholic Reformation period dealt with the conduct of the curé within his parish. He was supposed to be separate from his parishioners, to maintain his holy status.[80] That meant bishops and other administrators issued rules about clerical activities. Curés could not visit cabarets in their own parishes, for example.[81] They were not supposed to attend weddings or dances, play games of chance, or even socialize with their parishioners beyond what was absolutely necessary.[82] An order issued at a synod in Reims in 1669 had a section on the care curés must take with their exterior appearance. They were told that they must be "a visible example and a perfect model for all others, because their vocation is to preach publicly and to imprint piety." They were never to be seen in public without the ecclesiastical habit, soutane, and tonsure. Cabarets, hunting, and associating with gambling or gamblers was forbidden. Curés were also told they could not be involved in any business, trade, or servile employment.[83] All of these rules were designed to maintain a degree of separation between curé and parishioner and to emphasize curés' holy state and their status as representatives of the church.

When the curé of Chappes filled out his questionnaire, it seems clear that he had taken these rules about separation to heart. He wrote, "I do not know the dominant character of the parishioners, because I do not visit them."[84] He went on to add that his parishioners attended services regularly on feast days and Sundays, and a good number even attended on working days. His only problem with them was that in the summer some people went out to the cemetery during church services, and the youth had dances at the cabarets. This curé really did not know his parishioners, and he did not appear to feel that it was his duty to get to know them. His only concern was their attendance at services. Similarly, the curé of Nogent-l'Abbesse said that he could not say much about his parishioners because they were too good at hiding their true character. This curé was perhaps less disinterested than the curé of Chappes seemed to be, but his comments still indicate a sense of separation between curés and parishioners.

Other comments about both character and negative qualities demonstrate this separation as well. Fourteen curés indicated that they believed their parishioners were unsophisticated, and another sixteen said their parishioners were ignorant or uneducated. Even more telling is that thirty-one curés also mention something about the poverty of their parishioners. In some cases, curés lamented the fact that so many of their parishioners were poor and wished that something could be done to help them. The curé of Lagery used this opportunity to complain that the taxes on his parishioners were too high.[85] The curé of Mardeuil just noted that "there are poor in the parish that the prior-curé cannot relieve because of the modest nature of his revenue."[86] Others commented on poverty not just because they saw it as a problem, but because they viewed it as a character flaw. The curé of Germont wrote that "a little more activity would be good for them, they would be less poor."[87] In Montcy-Notre-Dame, an annex, the vicaire who served there indicated that "their great default is that they love the cabaret too much. They are poor, and often it is their own fault."[88] These curés may have perceived a significant social and economic distance between themselves and their parishioners, creating tension between them.[89]

Finally, the questionnaires reveal one more important item that may have led to conflict between priest and parishioner. Some curés' responses indicate that they had found themselves facing angry parishioners if they tried to implement some of the Tridentine reforms that had been inculcated into them in synods and seminaries. Twenty-five curés indicated that their parishes were difficult to govern, and this could easily have been because curés had tried to get the laity to change their conduct. If the parishioners had resisted such changes, they might have been labelled as difficult. The curé of Ventelay described his parishioners as insubordinate, but then said they were peaceful "if one can in good conscience say nothing to them."[90] This curé had presumably tried to encourage people to change their ways, probably through sermons or the confessional, and found that they resisted. Similarly, the people of Saint-Étienne-sur-Suippe were described as "always good when you do not attack their faults or combat their vices."[91]

The 1774 questionnaire thus gives us some additional context that may help present some possibilities for what happened between Vernier and his parishioners to make their relationship such a difficult one. Vernier was an educated man of a higher social status than his parishioners and a stranger to the parish. Perhaps he held attitudes similar to those of Aubriot de Boncourt and believed that peasants were backward and unworthy of much consideration. Perhaps he saw his parishioners as unsophisticated, or impoverished because of laziness. Those attitudes may have been enough to create tension initially, and if he had swept into Mareuil-sur-Ay and tried to reform what he saw as the villagers' vices and defaults, his actions could easily have led to conflicts. Then those conflicts could have resulted in twenty years of difficulties, a pact among the enemies of the curé to try to oust him, and a long and divisive court case.

At the end of chapter 1, it looked as though Nicolas Hyacinthe Vernier was guilty of multiple crimes against his parishioners, from neglecting the sacraments to sexual assault. His parishioners – or at least some of them – insisted that he was solely responsible for the religious scandal and disorder they were experiencing and hoped that the court would remove him from his benefice. The present chapter, however, has opened up some possible alternative explanations for what was happening in Mareuil-sur-Ay. While the extant documents of the case cannot explain exactly who was responsible for the broken relationship between Vernier and some of his parishioners, it does seem that the curé was not entirely at fault. Lay Catholics in rural areas disobeyed the rules of their religion often – of that there is no doubt. Most of their sins were expected and predictable. But they also lied, made up stories, and purposely tried to make their curés look bad. It is likely that neither Vernier nor his parishioners were entirely innocent.

Both Vernier and the people of Mareuil-sur-Ay believed they were doing the right things to further the cause of religion in their parish and to create and support social ties. They did not always agree on what was right, however, and this led to significant conflict. The next chapters will examine in more detail some of the major sources of conflict in Mareuil-sur-Ay: Vernier's performance of the sacraments and services, his relationships with women, and his image as curé. Three dozen additional *officialité* cases, from the dioceses under the jurisdiction of the archbishops of both Reims and Besançon, will provide additional context. These cases demonstrate how easily conflict could arise in the parish, and how, although not without difficulty, that conflict could be resolved. These incidents in Mareuil-sur-Ay, and those in other parishes as well, illuminate the great variety of religious experience in rural parishes and remind us that rural religion still mattered.

Fundamentally, however, the main story here is not about the guilt or innocence of Vernier or any of the other curés who went before the *officialité*. It is about the relationship between the laity in a rural village and their curé. When Philip Hoffman argued that increased education for parish priests led to an intellectual, social, and economic distance between laity and clergy, he was probably right. Evidence of strained relationships, even in rural areas, is found in both court cases and documents like the 1774 questionnaire. But to argue that this social disconnect led to a loss of devotion and a fundamental weakening of the power of the church that would be manifest during the Revolution of 1789 is going a bit too far. Neither Vernier nor his parishioners, when faced with the reality of their broken relationship, gave up on the church altogether. The very existence of the court case demonstrates this most clearly: if the laity had lost their faith as a result of conflicts with their curé, they would have just ignored him and other church leaders rather than spending months and years of their lives, and who knows how much of their money, in pursuing justice. Instead of distancing themselves from the church, they tried to repair the scandal by taking steps to remove Vernier and bring in a new curé who they hoped would live up to their ideals. They were surely unhappy with the verdict in the case, but even that did not lead to complete estrangement from the parish or the church itself. Mareuil-sur-Ay did not turn atheist, agnostic, or even Protestant just because they did not get along with their curé. And, as it turns out, even though the court declared Vernier innocent, the people of Mareuil-sur-Ay ended up getting their new curé after all.

# 3

# Scandalous Sacraments

THE COURT: Did you, about seven years ago, require Helain Coinon to give 24 *sols* to the *fabrique* for not having taken ashes on the first day of Lent, and, when Coinon said that he was not in a state to give those 24 *sols*, did you refuse him absolution for two years?

NICOLAS HYACINTHE VERNIER: Responded that he does not believe he has to explain, nor should he explain, what happens in the tribunal of penitence between him and his penitent. If Coinon did not do his Easter communion for two years, it was because he was not in a state to do it.[1]

There are seven sacraments in the Roman Catholic liturgy: baptism, confirmation, penance (confession), the Eucharist (communion), marriage, holy orders, and extreme unction (last rites). Since confirmation and holy orders could only be conferred by clergy with a rank of bishop or higher, parish priests like Nicolas Hyacinthe Vernier would have administered only five of these sacraments – but on a very regular basis.[2] In a parish like Mareuil-sur-Ay, rarely would a day go by when a curé was not asked to hear a confession, baptize a baby, or administer to a sick person. Just as parishioners expected their priest to provide regular religious services, like mass and vespers, they also expected him to be available to perform any of the five sacraments when the situation called for it. It was an essential part of his God-given duty as their curé.

When Vernier consulted the *rituel*, or diocesan handbook, for Reims (and presumably he had, since he mentioned it in his testimony),[3] he would have learned that the sacraments had been instituted by Jesus Christ as a conduit for His grace. Grace is given to the faithful to strengthen their spiritual life and acts as a remedy for all kinds of worldly ills: "This grace is the only hope for the faithful, who during the course of this mortal life are exposed to temptations, attacks, and assaults from their enemies." He also would have been made aware of his sacred and serious responsibility to perform the sacraments appropriately, to make sure that his parishioners were not cut off from the conduit of grace. Curés were to be careful not to "close the door to Heaven" because of their weakness, laziness, avarice, or any other sin; instead, "they must open it for those that God has committed to their care, and so as not to bring God's indignation upon them they must work to reconcile men to Him." Any curé who failed in this duty would be "chastised by God himself with all of the rigor of his justice."[4] We do not know, of course, whether God actually chastised Vernier for his problems with the sacraments – but his parishioners certainly did.

A significant number of the people of Mareuil-sur-Ay believed that Vernier had failed in this crucial aspect of his ministry. At the core of the disagreements between Vernier and his parishioners was his inability, or unwillingness, to perform the sacraments properly. This breach of confidence was so severe that they went to the courts to ask for Vernier's removal. They wanted another priest who would take his duty to administer the sacraments more seriously, so they told the court about every error and misstep Vernier had made with any of the sacraments. Other than the sacrament of marriage, which they did not complain about, they found a myriad of problems in his performance of the remaining four: baptism, confession, communion, and extreme unction.

However, it is possible that the villagers of Mareuil-sur-Ay might not have been entirely truthful in their testimony. Perhaps Vernier's actions were not quite as egregious as they led the court to believe. To examine the nature of the relationship between Vernier and his parishioners, we need to understand more about his performance of the sacraments, and how those sacraments could either unite him with his parishioners or divide them. Because the sacraments were so important – to both priest and parishioner – they could easily become a site of conflict, and thus studying them offers a way to gain a greater understanding of clerical–lay relationships and the nature of parish religion. Vernier's case, as well as others that deal with similar issues, demonstrate the complexity of these relationships as well as the depth of religious feeling in eighteenth-century rural parishes.

An examination of the role of the sacraments also sheds light on what Catholic reform meant in the eighteenth century. Seminary-

and university-educated priests had a difficult task during this period: their superiors expected them to make sure that their parishioners' behaviour matched the increasingly high standards set by the clergy, while those parishioners often had other ideas about behaviour and practice and expressed those ideas freely, resulting in conflict, misunderstandings, and even anger and violence.[5] Reforms were thus limited by multiple factors, and priests were beset by thorny practical problems that required constant negotiation and compromise. Even a ceremony as straightforward as baptism might cause unexpected problems for both the curé and the laity.

*We've Come to Baptize a Baby – Not Be Tested on the Catechism*

In the Catholic tradition, baptism was necessary to remove original sin, and it was the gateway to the Lord's grace and all other sacraments.[6] It was also the only way to become a Christian and a member of God's church. No one could possibly obtain eternal life without baptism.[7] Therefore, if an infant died before receiving this sacrament, its soul was effectively condemned to hell for all eternity. To keep this from happening, there were a number of prescribed safeguards in place. A baby born healthy would usually be brought to the church the day after its birth for baptism, but if the baby's condition seemed precarious a priest would be called in immediately to administer the sacrament. If a baby appeared to be in immediate danger of dying and a priest was not readily available, the midwife was authorized to say a prayer of temporary baptism for the child; this ceremony was known as the *ondoiement*.[8] That way if the baby died the body could still be buried in consecrated ground and the parents would have some solace; if the baby lived the priest would conduct the full baptismal ceremony at a later date.

Curés were in charge of making sure that midwives were instructed in the correct form of baptism, but the Reims *rituel* indicates that all of the parishioners should know how to properly baptize an infant in case of emergency. In fact, any person – including women, heretics, and infidels – could baptize a baby as long as they used the right words, had the right intentions, and administered water onto the head of the infant. Of course, it was always preferable to have a priest baptize a baby rather than a layperson, just as it was always preferable to have a man rather than a woman, or a Catholic rather than an infidel.[9] But baptism was important enough that literally anyone could do it. The only people who were advised against baptizing a baby in an emergency were the parents of the infant; by performing the baptism a parent would contract a spiritual affinity with their own offspring, thus creating a very complicated relationship tantamount to incest.[10]

In the pre-modern world, babies died with heartbreaking regularity. In most French parishes about a third of all babies born died before they reached their first birthday.[11] In one remarkable year, 1725, five sets of twins were born in Mareuil-sur-Ay; all ten infants died within a few days of birth. Families with single births were luckier that year: twenty-four out of twenty-eight of these babies survived the first few months, meaning the overall infant mortality rate in Mareuil-sur-Ay that year was 37 per cent.[12] Because infant mortality was so high, curés and vicaires needed to be ready to administer baptism at any hour of the day or night. Despite the fact that technically midwives and other lay people could baptize infants, parents always preferred to have a priest perform the full sacrament. Parents often did not believe temporary baptism was sufficient, and they worried about the state of their child's soul if the full ceremonies had not been performed; if neither the curé nor the vicaire was available, anxious parents might be very upset.

When Rémy Poncelet complained to the court that Vernier had been absent from the parish and thus unable to baptize his newborn twins, Vernier said that it was not his fault, because his absence from the parish had been legitimate and unavoidable. Neither Poncelet's complaint nor Vernier's response were at all unusual. Because parishioners were concerned about the availability of the sacraments, and especially the availability of their own priest to perform them, they expected their curés to be found within village boundaries as much as possible. In a very similar incident, Gabriel Mottet was also accused of being absent often from his parish, Ruffey (Besançon). A woman there also gave birth to twins, and she sent someone to the presbytery to ask Mottet to come and baptize the babies immediately in case they died, as death was always a significant risk with twin births. He was not at home, however; the messenger eventually found him in a nearby village but by the time he returned to Ruffey both babies had died.[13]

It was almost inevitable that parishioners would occasionally find themselves in need of the sacraments when their curé was absent from the parish, and it should not be surprising that this sometimes resulted in anger and resentment. But some of the other problems with baptism demonstrate that irregularities with baptism services could be a sign of larger conflicts. For example, it seems clear that curés believed in the efficacy of temporary baptism and often saw little need to perform the full service if the risk seemed slight but the inconvenience great. The laity, on the other hand, wanted the full service performed as soon as possible. It is also evident that in some cases parents believed their child's life was in greater danger than it actually was; perhaps long experience with anxious parents led some curés to act with less haste than their parishioners preferred. Parents might see a curé's postponement of a baptism service as callous and negligent, while curés might be more concerned with other issues, legitimate or not, and fall back on temporary baptism.

In Semide (Reims), for example, a family wanted a baptism performed on a specific day when the curé, Jean Baptiste Le Marie, had plans to go out of town. The family had chosen that day because they were waiting for an out-of-town godparent to arrive, but the curé wanted to leave the village as soon as possible. So, he went to the family's house and, against the wishes of the mother, performed a temporary baptism. He told her that since the child was doing well they could complete the full ceremony when he returned in a few days. The family, instead of waiting, brought in another curé to perform the baptism as soon as the godparent arrived.[14] The incident demonstrates two different and conflicting understandings of the baptism ceremony. The parents cared about being able to include this particular godparent and the larger occasion of the event, while the curé just wanted to fulfill his duty with the least amount of inconvenience possible.

Another incident occurred in the parish of Vigneux (Laon), and in this case it nearly led to violence. Curé Pierre Mercier arrived late to the church to perform a baptism, and the *seigneur*, who was attending the ceremony as a guest of the family, insulted him and told him that he should not have made people wait. They both became angry, Mercier said, and when he went back to the presbytery to prepare for the baptism the *seigneur* followed him, hurling insults, and both men picked up swords. The scuffle did not result in any injuries, and the curé told the court that when they had cooled off they worked to reconcile with each other and that "religion and time made them forget after awhile."[15] Neither party was guilty of anything egregious here – the *seigneur* just expected a little more respect from his curé and perhaps chose the wrong time and method to demand that respect. But it shows how easily a little bit of irritation could turn into a full-blown affair.

One of the biggest conflicts associated with the baptism service centred around the godparents. The choice of godparents was up to the parents of the infant, and they cared deeply about the matter. Godparents were responsible for the child's education and might be called upon to raise the child should the parents meet an untimely demise. Relatives were the most likely candidates, especially for a first baby. But non-related and prominent members of the parish were also commonly chosen. Important relationships could be cemented or forged through the choice of godparents.[16] Sometimes, recently married couples were chosen. Teenaged youths from notable families often served as godparents for families of equal or lower social status. Even young children, with their parents answering for them, could serve as godparents. For example, in 1733 Jacques Hennequin and his wife Claude Salmon chose the four-year-old son of Christophe Robert as the godfather for their son. The elder Robert stood in for the child at the ceremony. No one had any expectations that the young Nicolas Christophe Robert would actually help to educate his godson, but a social tie had been created that could last a lifetime.

Thus, the choice of godparents was no small affair, and if the curé tried to refuse the parents' choices, it could easily create tension. There were legitimate reasons why a priest might refuse to accept a particular individual as a godparent. The Reims *rituel* gives a list of several categories of people who were not allowed to stand as god-parents: clergy (unless the infant and its parents were residents of another parish); members of the religious orders; children who had not yet attained the age of reason; excommunicated Catholics; any-one who had failed to complete their Easter confession and commu-nion; anyone who was known for living a criminal and scandalous life; and anyone who was uneducated in the principal points of the Christian religion.[17] Sometimes, these rules were overlooked. In fact, they were probably ignored quite often. Not that a lot of parents were choosing excommunicates as godparents, but sometimes they did choose young children or people who were less educated in Christian doctrine than perhaps they should have been. Most priests, knowing that parents felt strongly about the godparents they had chosen, prob-ably ignored the irregularities to avoid arguments.[18] Vernier, it seems, did not.

For example, we have seen that the innkeeper Jean Blondeau was insulted when Vernier refused to accept his teenage children as godparents for the child of Philippe Genest. Blondeau told the court that he believed this refusal was the result of bad feelings between himself and Vernier after an argument over tithes. While such an argument could easily have taken place, Vernier put the blame squarely on Blondeau himself, arguing that as curé he was just trying to do his best with a difficult situation. The curé claimed that Blondeau's wife, Anne Billecart, had told him that she did not want her children to be the godparents for this particular family. Vernier would not reveal her reasons for this during his interrogation, since he did not want to betray Billecart's confidence, but he said they appeared well-founded and logical. He agreed to keep the children from being presented as godparents and assured her that he would not tell her husband about this arrangement since she was worried about his bad temper. When Vernier arrived at the church and discovered that Blondeau and Billecart's children were there, expecting to be the infant's godparents, he decided to test them on their catechism. Since godparents were technically responsible for the religious education of the child, priests were indeed permitted to test them before the ceremony.[19] However, this rule could easily get priests in trouble since adults had often forgotten their catechism and preferred not to be embarrassed during an important church ceremony.[20] Ignoring the potential for conflict, Vernier pressed the issue and claimed that he knew the children had not been attending catechism class regularly and that he was within his rights to refuse them.[21]

Vernier's testimony does not make it clear whether the Blondeau children were actually ignorant of the catechism or if he just did not want them to serve as godparents, but he made the same excuse when he refused Nicolas Billecart and Louise Joffrin as godparents for the infant son of Paul Billecart, an incident described in chapter 1. In his interrogation the curé gave a detailed account of what happened on that day in February 1750, and his version of the story differs significantly from that given by Paul Billecart. He said that although he knew who the chosen godparents were, since they were from prominent families in the village, they had not attended his catechism classes. Since he did not know if they had been instructed or if they had done their first communion, he believed that it was appropriate to make sure these young people were instructed in the obligations they were about to take upon themselves. According to his version of events, after asking just one question about the duties of godparents the godmother cut him off and said that they had not come to be questioned on the catechism. She and the godfather then began to walk out. Vernier put his hand on the infant and said to the midwife who was holding him, "Stop, I'm going to baptize the baby anyway," but the godmother took the midwife by the arm and forcibly pulled her and the baby out of the church. Vernier, after learning that they had taken the child to Ay to be baptized, crossed out the record he had previously made in the register. He gave these details to the court as proof that he had harboured no intention of refusing to baptize the child. Furthermore, Vernier told the court, he was insulted by Paul Billecart's claim that the baby had died soon after its baptism. He pointed to the parish register, which indeed showed that the baby survived for an entire year.[22] Billecart had conveniently omitted this detail in his testimony; there is no way that the child died as a result of his irregular baptism. It was the "blackest sort of slander" to suggest that it was his fault that the child had died, Vernier argued.[23]

Vernier thus told the court that his actions had been misinterpreted and that he was simply trying to uphold the rules of the diocese as well as encourage better religious education for the youth of the parish. His parishioners, unhappy with his attempts to meddle in their affairs, rebelled against him. This seems to have happened in the parish of Saint-Théodule and its annex, Labergement (Besançon) as well. In February 1743, the child of Pierre Renobert Defrasne was brought to the church to be baptized. The curé, Matthieu Faivre, refused to perform the baptism because he said the designated godfather was too young – only eight years old – and a "libertine" who did not attend catechism. The boy's father claimed that he was actually thirteen or fourteen and had taken his first communion the previous Easter, but Faivre still refused to baptize the baby unless another godfather was presented. After four days, Defrasne took the child to a nearby village where a vicaire performed the baptism.[24] This vicaire also gave testimony to the court, and said he believed that Faivre had argued with Defrasne and that the resulting resentment led to the botched baptism.[25] It is easy to see how arguments over just about anything, be it the level of education necessary for a child to serve as godparent, or an argument over tithes, or a myriad of other personal and secular matters, could overlap with the administration of the sacraments and create scandals. However holy they may have been considered, sacraments were administered not in some sort of spiritual vacuum but rather in the mundane world of human affairs.

None of these events by themselves were likely to lead to a court case; these curés were guilty of many other things besides arguments about baptism. But because parishioners testified about them, we learn a great deal about how curés interacted with their parishioners on a daily basis. The sorts of negotiations illuminated by these incidents were probably rather common in rural parishes. The sacraments were not rituals imposed upon a passive or resentful laity; they were living, variable, and flexible interactions between individuals and God's very human representatives on earth: the curés. The laity wanted and needed these rituals, and they made sure that their priests administered them. Both priests and parishioners had their own ideas about what exactly the sacraments should look like, and the result was constant negotiation and compromise. This is demonstrated even more clearly when we examine the sacraments of confession and communion, which often came with even higher stakes than baptism. Confession and communion had implications for the larger community – they might even be said to symbolize the spiritual health of the parish as a whole. Irregularities with these sacraments could easily lead to serious scandals.

### Confession and Communion in the Eighteenth-Century Parish

In 1768 Pierre Delacourt was curé of Ville-sur-Retourne and its annex, Bignicourt (Reims). Like every other curé, Delacourt held sole responsibility for the spiritual welfare of the approximately 250 souls in these villages, and a significant part of that responsibility was to hear the confession of, and then administer communion to, every adult in the parish. The church required this duty to be fulfilled each year at Easter and had steadfastly insisted on it since the original pronouncement at Lateran IV in 1215. If a person did not complete their *paques*, there could be serious consequences for the individual and for the curé.

According to court records, on 17 April 1768 Margueritte Hugot, wife of Bignicourt's miller, presented herself at the altar for her Easter communion. But when it came to her turn, the curé ignored Hugot and did not give her the Eucharist. He administered to the people kneeling on either side of her, but not to Hugot, and he did not even acknowledge her presence. As the curé moved further down the line of communicants, Hugot first quietly asked her neighbours, "Why did he pass me by?" Her anger growing, her voice soon rang through the church as she asked everyone attending to serve as witnesses that her curé had refused to give her communion. Delacourt was then forced to explain to the entire parish the reason for his refusal: the hate and enmity she had for her father-in-law, he said, was a scandal; he could not give her communion until she had repaired it. "God, and my *rituel*, forbids me," he said, "I don't want to damn myself to please the world." [26]

Five days later, Delacourt found himself on trial before the *officialité* for refusing communion to Hugot. Delacourt was asked if he knew that communion, and especially Easter communion, if demanded publicly, cannot be refused except to public sinners. Delacourt acknowledged this and said that since he regarded Hugot as a public sinner because of her treatment of her father-in-law, he felt justified in refusing her. He was then asked to provide his definition of a public sinner, and he responded that he understood it to be someone whom the majority of the parishioners recognized as a sinner. The court finally asked if Delacourt believed that on this occasion he had been a bit overzealous and excessive and if he recognized that he had not acted prudently enough. He responded that in the moment he had felt what he was doing was right but that if he had it to do over again he would have consulted the advice of his superiors first.[27] Despite this final admission and expression of regret, the court decided to permanently remove Delacourt as curé of Ville-sur-Retourne and Bignicourt.

The events of this case reveal something significant about the relationship between confession, communion, and the Catholic Reformation. It has often been assumed, both by early modern clergy as well as by modern historians, that the confessional would be an ideal way to persuade people to change.[28] It is reasonable to believe that if the laity wanted to be able to fulfill their Easter duty to confess and take communion – and it seems they did indeed want to do this – then they would have to submit to the will of the curé, their confessor. Sins would have to be given up, relationships mended, prayers said, and pilgrimages walked. Behaviour would have to change. And was that not the whole point of the Catholic reform effort? Delacourt believed it was his God-given duty to encourage Hugot to reform by denying her communion. The *rituel* for the diocese of

Reims states very clearly that public sinners could not receive communion until they had repaired the scandal they had caused.[29] But Delacourt's fate after he tried to correct the scandal in his parish demonstrates the limitations of trying to use the sacraments as tools of reform. The court took Hugot's side, presumably because the scandal the curé had caused by publicly refusing a parishioner communion was greater than that caused by Hugot's treatment of her father-in-law. Out of fear of disorder, scandal, and public outcry, the court bent the church's stated rules for confession and communion, surely causing curés like Delacourt to think twice before trying to use the confessional to change the conduct of their parishioners in the future.[30]

Much of the work that historians have produced dealing with confession and communion uses primarily prescriptive sources to examine how the clergy – and typically the most educated and elite clergy – felt about the sacraments.[31] Some of this discussion is centred around debates over Catholic reform, as well as the Jansenist conflict with the Jesuits involving confession and communion. This literature can tell us a lot about how clerical authorities thought about the sacraments and their administration, but in rural parishes like Bignicourt, where curé Delacourt and Margueritte Hugot squared off over the more practical aspects of communion, these erudite debates had little effect. Nobles and other elites in urban areas may have developed sophisticated beliefs about sin, conscience, contrition, and absolution, but most French Catholics looked at confession and communion quite differently.[32]

No matter how we approach it, confession is a tricky thing to study. By its very nature confession is secret, and there was no administrative organization associated with it that generated documents useful to the historian; this is why scholars have generally used only prescriptive sources.[33] *Officialité* records are by no means a perfect source for the study of confession either; most of the cases deal with priests who were either violent, womanizers, or drunks, and perhaps all three.[34] But there are some cases, like Delacourt's, that involve the more routine aspects of parish life, and those cases are particularly enlightening. Furthermore, even the cases involving the most dissipated priests often provide significant details about confession and communion as well. Court records, unlike prescriptive sources, also include descriptions of what actually went on in the confessional, in the words of both penitent and priest. These details allow the historian to add a degree of nuance to the information gleaned from the statutes, hand-books, and sermons – all written by the clergy – that make up the bulk of the usual source material on confession.[35] The fact that parishioners who gave testimony about curés who hassled their daughters or who were so drunk they nearly passed out during vespers still took the time to tell the court that those same priests gave them difficulties in the confessional tells us how important the proper performance of the rituals of confession and communion was. These sacraments were part of what made the priest–parishioner relationship work, and the laity were not shy about discussing this most private of matters in their depositions if it meant they had a chance to replace their troublesome curé with one who, in their view, performed the sacraments properly.

Historians generally agree that there have been three penitential regimes in the history of pre-modern Christianity.[36] The first regime primarily involved the upper classes, and the sacrament was performed only by the bishop. Sinners were transformed into penitents through rituals performed in front of the congregation, and once a person became a penitent they were essentially cast out of normal society. Penitents could not marry or engage in any sexual relationship (within marriage or not), participate in public life, or engage in business. The penitent remained in this state until their death, so this type of penance was done only once in a person's life. The second regime, beginning sometime around the seventh century, expanded penance to a larger segment of society and became less demanding and austere. Penance came to be something a believer participated in many times throughout his or her life. It was done with a priest, privately, and accomplished through the assignment of certain tasks described in manuals known as penitentials. The emphasis was on the restitution that needed to be made between the sinner, the community, and God, but there were no harsh public consequences, and the sinner was never cast out of regular society.[37]

The third penitential system was cemented by the Lateran IV pronouncement that all adult Catholics must participate in annual confession and communion. The major change in this period was that penance was internalized and focused more on the individual rather than the community. The process of confession, rather than the act of penance, was emphasized, as was the detailed examination of one's conscience. The fact that confessional boxes began to appear in churches is often seen as an important sign of this internalization;

confession and penance were supposed to be witnessed only by God and the priest who sat on the other side of the screen, not by the entire community.[38]

Some scholars have seen this shift in penitential practice after Lateran IV as placing a heavy burden on the soul of the sinner and even argue that the harshness of the system encouraged some people, like Luther and his followers, to lose faith in and abandon the system altogether. Certainly, these scholars have seen confession primarily as a tool for either reform or oppression.[39] Other historians have contradicted this view, insisting that for both spiritual and practical reasons the confessional was much more flexible and presented just as many opportunities for healing as it did for punishment. They also emphasize that the community was still an important factor in the rituals surrounding confession and communion; they had more than just a personal, individual value.[40] Most notably, communion became inextricably tied to confession during this period; anyone who wanted to take communion had to first receive absolution in the confessional. Confession was thus still linked to a very public, and community-oriented, ritual.

The material that follows will support the views of these historians, arguing that the practices surrounding confession and communion were not monolithic or inflexible. There were many practical limitations surrounding the confessional that allowed a great deal of lay control over the process. The men and women who testified about their experiences in the confessional showed a great deal of respect for the practice, and they believed that it was necessary for them to confess and receive absolution to be assured of their salvation. Some of them may have found the examination of their consciences on a regular basis to be overly demanding and upsetting, but they still participated and believed in the efficacy of the sacrament. At the same time, they insisted on having a say in how the process went. Curés simply did not have enough power or resources to control the confession and communion process entirely.[41]

The laity who wished to satisfy their Easter duty would need to go to their curé for confession, perform any appropriate penance, receive absolution, and then take communion. Often this meant at least two visits to the curé: the first to confess and the second to follow up and receive absolution after penance had been completed. The first visit might take place during Lent, or at the very beginning of the two-week Easter period, while the second might be put off until just before they took communion.[42] The penalty for failing to complete this obligation usually meant exclusion from other sacraments and ceremonies of the church and could lead to excommunication. The Reims *rituel* states specifically that anyone who did not take the Eucharist at Easter, and then failed to receive it at a later date set by the curé, was forbidden from entering the church. If the recalcitrant person were to die before rectifying this situation, he or she would be refused ecclesiastical burial.[43]

Yet this refusal to comply with the Easter duty rarely happened – by the eighteenth century the vast majority of French Catholics took confession and communion at Easter as the clergy expected them to. For example, a questionnaire filled out by priests in the diocese of Boulogne in the eighteenth century reveals that in rural areas all but a few individuals completed their Easter duty each year.[44] In Reims, only five of the 500 curés who answered their archbishop's questionnaire in 1774 said anything about people who had not completed *paques*.[45] Some curés noted that they would like more people to take communion at other times during the year, besides Easter, but most fulfilled the minimum requirement with little trouble. In urban areas there were more problems, largely because the number of parishioners was too great for the priests to ensure that everyone complied.[46] But in general, unless individuals were unrepentant Protestants, involved in serious and contentious lawsuits, or engaged in a known sexual relationship with someone other than their spouse, they confessed and took communion at least once a year, if not more frequently.[47]

Not everything went exactly according to plan, however; curés did not hold all of the power in the priest–penitent relationship and therefore these sacraments held a great deal of potential for conflict. Parishioners, for example, sometimes tried to use the confessional for their own benefit. In Saint-Théodule, Gaspard Defrasne was involved in a dispute with some people in his parish. Then, after an accident, he took to his bed and asked his curé, Matthieu Faivre, to come to his home to hear his confession and give him communion. Faivre told the court that Defrasne had fractured his leg but was in no danger of dying. He had asked for communion only because he hoped that if people knew he had received the sacraments, and thus could not have any sins on his conscience, they would be more likely to take his side in the dispute. Faivre told the court that he had recognized Defrasne's deceit and refused to give him the sacraments. To play a part in

Defrasne's scheme, Faivre noted, would have been an abuse of the
sacraments of the church.[48]

Curé Sauvageon of Sennely in the diocese of Orléans complained
in his memoir about another problem with confession – that his
parishioners routinely failed to confess all of their sins. This is, of
course, the great problem with using the confessional as a tool of
social control: if a person refuses to confess, there is very little that
the priest can do about it. Sauvageon mentioned that individuals
who had committed thefts of minor church property, like fruit or
wood, never mentioned it in their confessions. He noted, "And
when one is sure of this and even provides proof, they still deny it
and prefer to perjure themselves in the confessional rather than
declare themselves guilty."[49] A priest could only assign penance or
withhold communion for sins that were actually confessed; the curé
just had to hope that the weight on the conscience became heavy
enough that people would eventually see the error of their ways.
Sauvageon noted further that when people did come for confession,
they often refused to follow the established procedure for confessing sins. They approached the confessional without preparation,
and without the right attitude; they even fought with each other in
the line to see the priest. Then penitents spent their time with the
priest complaining about their misery and poverty, or giving excuses for the sins they had committed. Often, they complained about
their neighbours and accused them of sins while refusing to accept
responsibility for their own.[50]

An additional problem mentioned by Sauvageon was that people
preferred to wait until the point of death to confess their most serious sins. Deathbed confessions were understandably quite attractive
to some Catholics and probably happened regularly. Yet it was
church policies themselves that encouraged people to wait until
their last moments to confess their most serious sins. Handbooks
and regulations make it clear that curés were to be lenient with their
parishioners at the time of death, giving them the benefit of the
doubt and absolving them easily, rather than letting them suffer spiritual agony as well as the physical pain of death. The laity certainly
knew about this policy, probably from long-standing tradition. The
Reims *rituel* states that a person in danger of death could confess to
any priest, approved or not. At that time the priest could absolve any
sins – even those sins designated as reserved, which were usually only
absolved by a more senior authority. The *rituel* instructed curés that

they could absolve dying persons even if they had lost the ability to speak, as long as they could make a sign or gesture of remorse.[51] This attitude was certainly flexible and merciful, but it could encourage people to be less than forthcoming in the confessional when they were young and healthy.

Regardless of his complaints, Sauvageon gives no indication in his memoir that he ever refused communion to more than a handful of individuals. He may have recognized in his parishioners a multitude of sins but he was willing to absolve them of these sins (or ignore the fact that they refused to confess them). Another curé noted in his memoir that he had essentially done the same thing. Jean-Baptiste Raveneau, a curé in the diocese of Meaux at the end of the seventeenth century, regularly had a handful of non-communicants in his parish and spent a great deal of mental and spiritual energy trying to figure out ways to return them to the fold.[52] But Raveneau too was guilty of lowering his standards to allow the majority of his parishioners to take their Easter communion. For example, a conflict among the notable individuals in his parish produced a lawsuit and so much enmity that Raveneau feared he would be unable to give many of the individuals in question communion that year. Open conflicts or lawsuits between family or community members were seen as public sins, and unless the individuals involved agreed to arbitration and compromised, responsible and vigilant curés felt that they had to refuse absolution.[53] At the last minute Raveneau managed to have the case suspended so that Easter services could go forward as planned, but when his bishop visited, Raveneau was scolded for letting those involved take communion.[54] Caught between a rock and a hard place, Raveneau was trying to keep peace in the village while at the same time facing pressure from the bishop. Yet it is easy to see who had the advantage here: the bishop did not have the time or resources to intervene in every village dispute in his diocese, so it was much more likely that curés would continue to keep their standards somewhat lax for the sake of peace in the community.

Some of the difficulties with confession brought to light by the *officialité* were caused by curés who neglected the confessional. Curé Pierre Mangeut was often absent from his parish because he preferred hunting to fulfilling his duties, and that meant his parishioners were "left without the consolation of being able to approach the sacrament of penitence on the evenings of the great feasts of the year," as one witness put it.[55] François Jacqueney told his parishioners during Sunday mass that he had better things to do than hear their confessions, so they should go either to a neighbouring parish or to the Capuchins.[56] None of the witnesses indicated why Jacqueney was refusing them, but in another case, against Antoine Michel, it is clear that the curé was in the midst of several disputes with his parishioners and refused to admit them to the confessional as a result. Michel told one parishioner that he would sooner hear the confession of a dog than that of his parishioner.[57] In total, twenty-one parishioners testified that Michel had refused to hear their confessions.

Other curés withheld absolution from specific individuals out of resentment or revenge. A woman named Louise Dehu testified that her curé, Nicolas Hourblin, had purchased two pounds of fish from her for a sum of twenty-four *sous*.[58] He later complained that she had not actually given him two pounds and asked for a refund of nine *sous*, but Dehu insisted that she did not owe him anything. When she came to do her Easter confession, he refused to give her absolution. She presented herself three more times to the curé for confession, and he refused her each time.[59] François Maury, curé of Draize (Reims), took his resentment over a fairly straightforward dispute even further. In 1771 he lost a court case and was sentenced to pay a fine to his parishioner Antoine Wilmet. For the next five years he blacklisted Wilmet's entire family from the confessional, forcing them to find other priests to absolve them each Easter. This was not an isolated incident for Maury – two other parishioners testified that they too had been refused in the confessional after disputes with the curé.[60]

Even more problematic were the curés who used the confessional for personal gain. Priests were allowed to charge fees for certain types of services, like masses, marriages, and funerals, but they were expressly forbidden from charging anything for confession, communion, or any of the sacraments performed for the sick and dying. The curé was not allowed to ask for penance that would benefit him financially either.[61] But some curés, like Vernier, who asked one of his parishioners for fish in exchange for absolution, crossed this line. Jacques Philbert François, curé of Artemps (Noyon), was accused of requiring those who confessed with him during Easter to put a few *sous* in a collection box. Parishioners believed that he took this money for his own profit; François claimed he gave it to the poor.[62] Either way, this practice was considered irregular, as was curé Nicolas Hourblin's request that each child in his parish who confessed with him give him an egg.[63]

Two other curés asked for a lot more than a few *sous* or an egg, however. François Jacoulot was known for assigning his parishioners to work for him as penance for their sins, or he would ask for other things that he needed for his household, like a cart of wood.[64] Curé Matthieu Faivre refused to hear the confessions of, or give communion to, both André Defrasne and his aunt Claudine Defrasne because he claimed they owed him fifty francs. Faivre told Claudine that unless he got his fifty francs he would refuse her all sacraments, and that she would die "like an animal." She came to him to ask for confession many times anyway, and by the end of Easter she had finally worn him down; he begrudgingly heard her confession. André Defrasne continued to be refused, however, and opted to confess with the vicaire of a neighbouring parish.[65]

Vernier, as we have seen, also tried to use the confessional for his own benefit, asking especially for information, but for other things as well. In one instance, his parishioner Marie Jeanne Jacquot (Visse) argued with him over the funds collected for the patron saint of the parish, Sainte Radegonde. She claimed that the money was, according to long-standing tradition, to be used for decoration of the altar of Sainte Radegonde, while Vernier insisted that he could use the money for the church in any way he saw fit. Vernier went to a local court to try to force Jacquot to give him the money, but he was unable to obtain a sentence against her. Despite this, for years after this disagreement Vernier refused to absolve her in the confessional, claiming that she owed him for the court costs. She tried confessing with the vicaire of the parish in hopes of receiving absolution from him, but Vernier was still keeping tabs on her: whenever he saw her enter the confessional to confess with any other priest, he scurried over and interrupted, whispering to the priest that she was not worthy of absolution.[66]

The curés referenced above were guilty of breaking, or perhaps bending, diocesan and church rules with regard to confession. Many of them were chastised for it, and even if they were spared the indignity of being fired they still had to deal with the fallout from their actions with their superiors and their parishioners. In any case, their infractions kept them from using the confessional effectively as a tool of reform. And if the curé himself did not behave properly in the confessional, it was likely that his parishioners would lose confidence in him as their confessor. Any hope of reform trickling down from the top of the church hierarchy to the laity would by stymied by these

sorts of actions on the part of less-than-exacting curés, Vernier included. At the same time, curés who did try to uphold the letter of the law
might find themselves in greater trouble than those who ignored it.
Problems with confession and communion went much deeper than
a few misbehaving curés.

Additional information from Vernier's case demonstrates this
quite well. Although he was certainly guilty of significant lapses,
Vernier also received heavy criticism from his parishioners when he
tried to bring about reform through the legitimate use of the confessional. Two of these were women who, he claimed, had gotten
pregnant out of wedlock. Jeanne Louise Patron testified that the curé
refused her absolution and tried to get her to leave her parents'
home. In his interrogation Vernier explained that he had suggested
this for her own good, because her parents (butcher Jacques Patron
and Marie Madeleine Cognon) were such a bad influence on her. He
said that Patron had admitted to him that young, corrupt people
often stayed at her parents' home and that they were the cause of her
unhappiness as well as her pregnancy. Vernier told the court that he
only wanted to improve her situation by finding a place for her to
work that would take her away from such an environment. He also
told her that since her parents were not exact in fulfilling their religious duties and had not done their Easter communion in many
years, if they died he would be obliged to conform to the rules of the
church and bury them on the outskirts of town instead of in the
parish cemetery. He told similar things to Elizabeth Trouson, who,
he claimed, had also become pregnant by a man staying at her parents' home; out of duty and charity, he claimed, he had tried to find
a place for her elsewhere.[67]

Patron did, in fact, have an illegitimate daughter, born in 1765.
Four years later, the parish registers show that she married Jean Baptiste Batillet and had another child only seven months later.[68] Pregnancy before marriage was not unusual; in Mareuil-sur-Ay during the
eighteenth century 14.3 per cent of brides gave birth to a child within eight months of their marriage.[69] But the fact that Patron was one
of these does suggest that Vernier may have been right. His attempts
to use diocesan rules to change her behaviour were not successful,
and perhaps he went about things in the wrong way, but knowing
these details does make him seem less callous and arbitrary. There is
no record of a marriage or a child for Elizabeth Trouson in the
Mareuil-sur-Ay registers, but it is possible that she had also been preg-

nant and either gave birth in another parish or suffered a miscarriage. Vernier insisted that he had the best interests of the women at heart when he refused them absolution and tried to get them to leave their parents' homes.

Vernier also tried to deny absolution to anyone in the parish who sold alcohol. He vigorously defended his actions in the confessional on this point, claiming quite rightly that diocesan regulations specified that people who were not willing to put the circumstances of sin behind them should be denied absolution, as should those who had promised to change but never had. The *rituel* explains that it is the confessor's responsibility to help those who have been in a state of mortal sin for a long time to change their ways.[70] This would certainly apply to the women who were living in the same household as their sexual partner, without being married, and it could apply to those who sold alcohol – at least, in Vernier's mind it did.

Vernier saw alcohol as the main reason for disorder in his parish. Many priests probably ignored the stricter sections of the *rituel* about confession and absolution because they did not want a rebellion on their hands,[71] but when it came to the evils of alcohol Vernier was unwilling to compromise, and he earned the enmity of many of his parishioners as a result. This shows that the confessional was often ineffective as a tool of reform because the laity pushed back against it when curés crossed the boundaries put in place through long-standing tradition and practice. Parishioners from Mareuil-sur-Ay, knowing that their previous curé had never withheld absolution from anyone for selling alcohol, and seeing that their counterparts in nearby villages sold alcohol and still took communion, refused to accept this aspect of Vernier's reform agenda. When he denied them absolution, they did not simply accept their fate and either change their ways or live without the benefits of the sacraments; they brought in the authorities to try to find a curé who would perform the sacraments in the way that they wanted. Parishioners knew that they were not powerless in their relationship with the curé, even when it came to confession.

Perhaps Vernier was overly harsh in the confessional, and his strict adherence to prescribed church and diocesan rules was really the problem here. His harshness may in fact be connected to larger debates about the nature of confession that had been taking place in France for nearly a century. Confession, penance, and absolution were the major issues involved in Jansenism, one of the primary theological controversies of the latter half of the early modern period. Jansenism was a controversial interpretation of the writings of Augustine on grace and works, original sin, and predestination.[72] The theology had its roots in the mid-seventeenth century, but its influence continued to be felt in the eighteenth century after the papal bull *Unigenitus* condemned its major tenets in 1713. Several prominent eighteenth-century bishops were notorious for their open support of Jansenism, while others were known for having Jansenist leanings. One of the most basic disputes between Jansenists and traditional Catholics (most notably the Jesuits) involved the sacraments of confession and communion. Jansenists, with their strict belief in humanity's inability to earn grace, believed that communion should only be taken when the penitent was in a state of complete worthiness. They discouraged frequent communion and preached about the dangers of communing unworthily. The Jesuits, on the other hand, promoted and encouraged frequent communion and saw the sacrament as a necessary conduit for earning and receiving God's grace. They argued that the true danger was found not in unworthy participation in the Eucharist but in avoiding it and leaving the soul open to temptation and the weaknesses of the natural man.

Is it possible that Vernier was a secret Jansenist, and thus excessively strict with his parishioners in the confessional? I think not. To a curé like Vernier, Jansenism would have appeared to be less about doctrine and more about rebellion against the church leadership. We have no indication that such a rebellion was among his infractions; Vernier's problems were with his parishioners rather than his superiors. But that does not mean he was completely ignorant of Jansenist ideas about strict confession. It is certainly possible that Vernier could have been attracted by the idea of using the confessional as a tool to promote social discipline and conformity. This was one of the primary goals of church leadership, after all, and a bit of social discipline would have made Vernier's life much easier.

At the same time, we cannot assume that it was only excessive harshness or commitment to the church's rules on the part of Vernier or other curés like him that led parishioners to rebel, either openly or behind the scenes. Most of the time curés were not trying to uphold strict or extreme standards in any way; in fact, they often had a hard time just following the basic rules and regulations involving confession. One of the primary reasons for difficulties in the confessional comes from loopholes in the confessional system itself. In an ideal version of this system, each Catholic would confess with his or her curé, and only that curé. A relationship of understanding and self-respect would develop between priest and penitent, and the curé would be able make sure that his parishioners were not living with the condemnation of mortal sin upon them. Through the careful assignment of appropriate penance, a few well-placed suggestions in sermons, a bit of prodding in the confessional, and then refusal of absolution if need be, curés would be confident that their parish-ioners were not committing sacrilege when they took communion.[73] But eighteenth-century rural parishes were far from an ideal world, and the system that looks so clear and straightforward actually con-tained significant loopholes.

One of these loopholes was the distinction that the church made between public and private sinners. In their texts, church leaders made it clear that they placed the good of the community over the sacred nature of the Eucharist in one specific and important case: the private sinner. As we saw in the Reims *rituel* and the Delacourt case, priests knew that if a public sinner approached the altar during a church service and demanded to receive communion, he or she was to be refused. However, if a private sinner – someone whose sin was known only to the curé – asked to take communion in front of the whole parish, he or she was not to be turned away. By asking for an unworthy communion the communicant would be committing a sacrilege that would have to be confessed and absolved later, but the priest was told to allow it for the good of the community. Public sin-ners had already disrupted the unity of the parish, and their sins had caused a scandal that would only be compounded if the person was seen taking communion with the rest of the community. But a private sinner had not created any such scandal because his or her sins were as yet unpublicized. If communion were withheld from this individ-ual, in fact, it would make a private sin public and cause additional disruption. It was thus better for the community to remain ignorant of the sin, even at the expense of the additional offence charged to the soul of the sinner.

What exactly was a public sin, and who defined it? Another curé who struggled because of this distinction between public and pri-vate sins was Jean Pelletier.[74] Sometime before Easter in 1740, Pel-letier gave his parishioner Nicolas Galichet permission to confess with another priest. But he also told him that he could not take

communion until he provided proof that he had been absolved.
Galichet refused to do this, and he asked people from other parishes in Reims to attend the mass on 18 April when he planned to present himself for communion. He wanted them to serve as witnesses
for whatever happened next. Sure enough, Galichet asked Pelletier
for communion three times, saying, "Monsieur, I am Nicolas
Galichet your parishioner, and I ask for Easter communion." Pelletier responded, "My friend, I have nothing to give you."[75] According
to multiple witnesses this refusal caused a great tumult in the
church. People were murmuring and a few even shouted that this
action was dreadful and unheard of.[76] Pelletier insisted that he had
been correct to refuse communion to Galichet because his sin was
public. Strangely, he would not tell the court what that sin was, only
that it was not concubinage, usury, or any other sin that a priest
would have to prove was public. Furthermore, Pelletier argued, the
real scandal would have been if he had given communion to
Galichet, because the true Catholics in the parish would have been
outraged to see a sacrilege committed.[77] Pelletier's testimony shows
the fine line that curés had to walk when administering the sacraments of confession and communion. One step too close to a strict
interpretation of Catholic doctrine could be the step that led the
parishioners to rebel against the curé.

Other curés gave communion to unworthy parishioners instead of
refusing them publicly, but they found other ways to make their frustration with irregular confessions and communions known. For
example, on Easter in 1736, Nicolas Vauquelin, curé of Saint-Pierre de
Crépy (Laon) stopped the mass just at the point when his parishioners were kneeling in front of the altar, waiting to receive communion. The kneeling parishioners included the mayor of the town as
well as many other people with whom he apparently had a conflict.
According to witnesses, Vauquelin began hurling invectives at them,
saying that there were four or five among them who were Judases,
about to take communion unworthily. He wished aloud that it was
the will of God that the earth would open up and swallow them so
he would not have to give them communion. The parish was scandalized, and this event triggered the court case that cost Vauquelin his
job.[78] Vauquelin had already been accused of sexual assault against
one of his parishioners, as well as several other infractions in the performance of his duties, but it was this irregular communion service
that finally got the attention of the authorities.

Perhaps even more relevant for curés than the distinction between public and private sins was the second loophole in the confessional system: the fact that having just one priest to make sure that hundreds of parishioners had confessed and repented was highly impractical. Even in small parishes in the countryside there were simply too many people for curés to keep track of. Raveneau counted 215 families and around 500 communicants in his parish in 1676. That year, his first as curé, he noted that the crowds at the confessional began on the Thursday before Easter, early in the morning. On Friday, he had to preach and then teach catechism in between hearing confessions, while on Saturday he was in the confessional from early morning until late at night. In his memoir he wrote, simply, "This is too much; I need to get help."[79] Curés brought before the *officialité* also gave hints that they were burdened by long lines at the confessional during holy seasons as well, not to mention all the time it took for them to bring the sacraments to the sick and dying of the parish at any time of the day or night. This could easily lead to problems, since overburdened curés might have to be less than thorough in the confessional; savvy parishioners might have tried to take advantage of their fatigue.[80]

The most obvious solution to this is the one that Raveneau eventually employed: he brought in additional priests to hear confessions. Vicaires, members of religious orders, and even local unbeneficed priests could be engaged to hear confessions as long as they had a certificate of approval from diocesan officials. The Reims *rituel* also suggested that because of the intimate nature of confession, the laity should be allowed to choose their own confessor if their conscience demanded it, including during the Easter season. The *rituel* includes text from Lateran IV, which explains that if a person has a good reason for not wanting to confess with his or her own pastor, then they should ask permission to confess elsewhere and the pastor should freely give that permission. Curés were told that they should "rid themselves of all spirit of self-interest and domination," and willingly accommodate the needs of their parishioners.[81] So once again, the liberal rules of the church created difficulties for any curé who might want to use the confessional as a mechanism for reform. The only way confession and communion could be used to change behaviour in recalcitrant individuals was if the curé had complete control over both sacraments. Because of this loophole – the ability of parishioners to choose their own confessors and the proximity of the religious orders – the curé had little recourse if the laity chose to confess to a

priest whom they knew was going to absolve them with little difficulty.[82] He would still have no choice but to give that person communion if he or she asked for it.

That was exactly the situation Jean Fay, curé of Harricourt (Reims)
found himself in, according to his testimony in the case against the
curé of nearby Buzancy, Jean François Person. Fay testified that Person
was giving absolution to people from his parish too easily; Fay complained that this was making his efforts to reform behaviour difficult,
since sinners knew they could just go to Person if Fay refused them.
Most notably, Person had given absolution to a young couple who had
scandalized the parish because of their sexual relationship, resulting in
the woman's pregnancy; Person heard their confessions and gave them
absolution. They took communion the next day.[83] Another curé complained during his court case that one of his parishioners did not
attend mass or parish services and was separated from his wife. This
should have been a reason to deny him communion, but by carefully
choosing different confessors from villages and towns in the vicinity,
he was able to hide his sins and receive absolution.[84]

As might be expected, the free-confession loophole caused no end
of difficulties, as curés tried, rather unsuccessfully, a myriad of ways
to maintain control over the confessional. As we saw in the Vernier
case, permission to confess with another priest was granted in the
form of a *billet*, filled out and signed by the curé. The penitent
would show that *billet* to the priest before the sacrament could be
administered and then bring it back to the curé. This was supposed
to help give the curé some degree of control over the process, and
curés did refuse to grant *billets* in some cases. Curé Vauquelin, for
example, was accused of refusing his parishioners the permission to
confess with priests other than those he named himself.[85] He was
within his rights to do this, but the fact that his parishioners still
brought it up as evidence against him shows that this was a rule they
did not expect their curé to follow very strictly. Most of the laity
demanded that curés hear their confessions on their own terms, and
those curés who did not were likely to be resented, criticized, and
even taken to court.

Multiple witnesses in the Vernier case testified of his unwillingness
to allow outside priests to hear confessions in his parish. His attempts
to control both confession and communion even led him to have a
colleague preach a sermon about it. This colleague was described as
either an ex-Carmelite or an ex-Jesuit and was thought to be Vernier's

relative, perhaps a nephew (which was later confirmed during the interrogation). Fourteen individuals testified about this so-called Carmelite's sermon; they explained that the message of the sermon was that Easter confession was not free and that anyone who confessed with a priest other than the curé was damned, as was the priest who heard the confession. Witnesses reported that the preacher used the word "damned" many times and that everyone was scandalized by his words and his tone. Everyone, that is, except for Marie Jeanne Bellot, who testified that she could not hear what was preached because of the noise made by so much murmuring.[86]

Jean Réné Blaudinne de Marassé, a local military officer, attended this sermon as well. His report corroborates what the other witnesses said about the preacher: that he had asserted that individuals cannot confess with other priests besides their own curé at Easter, even if they have been given permission to do so at other times. De Marassé indicated in his testimony that he believed this went against the liberties of the Gallican church and the liberty of confession. Concerned, he went to speak with Vernier after the sermon and was surprised to hear the curé say that he thought it had been a very good sermon. In fact, Vernier then boasted that he had written it himself and ordered the Carmelite to preach it![87] Vernier claimed that what his nephew had actually preached was that it was dangerous for parishioners to ask for a *billet* to confess with a priest that they did not know, because such a priest would not be able to give them the best counsel. Only their curé could provide the help they needed to truly rid themselves of their sins, because only he knew and understood them. He did not say, he claimed, that Easter confession was not free. Nor had he written the sermon himself, as De Marassé had testified.[88] No matter who was telling the truth, it seems clear that Vernier was attempting to use the confessional to change the conduct of his parishioners, and it had backfired.

Pierre Sellier, curé of Suzanne (Noyon), also gave his parishioners difficulties when it came to granting *billets*. A complaint was made against him at some point during the first half of 1730, and the bishop visited the parish on 2 June that year, but the court did not hear depositions until September. Between the time of the complaint and the beginning of the court proceedings, Sellier refused to grant people who had signed the complaint any *billets* for confession, and this created quite a bit of difficulty since a number of people had wanted to receive confirmation during the bishop's visit. Bishops were the only clergy who could administer the sacrament of confirmation, and confession was a prerequisite for that sacrament. Bishops might only visit rural parishes once or twice in a person's lifetime, so it was a chance they would not want to miss. Sellier's refusal to grant *billets* was therefore especially problematic. When the court questioned Sellier about this, he first insisted that he had not refused a *billet* to anyone. However, the court pressed him, and he eventually admitted it. He said he thought he had done the right thing when he refused to issue *billets*. The court told him that he had not.[89]

Another curé who believed he was acting correctly as far as confessional practice was concerned was Jean Baptiste Lanneau, who refused to hear the confessions of parishioners who had been part of a dispute over the choice of churchwardens. He even went so far as to announce from the pulpit that he would not confess anyone who had signed a complaint against him. But the testimony in the case shows that Lanneau's infractions had begun years earlier, when he had created a system to try to regularize confession in a way that was making his parishioners angry. He gave his penitents specific days and times for their Easter confession and, according to witnesses, if anyone missed their assigned time then they were out of luck. For example, Jacques Gérard testified that on the day his wife was assigned for confession she was ill and could not go to the church. After she recovered she presented herself for confession but the curé declared that she had missed her day and thus damned herself. Another parishioner testified that he had been unable to complete his Easter duty for four years because he had missed his assigned day for confession just one time.[90] Lanneau told the court that he had never turned away anyone just because they missed their assigned day, so perhaps there was more to the story than the witness testimony reveals. Lanneau was probably within his rights to do these things if he was obeying the letter of the law, but his parishioners resented his strict interpretation of the doctrines and rules surrounding confession and communion.

Curé Matthieu Faivre was criticized even more severely for trying to make his parishioners follow the rules. Faivre was notorious for refusing to administer sacraments to parishioners who did not follow proper procedures. Multiple men and women testified that they had approached the curé to tell him that they had confessed elsewhere and wanted to receive communion during the mass. He routinely told them that they should take communion where they had confessed instead. Once he told three men who had presented their *billets* that he would administer to them but only because he wanted to follow the example of Jesus, who had given communion not only to his eleven faithful apostles but also to Judas his betrayer.[91] In another instance Faivre refused to hear the confession of Marie Joseph Nicod because she had not attended a mass one Sunday. She tried joining the line of people waiting to confess in the confessional, but as soon as Faivre saw that she was next in line he simply left. Nicod finally went to a nearby parish to confess, despite the fact that the roads were icy and she was just a dozen days away from having a baby. It was common for pregnant women to confess when they were almost ready to deliver, in case they died during childbirth, so Nicod would have felt Faivre's refusal to hear her confession very keenly.[92]

All of these attempts to keep his parishioners in line were a significant part of the case against Faivre. But refusals and postponements were nothing compared with what he tried during Easter of 1746. Faivre was curé for two villages: Saint-Théodule and its annex, Labergement. Faivre was not required by his benefice to say two masses on Sundays and feast days, so parishioners from the two parishes often met together, at one of the two churches. Three weeks before Easter Faivre announced that on the next Sunday the only mass would be in the church at Saint-Théodule. But apparently not enough people from Labergement attended this mass – they either missed the mass entirely or they went to a nearby parish. It was not unusual for rural parishioners to miss the mass for legitimate reasons, like illness. Most commonly, however, people missed the mass because someone had to stay home to look after the household. Thieves were known to strike when everyone was at church for services. Perhaps people from Labergement had not wanted to leave their property, or maybe they just did not want to make the journey to Saint-Théodule. Whatever the reason, it angered Faivre and he decided to do something about it.

From the pulpit Faivre declared his parishioners mutinous subjects, and he later refused to hear some of their confessions. Then, on Easter Sunday, Faivre made an announcement. He told his parishioners he was unhappy with the financial compensation he received from Labergement and believed they owed him a greater allowance of wood. Unless he received more wood, he said, he was going to pack up his things that night and go stay at the abbey across the river. Anyone who wanted to do their Easter confession would have to find him there, and then he would give communion in Saint-Théodule on Sunday. And to make sure that everyone came to do their Easter communion in Saint-Théodule, he had decided that he was going to eat all of the consecrated hosts in Labergement. He then proceeded to do so, in front of all who were assembled at the church. Multiple witnesses gave details of this, saying that he ate every host in the tabernacle and even the one in the *lunette* – the reserve host saved for anyone who might fall sick.[93]

This event caused a tremendous uproar among the people of Labergement. Some were even crying in the church because they were so upset. During the court proceedings Faivre tried to convince the court that the church in Labergement was so humid that the hosts were at risk of rotting, so he ate them to avoid sacrilege.[94] But this seems a flimsy excuse, and multiple people reported in their depositions exactly what Faivre had said from the pulpit before he ate the hosts. The fact is, Faivre tried to force his parishioners to follow the rules for confession and communion by taking away their opportunity to take communion on their own terms. He went to the extreme of actually consuming all of the consecrated hosts – the Lord's body – one by one, in full view of his parishioners. This scandal then resulted in a court case.

However, perhaps Faivre would consider himself lucky if he could have known what would happen to one of his colleagues in the diocese of Besançon, Antoine Bullet, when he tried something similar. Bullet was the curé of Mouthier and its annex, Lods.[95] As we saw in chapter 2, a dozen men of Lods ended up on trial because they had locked Bullet in the sacristy for several hours and threatened to break his arms, nail his hands to a board, or attack him on the road and kill him. What is especially interesting about this case is that the reason the people of Lods were so angry with their curé was directly related to Easter communion. It appears that the people of the annex wanted to take communion in their own church, with a local priest instead of the curé. This local priest was a communal, or familiar, priest, and had no specific assignment or benefice. Communal priests were not supposed to perform the sacraments, but they did earn money by saying masses and making sure that the conditions of founded masses in the parish were fulfilled.[96] This particular communal priest was well-liked by the parish-ioners of Lods but was at odds with the curé, as communal priests often were. He encouraged people to take communion at his mass, held at the church in Lods.

Upset by this breach of diocesan rules, Bullet decided it was time to regain control over his parishioners' communion. Just before Easter in 1744, he reminded everyone at the mass in Lods that they were required to do their *paques* in Mouthier with him and not with any other priest. To make sure that this happened, he said, he was going to lock up all of the consecrated hosts in the tabernacle and take the key with him. Bullet then retired to the sacristy, but he was followed by parishioners who demanded the key to the tabernacle and told him that he could not leave until he gave it to them. Luckily for Bullet, the parishioners failed to follow through with their threats to injure or kill him and settled for tackling him and forcibly taking the key. From that point on, Bullet refused to come to Lods for any reason, whether it was to say the mass, hear confessions, or administer the last rites, unless he was accompanied by at least four village notables who would guarantee his protection.[97]

Bullet's circumstances were perhaps extreme, but the situation was not entirely unique. Curés had to allow their parishioners to confess with other priests, deal with unrepentant subjects, and follow a somewhat lax interpretation of diocesan rules. If they did not, they were opening themselves up to disorder and scandal in the parish, open rebellion, lawsuits, and perhaps the loss of their benefice. They could not even count on church authorities to back them up. It appears, then, that the confessional was not the tool that the clergy hoped it could be. Each Easter the most effective priests went through perhaps dozens of small negotiations to make sure that the vast majority of their parishioners were able to participate in the sacraments. Rarely could they use the confessional to change people's behaviour, if those people had no desire to change. Instead, the process of negotiation clearly shows that church standards were seldom upheld completely, in the interest of maintaining functional relationships between all the members of the rural community.

Many of the examples cited above demonstrate that confession and communion were central to the religious life of rural parishioners. Yes, parishioners had to tick the box and fulfill their Easter duty each year, and for some of them it may have been mere routine. But they still expected the rituals to be available to them and to be performed correctly. This was important both for their own sense of personal spirituality and relationship with God and for their conception of a functioning community. When the laity entered the confessional or knelt at the altar for communion, they knew exactly what to expect.

When they did not find the kindness, solace, and absolution that they anticipated, along with the familiar prayers and rituals, they often took matters into their own hands. As we have seen, lay Catholics were willing to change confessors, complain to authorities, or even take their curé to court when he failed in his duty to provide a satisfactory confessional experience. This is most obvious when curés were guilty of a clear violation of the rules of the confessional. For example, some women spoke out when their curés solicited them for sexual favours during confession.[98] But others also felt they could ask for and expect some give-and-take in the confessional process even in less extreme circumstances. Sometimes, they simply negotiated with the curé one on one, letting him know what they expected and how he had erred. Testimony recorded by the *officialité* fortunately gives rare evidence of this, in the voices of the penitents themselves. The best examples of this strategy all come from female penitents, interestingly enough – even women, and perhaps especially women – felt they were entitled to a proper confession.

For example, one Easter Constance Coqueteau went to her curé, Nicolas Hourblin, to give her confession. She knelt in the confessional and confessed her sins as she usually did. But soon she realized that Hourblin was not asking her any questions or expressing any sorrow for her sins. Confused, she took him to task and demanded that he interrogate her![99] It was at that point she discovered that he had been drinking and was not in full possession of his faculties, but even then she was not shy about asking her curé to follow appropriate confessional procedures. Less scrupulous parishioners might have taken advantage of the situation and just accepted absolution when the tipsy curé offered it, but clearly some Catholics believed in the efficacy of confession and they wanted the ritual performed by a competent priest. Similarly, Marie Nicolle Malte argued with her curé, Pierre Mangeut, in the confessional over a financial matter. As a result of the argument Mangeut sent her away without absolution, and she decided to confess with a neighbouring curé since she was close to the end of her pregnancy. Following her confession, she went back to Mangeut and asked for communion. He asked her where she had confessed, and she retorted that it should not matter to him, since he had not wanted to hear her confession in the first place. Mangeut took her by the arm and dragged her rudely out of his courtyard, but despite this Malte presented herself at the altar for communion anyway. Mangeut had no choice but to give it to her.[100] A woman in

Matthieu Faivre's parish employed a similar strategy in wearing her curé down until he performed the sacraments for her. Marie Françoise Parrin Pianée was also about to have a baby, and she was anxious to confess her sins before she delivered. For at least a week she tried to get the curé to hear her confession, but Faivre, for reasons not stated in the deposition, was avoiding her. Pianée tried to track him down, even speaking to his valet and asking him to let her know when the curé would be in the church. Finally, after eight days, she cornered Faivre and said to him that if he did not want to hear her confession at the church, she would send for him when she went into labour and he could hear it then.[101] Apparently the prospect of administering to a woman in childbirth was too much for Faivre, so he admitted her to the confessional.

The Vernier case provides examples of several of his parishioners who were unafraid to express their dissatisfaction directly to their curé – even within the confessional itself. Many people in Mareuil-sur-Ay expressed outrage that Vernier often asked them for inappropriate information about other parishioners when they came to the confessional. During his interrogation Vernier was asked if he had tried to "profit from his position as confessor and thus trouble the peace of families and corrupt the servants by threatening them with damnation if they would not give him an exact account of what was happening in the homes of their masters and mistresses." He denied this accusation by simply saying no, but the parishioners argued otherwise.[102] For example, just a few months before the court case began, Claudette Gérard, a servant of Nicolas Christophe Robert, went to confess with the curé and before she could begin he asked her if her master was holding meetings at his house. These meetings probably referred to the plans for the complaint against Vernier, since Robert was one of the plaintiffs in the case. She told him that she had come to confess her sins and not to give an account of her master. As a result, the curé refused to hear her confession and sent her away, telling her that unless she quit her job she would be damned. However, it is important to note that he got no information out of her. Gérard knew that what Vernier was asking went beyond the purpose of the confessional and refused to comply with her curé's orders. Nicolas Vilmot, the servant of another plaintiff, Pierre Trubert, testified that the curé had done something similar by asking him questions about what his master was doing with his fields. Vilmot did not tell him, nor did he submit to the curé when he asked him to leave his position with Trubert and work for him instead.[103]

Vilmot's testimony about these incidents is light on details, but that of another of Trubert's servants, Marie Thomas, is not. On Holy Wednesday in 1769, Thomas went to confess with the vicaire (Jean Louis Harlin) and in the middle of her confession the curé left his own confessional box and interrupted the vicaire to speak with him. There must have been quite a path worn between the two confessionals, since it seems Vernier could hardly let a day go by without interrupting his vicaire. Vernier left after a few moments and Thomas continued her confession, until Harlin stopped her again because the curé was signalling him from across the room. The vicaire left his post yet again and spoke with Vernier before returning to hear the rest of Thomas's confession. When she was finished, Harlin told her that she needed to get her master to remove his signature from the complaint that had been made against the curé. Thomas responded that as a servant she had no power over her master and that she did not dare speak to him about it. If he or Vernier wanted to get Trubert to take his name off the complaint, she insisted, they should ask him themselves. So, the vicaire sent her away without giving her absolution.[104]

These were not isolated incidents, nor were they limited to servants. *Laboureur* Pierre Blondeau testified that he went to confess with Harlin and was refused absolution because he did not want to divulge what was being said about the affair between the curé and the parishioners. Harlin told him that Vernier had given him specific questions to ask Blondeau in the confessional and that if Blondeau did not answer them he should be denied absolution. Blondeau decided to forgo his Easter communion that year rather than answer. Agnes Jacquot also testified that twice Vernier tried to get her to give him details about the goings-on in the parish, and specifically about affairs with which he was involved; she refused to provide any information. Instead, she told him that the care of her own house kept her busy enough that she had no need to occupy herself with the business of others.[105]

Vernier did not treat Catherine Adam any better one year when she tried to receive absolution from him. In 1760, Adam went to Vernier to give her Easter confession. Vernier heard her confession, gave her penance, and told her to return for absolution in about a week. She did, but as soon as Vernier saw her kneeling in the confessional he said, "How your mother wishes to cast you off," and then slammed the screen shut in her face. Presumably, he was referring to the church, indicating that because Adam was still selling wine she would not be able to receive absolution and take communion with the other members of the parish. After this outburst, she left the church in shock; she told the court that if that was going to be the way the curé received her then she would not go to him for confession again. A couple of months later she was passing by the presbytery when Vernier called to her, reminding her that she had not yet done her Easter communion. She responded that it was his fault – that when she had come to the confessional she had "expected to find a priest but found instead only a furious man." She insisted that she would not return to him for confession.[106]

From all of this it is clear that the sacraments of confession and communion were so important to the laity that when they felt their curé was not performing them properly, they let him know, sometimes within the confessional space itself. These parishioners believed that the curés were there to serve their needs, and they did not hesitate to complain if those needs were not met. Sometimes these expectations were communicated locally, one on one, and if that did not work then parishioners had opportunities to use the court system to take their curés to task. Another thing that *officialité* records reveal is that although the church focused a great deal on confession and communion at Easter, the occasions when these sacraments were performed at the sickbed in the moments before death were perhaps even more important to the laity.

### Parading God through the Streets: Sacraments at the Sickbed

French Catholics believed that the events surrounding the moment of death played a key role in what happened next, in the afterlife.[107] During those final, crucial moments, wills were made out or approved and last wishes were made known. Sins had to be confessed and forgiven or the soul would be confined to hell and everlasting punishment. All of these events required a priest. Curés thus had to be ready, day or night, to wade through mud or snow and make haste to the bedsides of dying souls, carrying the Eucharist and words of comfort. Just as with the annual confession and communion, parishioners insisted that these deathbed rituals be performed correctly, and on their own terms.

If a person was sick or injured and in danger of dying, the curé would be called to administer three distinct sacraments. First, if the person was conscious and able to speak they would be given confession and absolution. Once absolved, the person could then receive their last communion, known as the viaticum. The curé would carry, in ritual fashion, the consecrated host from the church to the sickbed, accompanied by as many family members and parishioners as were available; these worshipers might follow the curé back to the church after the ritual in reverence for the sacrament as well. Finally, the curé issued the last rites, or extreme unction, and the person could face death with a clear conscience.[108]

Lay people in rural areas insisted on being administered to at the moment of death. This was not a ritual that the clergy had to prod people to participate in – they willingly submitted to the ministrations of their curé when he visited their sickbeds and demanded those services when they were not offered. They requested them for their family members and fellow parishioners too.[109] The vast majority of the parishioners who testified before the *officialité* court were adamant about having their curé available to perform these last sacraments, multiple times if necessary. One of the most common complaints about curés was that they failed in this duty, either out of negligence, resentment, drunkenness, or absence from the parish. Parishioners also expected curés to be available to administer to everyone in the parish, rich or poor, notable or obscure, nearby or far away.

Nicolas Desboeuf expressed his fears for his fellow parishioners when he learned that his curé, Lanneau, was refusing to administer to a man who lived next door to the curé himself. Desboeuf told the court, "If he lets his neighbour die without the sacraments, what will happen when it's someone at the back of the parish?"[110] Similarly, Vernier was criticized for not wanting to minister to an eighty-three-year-old woman who was staying at the home of tavern-keeper Joseph Baudoin and his wife Marie Hardy. Hardy went to the curé to ask if he would bring the widow the last rites. She found him in the middle of a card game, which he refused to leave.[111] He said that since she had received the last rites from the vicaire the day before, she did not need them again. Vernier was in the right in this case: the *rituel* states that extreme unction should not be repeated during the same illness unless it is a very long illness.[112] But Vernier did not stop there; he berated Hardy and said that she should just "let her die," as her death would be "good riddance" for her and her family. Realizing that Vernier was not going to administer to the widow, Hardy warned him that she would die soon, and he should be ready to do the burial the next day. Vernier responded that he did not care and again repeated that she should just let the woman die. Multiple parishioners testified of the horror they felt when they heard Vernier's callous statements.[113]

Vernier argued in his interrogation that the sick woman had received the Eucharist the day before and had not gotten out of bed since then. A surgeon, Pierre Jerome Leclerc, who was visiting Vernier at the time, gave testimony to corroborate this story. He said that the curé had explained to the messenger that she had received the Eucharist the previous day and that because his vicaire was absent he did not want to leave the presbytery, presumably in case he was called away on a more urgent case. Leclerc also noted that Vernier told him that the woman had been sick for a long time and that a great burden would be lifted from the family when she finally passed away.[114] In this context, his words do not seem quite as heartless as Hardy testified. His actions toward Jean Jacquot and his family seem less severe as well. Marie Nicolle Jacquot testified that Vernier had refused to administer to her father-in-law, despite repeated requests.[115] Vernier told the court that Jacquot had in fact received the last rites and had given his confession, but that because he was vomiting nearly continually the curé had not felt comfortable giving him the Eucharist.[116] This too would have been against the policy of the diocese – priests were not supposed to administer communion if there was any chance that they might be sick and vomit the body of the Lord back up.[117]

Once again we see a fundamental difference in the way that the clergy and the laity saw the sacraments. The laity wanted the curé to be available to administer the last rites at any time of the day or night, and as often as they wished. This could create significant conflict between priest and parishioner, either because the priest was negligent or simply because he was busy and tired. In one case, several parishioners testified that they were visiting their curé, Aubriot de Boncourt, at the presbytery when a messenger arrived asking him to administer to a sick person. The curé refused to go, saying he was busy. The messenger returned three times, and finally his visitors left the presbytery because they did not want to be blamed for contributing to the curé's negligence.[118] In another case, there were

complaints that curé Gabriel Mottet had let several parishioners die
without the sacraments. It was said that he had announced from the
pulpit that his parishioners should stop asking him to bring anyone
the sacraments after dark, telling them that he was not "a wolf running in the night." His parishioners rightly found this offensive and
told the court as much.[119] Others testified of curés refusing to get
out of bed or to leave their dinner guests when asked to visit sick
parishioners. When confronted with these accusations, curés often
insisted that these individuals had not needed the sacraments, either
because they were not actually in danger of dying or because they
had already been administered to. Many sick people and their families asked for the last sacraments multiple times during one illness,
and curés were perhaps feeling a bit beleaguered. But this only
shows how important these rituals were to the laity: they wanted to
participate in them even more often than what the clergy prescribed. They wanted their curé there, as close to the moment of
death as possible.

They also expected these sacraments to be performed with dignity
and decency, following the traditions of the parish. Curés were supposed to conduct themselves with kindness at the sickbed; curés who
did not were regularly criticized. For example, the parish of Volon
was scandalized by the fact that their curé, Antoine Michel, administered the last sacraments when he was drunk.[120] Another curé, Jean
Drouin, was criticized for sitting and drinking with family members
in the kitchen while a woman was in the next room on her
deathbed.[121] Vernier was disparaged for his treatment of Gérard
Thierry's father when he was dying. Instead of hearing kind counsel
that would calm the conscience of the dying man and his family,
Thierry testified that he and his mother had had to listen to harsh
words from the curé: Vernier called Thierry miserable, because he
had persisted in selling alcohol in the parish.[122] Lanneau was accused
of similar infractions in his treatment of Jacques Poincenet. When
the sick man complained that he was hot and burning with fever, the
curé heartlessly told him he should just sit in the river to cool off.
Lanneau claimed that this was a legitimate suggestion, but the
friends and family who were attending Poincenet's sickbed testified
that the curé's tone said otherwise.[123]

Finally, curés were supposed to be lenient and forgiving to dying
parishioners, as outlined in the diocesan handbooks. When they were
not, witnesses made sure that the court heard about it – even if the

curé was technically within his rights to refuse absolution. According to the wife of Nicolas Fleury, she was scandalized when her husband was dying and their curé, Aubriot de Boncourt, would only give him the viaticum after initiating a prolonged debate over some financial matters. She thought he was taking advantage of a sick man to extract promises from him. The curé claimed that Fleury was following his conscience and had confessed freely but witnesses still believed the curé had not treated the dying man compassionately.[124] Curé Jean François Fouchard was questioned about the death of one of his parishioners, a man named Poissonat, because witnesses were claiming that he had died without sacraments and been denied a church burial. Fouchard said that Poissonat, injured but conscious and in full possession of his faculties, failed to give any signs of remorse for having offended God, so he felt he had to refuse him the last sacraments.[125] The people of the parish felt otherwise. Similarly, the family of Nicolle Minel was scandalized by the fact that their curé, Drouin, failed to absolve her on her deathbed. Drouin claimed that Minel had a public sin that had gone unconfessed – another case of a well-known conflict with her father-in-law – and he was waiting until said father-in-law arrived so that she could make her peace with him.[126] Witnesses would have preferred that he absolve her even without this reconciliation, so that she could receive the viaticum before she died.

Interestingly enough, many of the witnesses in these types of situations noted that they were scandalized by the actions of their curés, but they still wanted him to be there to administer to the sick and dying anyway. A case involving curé Pierre Mangeut shows this particularly well. On one occasion, Mangeut heard the confession of one of his parishioners but then said aloud, in front of the people gathered at the man's deathbed, that he would not give him absolution. We might think that after the curé had insulted the sick man so grievously and so publicly, no one involved would want to see or hear from him again. But the next day when the man's condition continued to deteriorate his son-in-law, Pierre Hanzat, was dispatched to request the curé's aid once again. Hanzat knocked on the door of the presbytery for a long while, receiving no answer. So, with the help of another parishioner and a ladder he went over the presbytery wall, extracted the curé from his room, and took him back to administer to the sick man.[127] This incident shows the lengths people would go to in order to have their curé present at the moment of death. It was important for both the individual and the community that the curé be present to administer the last sacraments. It was his job, and his responsibility, and the laity did everything in their power to hold him accountable.

In 1715, the people of Lizine, a parish in the diocese of Besançon, testified in a court case against their curé, Claude Antoine Monnier. The curé's sins were straightforward: he had carried on a public affair with a woman of the parish for years. One witness reported that Monnier was at his mistress's house so often that whenever he was needed to perform the sacraments they sent messengers to her without even bothering to check the presbytery.[128] But the affair had gone on for so long, and had caused so much scandal, that several witnesses reported that they, and the parish in general, had lost confidence in their curé, to the point that they no longer wished to receive the sacraments from him. One woman testified that Monnier had such a bad reputation that no one wanted to confess with him and no one was attending catechism because he was committing more wrongs than the people he was supposed to instruct. Two other parishioners said that everyone was so scandalized with Monnier's libertine morals that they could not attend the mass without horror. Another witness told the court that he would rather die without confession than resort to confessing with a priest as scandalous as Monnier.[129] In another parish, half a century later, Jean Baptiste Lanneau was also told he had lost the confidence of his parishioners. He had been curé of Louvercy and Mourmelon-le-Petit (Reims) for fourteen years, but after a lawsuit involving the choice of churchwardens Lanneau began refusing to hear the confessions of more than two dozen parishioners, preventing them from fulfilling their Easter duty. One of his parishioners expressed her fear about this, telling the court that Lanneau showed so little interest in the salvation of his parishioners that if he remained any longer as curé she was afraid the parish would become Lutheran.[130]

The curés in both of these cases originally found themselves at odds with their parishioners for reasons unrelated to the sacraments. But it did not take long for these important rituals to end up becoming central to the conflict. Confession and communion were so important to parish life that the rituals inevitably became caught up in the relationship between the curé and his parishioners. If the curé had lost their confidence, they did not feel comfortable receiving the sacra-

ments from him. The administration of the sacraments – especially
the sacraments of confession and communion, either at Easter or on
the sickbed – was central to the parish community. The laity participated in a variety of devotional activities throughout their lives, from
sermons to pilgrimages to confraternities to missions, but more
important than any of these were the sacraments. Without a competent curé, those sacraments could not be performed. In this sense, the
parish community, even in the eighteenth century, placed the parish
curé solidly at the centre of their religious and social lives, because he
was their primary access to the sacraments of confession and communion. Having a curé who willingly heard confessions, administered communion, and visited the sick and dying was symbolic of the
unity of the parish itself. The sacraments were important to individual spirituality as well, there is no doubt, but their value for the community was just as great.

At the same time, the laity did not accept the administration of confession and communion if performed inappropriately. Bishops and
curés might have hoped that they could use pressure in the confessional to solve disorders in villages and towns – to keep marriages
together, to stop the abuse of alcohol, or to get people to improve
their observance of various rules. But if they went too far and
attempted to reform the laity's behaviour in ways that did not suit the
laity themselves, they were likely to experience some form of rebellion. The Catholic Reformation had been effective in that parishioners recognized and followed through with their duty to confess
and take communion at Easter. In fact, it had worked so well that
sometimes parishioners were the ones who took their curés to task if
they did not perform the sacraments according to their standards.
Sometimes, those standards aligned well with the church's rules –
many parishioners expected a curé who was a patient and kind healer of their souls, for example. They also knew the various rules about
public sins and private sins, and many others. When curés broke those
rules, they were not afraid to let him or the authorities know about
it. Whether their curés were too strict, too lax, or simply negligent,
parishioners demanded change. They clearly believed that curés were
there to serve their needs, and they felt free to dictate exactly what
those needs were. They negotiated, compromised, badgered, complained, appealed, and finally used the church court system to make
sure they had a curé who met their standards. In many cases, the

church hierarchy supported them in their efforts. Confession and communion acted, then, not as tools for social control but rather as symbols of local identities and communities. The meanings of those symbols were dictated through a process of negotiation and compromise between parish priest and parishioner, within the confessional, at the altar, and at the sickbed.

# 4

# The Holiness of the Place

During sermons and at the foot of the altar, [the curé] called them miserable and unhappy. He even dared to say to them that he wished the malediction of God would fall upon them and their goods, even though the supplicants have never strayed from the rules of Christianity, and they lived in peace for forty years with his predecessor, without any reason for complaint on either part. And, even if the supplicants had done something worthy of his discontent, his words were incompatible with the holiness of the place where they were said.[1]

In August 1713, the two Moignat brothers suffered the loss of their father. They were living in Saint-Dizier-l'Évêque (Besançon), where their father had died, but their ancestral home was the parish of Grandvillars about fifteen kilometres to the north.[2] Since their mother was buried in Grandvillars, they wanted to take their father's body there for the funeral mass and then bury him next to her in the cemetery. One Moignat brother was the curé of Saint-Dizier-l'Évêque, so they invited several other curés from the surrounding region to attend the funeral mass, procession, and burial in Grandvillars. When these curés, as well as family members and other residents of Saint-Dizier-l'Évêque, arrived at the church, however, they found that the curé of Grandvillars, Jean François Fouchard, had not agreed to do the mass or the burial. He did not meet them on the outskirts of town to carry the body in procession to the church, as they had expected. He refused to allow them to ring the church bells or use any of the usual linens and ornaments that were needed for burials. The body was taken to a nearby house while family and friends tried to get Fouchard to change his mind, but he only locked the sacristy and went home, shutting himself up in the presbytery.

The reason that Fouchard did not want this burial to take place was because of the poor state of the cemetery. Grandvillars had a new parish church, but the cemetery next to the old church was where Moignat's wife had been buried. Fouchard told the court that the cemetery had been closed four or five years previously because the parish was too poor to provide the upkeep for two cemeteries. One of the major efforts of church administrators in France in the early modern period was to enclose cemeteries and make sure that animals could not get in and desecrate the graves.[3] Clerical leaders wanted the cemetery to be an extension of the sacred space of the church itself and ordered parishes to pay for their cemeteries to be enclosed with some combination of walls, fences, hedges, and, as a last resort, ditches. This was often difficult and expensive to do properly; it could easily lead to arguments between curés and parishioners about who was responsible for the work and expense. Fouchard, probably wanting to avoid a financial battle with his parishioners about the state of the old cemetery, abandoned it. But when Sieur Moignat and his brother, the curé of Saint-Dizier-l'Évêque, arrived and wanted to bury their father there, he found himself in the middle of a fight anyway. Sieur Moignat tried to convince Fouchard to do the burial, saying that if his mother had been buried there it should still be fine. Fouchard said it had deteriorated since then; Moignat said it had not. Then Fouchard suggested that perhaps a wrong had already been committed when Moignat's mother had been buried there, and he did not want to commit another. It was at that point that he left the church and hid behind the walls of the presbytery.

Meanwhile, the curé of Morvillars, the village closest to Grandvillars, sent someone to his church to get the items usually used for burials. Then the curé of Bourogne knocked repeatedly on the door of the presbytery and shouted that he would break a window if Fouchard did not come out. Fouchard still refused to leave the house but appeared in the garden and told them that if they wanted the ornaments necessary to celebrate the mass, they could find the schoolmaster and get him to use his keys to open the sacristy. The curés did this and then met together inside the sacristy to decide what to do. The Moignat brothers agreed to engage people from the village to have the cemetery enclosed that very day, so the curés decided they would perform services and the burial themselves. They even got Fouchard to agree to this, reluctantly, still communicating from behind the walls of his garden or through the window of the presbytery. Several men, from both Saint-Dizier-l'Évêque and Grandvillars, testified that they themselves repaired the considerable gaps in the ditches and hedges that enclosed the cemetery that very day. Fouchard did not preside at or even attend the service.

In his complaint to the *officialité*, Sieur Moignat claimed that Fouchard's refusal to bury his father was "an insult without equal"; he had created a scandal so great that "all the people, *grand et petit*, cried out against the bad faith and malice of the curé." Unfortunately, the outcome of this case has been lost, so we do not know if the court agreed with Moignat or the curé. Either way, the argument over the cemetery is instructive. Fouchard had tried to carry out the reforms regarding the enclosure of cemeteries that his superiors had insisted on, but his worthy actions only got him in trouble. Another curé might have ignored the rule, especially since the two Moignat brothers had significant social standing in the area, and avoided the conflict. In fact, Fouchard's own colleagues, the handful of curés who were attending the services, urged him to do just that: ignore the rule and allow the burial to take place. Yet Fouchard still refused. Services like this were where curés might draw their line in the sand and refuse to give in, even when all logic seemed to suggest a less scandalous plan of action. The conflict became not just about a burial but also about who held the ultimate authority in the parish. This was about the status of the curé, and his position in the community. Holy places like churches and cemeteries were thus sites of conflict as well as sites of religious ritual. Struggles involving parish services like burials, but also sermons, processions, catechism class, and the mass itself, demonstrate the limits of Catholic reform as well as the complicated but vital relationship between curés and their parishioners.

### Public Spaces, Public Problems

In another instance involving a burial, curé Nicolas Quentin of Vaudemange and Billy (Reims) found himself at odds with his parishioners over the vestments he wore for a funeral procession. The argument, over such a trivial matter, shows just how troubled the relationship between Quentin and his parishioners had become. The difficulty started because Quentin was known for being absent from his parish on a regular basis. According to his parishioners, his absences led him to neglect parish services and the sacraments, specifically the last rites. Quentin admitted in his testimony that he often had to visit neighbouring villages because of family issues but said that he had never neglected the sick of the parish.[4] If we believe Quentin was being truthful about that, it seems his parishioners felt he could still do more for the sick and the dying. If in fact he was less than forthright in his testimony, then he probably had let people die without the sacraments. Specifically, many of the people who testified in the *information* mentioned the fact that they believed Nicaise Pierre had died without confession because the curé had failed to visit him in a timely manner.

Quentin told the court that as soon as he was told about Pierre's illness he had gone to the sickbed to hear his confession, but Pierre decided that he needed to examine his conscience more carefully and asked if he could put it off until the next day. Quentin agreed and told the family to let him know if his condition worsened. Early the next morning a messenger came to the presbytery and told Quentin that he was needed immediately; when the curé arrived, he found Pierre at the point of death. He was not in a state to confess, presumably unable to speak, so the curé was only able to administer the last rites; Pierre died about fifteen minutes later.[5] From the available testimony, it is difficult to know who was at fault here. Should Quentin have insisted on hearing Pierre's confession when he was still able to speak? Should he have stayed with the sick man overnight instead of waiting for a messenger? If we give Quentin the benefit of the doubt, then Pierre's death without confession seems to be nothing more than an unfortunate accident. But that is not the way his parishioners saw it.

Just a few months after Pierre died, his wife passed away as well.[6] Quentin performed the funeral mass and then left the parish to go to his father's house to deal with some family issues. He was supposed to return for the funeral procession and burial at four in the afternoon but was at least an hour late. This, after the difficulty with Pierre's confession months earlier, must have put the family on edge. Then when Quentin did arrive to lead the services, he was not wearing the traditional black cope (a clerical vestment also called a cloak, or mantle). The family questioned him about this, and an argument broke out. Quentin believed the ceremony could go forward without the cope, since it was not against the customs of the diocese, but the family insisted that he not do the procession or the burial without it. It is possible that Quentin's refusal to wear the cope was an insult to their status in the parish, as curés often wore their nicer vestments for

funerals of village notables. On one side, then, we have a family who
believed that their curé had insulted and offended them on at least
two occasions and wanted to make their displeasure clear. On the
other side, we have a curé who felt his authority was being threatened,
whether he was guilty of those insults and offences or not. Both sides
dug in their heels.

Quentin continued on his way to the cemetery, but the family did
not follow. At some point soon after this, incredibly enough, an
injunction from one of the vicars-general appeared, instructing the
curé to proceed with the services after acquiring the black cope. Why
would a diocesan official have intervened in such a trivial matter?
How would he even have known about what was happening? These
were apparently questions that Quentin asked himself in the
moment, because he did not believe that the injunction was real and
refused to comply with it. He later told the court that he thought it
was a forgery and thus felt justified in ignoring it and continuing to
insist that he did not have to wear the black cope. The case materials
do not make it clear if the injunction from the vicar-general was a
forgery or not, unfortunately. According to Quentin's testimony,
everything happened very quickly, and he tried to tell the family to
calm down and then come and see him at the presbytery so that they
could work things out, but instead they incited a crowd of parishioners, primarily women, to approach the curé and demand that he
give them the injunction so that they could read it for themselves. He
finally handed it over before leaving, and the burial was put off for
four days, when the curé of a neighbouring parish was finally brought
in to do it. Quentin said that there was too much enmity between
him and his parishioners, so he was not in a state to do it himself.
What happened here was about much more than clerical vestments.
The burial services for this particular parishioner became more than
just a ritual, but a site where dissatisfaction with the curé, and the
curé's dissatisfaction with his parishioners, could be made public.
The resulting scandal showed the underlying tension in the parish,
and the court case was a last-ditch attempt to repair that scandal and
restore the relationship between the curé and his parishioners.

Another public event that could easily display tensions between
curés and parishioners was the procession.[7] Processions were held regularly throughout the year in every Catholic parish, both rural and
urban. Some were associated with certain holy days, and others were
done to either celebrate specific events or in supplication for bless-

ings from God. Processions were a way to sacralize territory that was normally secular: village squares, city streets, and even the long roads that connected one village to another. The clergy took the Eucharist – the bread that had been transformed through spiritual power into the body of Christ – and brought it outside of the church, extending the holy space and publicizing the miracle of the mass. Processions were also a ritual that everyone in the parish could participate in, either by marching in the procession itself or by watching it from the sidelines.

So, while there was great unifying potential in processions, there were also many opportunities for conflict. Participation in the procession was associated with status; people who walked nearest to the clergy and the Eucharist, or carried candles or holy objects, were privileged to be able to do so. These were coveted roles, and village notables guarded them carefully. Village tradition was also of supreme importance here; people wanted processions done in exactly the same way as they had always been done and did not take kindly to changes instituted by curés or churchwardens without consent. Finally, processions were supremely public events, the whole point being to bring out the parish's best ornaments and vestments and show them off to everyone in the village and anyone else who might attend. The public nature of the event meant that small disagreements could become scandals.

For example, in 1761 Jean François Coyer announced during his *prône* that for the Fête-Dieu procession that day he did not want the girls who usually carried the candle in honour of the Virgin to accompany him. Coyer had had many disagreements with his parishioners, and they appeared to be constantly involved in lawsuits with each other. Unfortunately, the records of the case do not explain why Coyer did not want the girls to march in the procession with him, but we can imagine that it upset the parishioners that one of their long-standing traditions had been suppressed. When Coyer arrived at the church to begin the procession he found the girls assembled in their usual places, with their usual candle. Seeing that his parishioners had ignored his orders, he simply turned on his heel and left the church. There was no procession that day, and parishioners noted that Coyer seemed angry when he said the mass a bit later.[8] A similar event happened in Muizon (Reims), when Nicolas Hourblin was the curé and he disagreed with the parish's choice of churchwardens. He tried to make a statement about this by asking the previous churchwarden,

Rémy Rouvroy, to carry the cross for the procession on the feast of Notre Dame. Rouvroy told Hourblin that he would not do it, and then when the new churchwarden presented himself with the cross the curé refused to do the procession at all.[9]

In Saint-Théodule, Matthieu Faivre managed to use a procession to make a statement about his unhappiness with several parishioners, all in the name of avoiding a scandal, strangely enough. One August he was upset with Jean Baptiste Deniset and several of his friends in the parish. At that time, there was supposed to be a procession performed for a specific purpose: the excommunication of the insects. Priests performed a procession like this in the belief that excommunicating insects would keep them from eating the crops. A few days before the procession Faivre sent one of his friends in the parish, the warden of the confraternity, to tell Deniset and the others that they should not attend the procession. If they did, he said, they would be the ones excommunicated and would be the cause of a scandal. The men decided not to irritate the curé further and stayed away.[10]

Nicolas Hyacinthe Vernier also chose to use a procession to publicly air his grievances with his parishioners. As we saw in chapter 1, he insulted Jean Baptiste Billecart and his family by refusing to use the special canopy that Billecart, as warden of the confraternity, had provided to cover the Eucharist. The whole parish was scandalized when Vernier angrily rebuffed the four men who had been chosen to carry the canopy (especially because Vernier had been holding the consecrated Eucharist at the time) and then used the small, everyday canopy carried by two altar boys instead. Witnesses and the plaintiffs said that Vernier had done this just to upset the Billecart family, since they were most closely associated with the canopy itself. In his testimony Vernier acknowledged that his actions were tied to the Billecarts, but for entirely different reasons. He explained that the responsibility for carrying the canopy was supposed to be rotated through the members of the confraternity so that each would get his share of the honour associated with participation in the procession. Processions were an opportunity for the community to display solidarity in an open and conspicuous way, both within their ranks and within the church. But for three years in a row, Nicolas Billecart had always presented himself to carry one of the corners, each time excluding someone else from being able to carry it. This could be viewed as a public insult to his brothers in the confraternity, as well as Vernier himself. Vernier also indicated that Nicolas Billecart was one of his primary adversaries in the parish, and he was tired of having to walk beside someone whom everyone knew was his sworn enemy. He felt it detracted from the spirit of reverence that was supposed to permeate the occasion. So, he had decided of his own accord to prepare the common canopy for the procession instead of the special one. To preserve the dignity of the holiday, however, he had it decorated in a distinguished fashion, and it was brought to the sanctuary by two altar boys wearing surplices. According to the vicaire, when Vernier saw that the special canopy had been prepared anyway, he said to those who carried it, "Please be so kind as to withdraw, if you would, so that I can lead the procession – your canopy is causing me inconvenience." The men withdrew as requested, and Vernier said that the procession carried on as normal.[11]

So, according to Vernier's testimony, he had used the occasion of the procession to make his displeasure with his parishioners known and, as he explained to the court, that displeasure was warranted because it was Nicolas Billecart, and indeed the extended Billecart family, that was in the wrong.[12] Whether this was the complete truth or not, it still shows how religious rituals could easily be caught up in village arguments. It also demonstrates how limited curés could be in the reforms they could make, if something so simple as requiring a more equal rotation in processional duties could lead to a public scandal. Vernier continued to insist that he had not been trying to cause a scandal but simply trying to enforce conformity to religious rules. This was the same excuse Vernier gave when it came to his actions surrounding catechism class and the first communion ceremony for the young adults of the parish; he insisted that he was just trying to uphold the church's standards for religious education. His parishioners, he claimed, were the ones responsible for any scandals involving their children, because they had not taken enough steps to ensure that those children were sufficiently educated.

Catechism class and first communion could easily be another site of conflict between priest and parishioner. During the Catholic Reformation, church officials believed that better education through catechism would solve many of the problems with the laity's behaviour. Bishops issued new catechisms for their dioceses and then instructed their curés to teach the catechism to children and young adults every Sunday and feast day. Children were expected to memorize pages and pages of material, which contained the answers to the questions that their curé would ask them before he would allow them to take their first communion and be admitted to the community of adult parishioners. Bishops felt so strongly about catechism that some of them even tested the children themselves during visits, just to make sure that both parents and curés were doing their jobs and educating the children satisfactorily. But even if bishops did not perform these examinations often, catechism had become an important part of parish life simply because it was a prerequisite for first communion. If it was ignored, by either the laity or the curés, there would be serious consequences.[13]

The most common complaint about catechism found in court cases was that the curé did not teach it – either not often enough, or not at all. As a result, parishioners lamented, the young people of the parish could not do their first communion. For example, curé François Jacqueney was accused of failing to teach catechism or do any kind of instruction. In fact, some of his parishioners said that they had never seen him teach a single catechism class. The class was instead taught by the vicaire, but he had been sick and the curé still had not taught any classes. The schoolmaster and his son taught the class a couple of times during the vicaire's illness, but, as one parishioner put it, this had probably done more harm than good. As a result of the lack of instruction, there were young people who were taking first communion without knowing either the truths of their religion or the proper way to approach the sacrament. One young person took communion right after eating lunch, for example, and another after smoking tobacco, because they were not aware that fasting was a prerequisite for participating in the sacrament.[14]

Other curés seemed to disagree with their parishioners on who was responsible for holding catechism class. Curé Pierre Mangeut did not teach catechism very often, and the village schoolmaster testified that in fifteen years the curé had only held first communion ceremonies four or five times.[15] Many people had to send their children to other parishes to be instructed, including Jean Delagloye, who testified that the curé had told him that it was the parents' responsibility, and not his, to prepare their children for first communion. After hearing that, Delagloye decided to send his fourteen-year-old daughter to live with his sister in another parish for awhile so that she could receive instruction.[16] Another curé, Jacques Philbert François, complained to the court that it was the responsibility of the parish clerk, or schoolmaster, to teach catechism, and since there was no clerk in the parish, there was no catechism class. When the court pressed him on this, he claimed that he had tried to teach catechism himself but no one had attended his classes. He was then asked if it was the duty of a clerk or a pastor to make sure that people attended instructions; he responded, "A pastor can do nothing without his clerk."[17]

When curés did teach catechism classes themselves, the class itself might become another public space where disagreements between priests and parishioners might come to light. As we saw in chapter three, curé Matthieu Faivre had a dispute with his parishioners at Easter in 1746 when he ate all of the hosts in an annex church to try to force the people to take communion in the parish church. That year he also refused to do any special instructions for the children who were preparing for first communion, as he had done in years past. Multiple people testified that there were a good number of children who were old enough to do their first communion, but when their parents asked about instruction the curé told them to send their children to the schoolmaster. In his interrogation Faivre claimed that he had not done a first communion ceremony that year because there were no children of appropriate age who were sufficiently instructed, but it seems clear that his conflicts with the parish had led him to neglect, perhaps purposely, this duty.[18] It was a way to show that unity in the parish had broken down, as well as his displeasure with the way that his parishioners were behaving.

Underlying tensions were probably also responsible for the difficulties that Jean Baptiste Lanneau encountered with the catechism in his parish. Curés were supposed to teach the approved diocesan catechism so that no matter where a person went in the diocese, they would all know and be able to recite the same text. But Lanneau was using an abridged version of the diocesan catechism, and he told the court that he had received permission for the substitution from one of the vicars-general. The full version was too long for the children to learn, he claimed, and he liked this shorter version. But his parishioners presumably did not like it because it was different from the one they were used to and because, as one parishioner said, it was in manuscript form and had to be copied out by hand. The handwritten copies were often difficult for peasants to read, making it hard for parents to make sure that their children were learning the correct material.

Whether this was the case or not, Lanneau's responses to his parishioners when they questioned him about the difficulties with this catechism reveal the tensions between the curé and the laity. Other disputes had created bad feelings, and those feelings had spilled over into catechism class. Evidently, Lanneau had drawn his line in the sand over this issue, and if children did not provide the responses found in this abridged version of the catechism when he tested them, he would refuse to admit them to first communion. Furthermore, when a *laboureur* named Louis Gérard asked Lanneau why they had to use this catechism, the curé simply told him that his catechism was better and that he was the master in his church. When the court asked him about this, he responded forcefully that indeed he was the master in his church – at least, he conceded, if there were no other clerical authorities present. Once again, we see that parish services, including catechism class, could easily reflect existing tensions within a parish.[19]

This incident also reveals that curés had to walk yet another fine line when it came to catechism. They had to be as flexible as possible when it came to educational standards; if they asked for too much, the laity would surely push back, thus limiting the amount of reform they could expect to accomplish. This was especially true for the adults in the parish. Although bishops and other church leaders initially believed that adults should know their catechism no matter how old they were, over time catechism became associated with childhood only. Adults balked when curés tried to ask them questions from the catechism when they were ready to get married or when they were presented as godparents. Catechism came to be seen as a childhood ritual and nothing more.[20] Even when it came to children, curés still could not push too hard. They had to make sure that the children were educated enough to take their first communion, but they had to know when to be lenient and when to be strict. Vernier seemed to have difficulty distinguishing between those occasions.

Vernier's attempts to change his parishioners' conduct can be seen in the way he handled catechism and first communion. For Vernier, this was when he could make sure that his parishioners knew exactly what was expected of them and instill in them a reverence for the sacraments of confession and communion. Vernier seemed to take his responsibility as the primary catechist, and as the gateway figure to first communion, seriously. This is why, he insisted, he taught extra catechism classes at his home specifically for the children preparing for first communion, even though holding classes in the presbytery was against the rules. Knowing that the court would be concerned about the separation of the sexes during instruction, he told the officials that he put boys on one side of the room and girls on the other.[21] He said he even taught classes beginning at four in the morning, so that the children would still be able to put in a full day's work afterward. Vernier did admit that he sometimes made fun of children if their bad behaviour warranted it. He also said that if he was not satisfied with the responses of one of the older children on their catechism, he might ask them how old they were and then say that someone their age might be married by now – implying that they should be ashamed for not knowing their catechism. He said he never meant anything improper or sexual in his comments.[22] He probably beat children for various infractions too, as his parishioners had testified, but this was entirely normal. Parents, masters, and schoolteachers all regularly used corporal punishment for children and servants, and it should be no surprise that curés did too. The court did not even ask Vernier anything about whether he hit his catechism students – the officials presumably had other things to worry about.

Vernier's most serious offence dealing with religious education was that he charged fees for each child who wanted to take first communion and for places to sit on one of the church benches during the mass. Each student, rich or poor, had to pay thirty *sous* to participate in the ceremony. Vernier claimed that the money was to pay for a candle for each child to hold, and for the mass that was said as part of the ceremony. This was not an insignificant amount of money – parents paid the village schoolmaster about the same amount for five or six months of instruction in reading.[23] Twenty-seven of the witnesses complained about this fee in their testimony, but even more egregious was the fact that the curé also charged each child's parents a fee for a spot on one of the church benches.

It was routine in French parishes for families to pay for the right to sit in specific benches during church services; these fees were an important source of income for the parish, and usually it was only the wealthy families who could afford to make this type of "contribution."[24] They could easily become a sore spot between curés and their parishioners, especially since they were just one of many types of fees people had to pay. The practice of assessing surplice fees for various church services, including processions, publication of the banns, weddings, funeral masses, and burials, was well established at the time; dioceses often published specific lists of fees that priests were allowed to charge for their services.[25] People hated these fees because they felt that the money they paid in tithes should be enough to cover the full salary of curés and vicaires without any extra fees.[26]

As might be imagined, conflicts over these surplice fees were quite common. Parishioners who could legitimately afford to do so paid the fees grudgingly, but only if the curé charged the correct amount – and that meant the amount that had always been charged, according to tradition. Diocesan officials might have paid attention to the list of set fees published in the *rituel*, but the parishioners knew what their forebears had been charged in times past and what their neighbours were currently being charged. They even knew what people in other parishes were paying, and if their curé asked for more, they complained. For example, in the parish of Suzanne (Noyon) parishioners told the court that many people had withdrawn from a confraternity in the parish because their curé, Pierre Sellier, was charging five *sous* to join and two *sous* for the yearly dues, whereas previously they had paid half as much.[27] Many people made similar accusations during the trial of Gabriel Joseph Blondeau, curé of Courcuire (Besançon). One woman claimed that Blondeau had charged her more than the usual fee for the burial of her husband.[28] Others said he charged more for marriages.[29] Another parishioner said that Blondeau had refused to do a burial unless he was paid more money than required, and he still did not say a mass, which was normally part of the service.[30] Anne Françoise Ethier testified that she went to the church for her *relevée*, or churching, after she had a baby. She brought the usual fee and a little extra, but the curé still asked for more, and he left her standing at the door of the church when she refused.[31] Another mother, Claudine Vaultier, testified that Blondeau refused to bury her child until he had been paid, so she had to take the child to Besançon for burial.[32]

This was another common complaint about surplice fees – parishioners did not like to be asked to pay for the service in advance. It was assumed that curés would be lenient when it came to the fees for burial services, which were often unexpected and therefore unbudgeted. A considerate curé would do the service even if he had not been paid up front, especially if the family was poor, and just hope that the fees would be forthcoming. Unkind curés, like Blondeau and Nicolas Quentin, refused to do burials unless they were paid before the service. According to his parishioners, Quentin regularly charged more in fees than neighbouring curés and "is so self-interested and has so little charity that he exacts from the poor the payment in advance." Quentin claimed that the reasons he charged more than neighbouring curés were that he gave some of the money to the schoolmaster instead of having the family pay a separate fee and that he actually buried the poor without any payment.[33] No matter who was telling the truth, it shows that parishioners expected a certain amount of leniency when it came to surplice fees.

Vernier showed little leniency when it came to fees; in fact, he tried to maximize the profit from the benches in his church, asking for anywhere from fifteen *sous* to five *livres* from each young person as soon as they became officially recognized as a member of the community, no matter the economic situation of their families. According to the parishioners, the amount Vernier charged for these seats on the benches varied widely. His fee for the candle and the first communion mass was always the same (thirty *sous*) but witnesses reported all kinds of different amounts charged for spots in the church. Some paid only fifteen *sous*, but widow and *vigneronne* Jeanne Lemaitre said she had to pay forty *sous*, while *laboureur* Pierre Blondeau reported that he was charged 100 *sous*, or five *livres*.[34] Almost everyone else seems to have been charged somewhere between these two extremes. Added together, this could mean that Vernier made a significant amount of money each year. Rémy Poncelet and Scholastique Duval both testified that their son had been asked to collect the fees from the villagers one year; he collected seventy-two *livres*, which he gave to the curé.[35] No one seemed to be quite sure what he did with the money.

Witnesses testified that nothing else mattered to Vernier about the first communion ceremony except his collection of these fees. Children who were unprepared for first communion but had paid their fees were admitted; children who were prepared but whose parents had refused to pay were not – it was as simple as that. Jean Jacques Blondeau testified that when he was preparing to do his first communion the curé told him that he regretted clearing him to participate in the ceremony, because he did not know his catechism well enough yet. But because he had paid the thirty *sous*, as had each of his two sisters, he told the boy that they would all be admitted. Claude Eloy Mayeux testified that his father refused to pay the fees, arguing that he should not have to pay fifteen *sous* for a place in the church since Claude was an altar boy and would not need anywhere to sit during the mass. His mother went to the curé to try to explain this, but Vernier chased her from the church and Claude was not allowed to do his first communion that year or the next.[36]

Other prominent families refused to pay the fees as a matter of principle, and they often ended up sending their children elsewhere to learn the catechism and take their first communion, usually at even greater expense. Denis Pierre testified that he sent his son to Châlons-sur-Marne and then to Paris for his religious education, rather than paying the thirty *sous* to the curé. He did the same thing with his daughter, sending her to a convent in Avenay; however, this turned out to be a much greater expense than he had anticipated, because while she was there a fire broke out in the convent and she lost all of her belongings. Pierre then blamed Vernier for this loss. Jean Blondeau also tried to refuse, out of principle, to pay the fees when his son Pierre was about to do first communion. On the evening before the ceremony, Pierre went to his mother and begged her to give him the money so that he would be able to take his first communion the next day. She gave in and paid the fees, keeping it a secret from his father, and the boy was admitted to the ceremony. Plaintiff Pierre Trubert had two sons, and when they were of an age to do their first communion he told the curé that he would buy the required candles himself instead of paying the fees. Vernier refused to admit them anyway, so Trubert had to send them to study with a schoolmaster in another village. Vernier was not satisfied with this and sent a letter to the curé there, instructing him not to admit the Trubert boys for first communion, so the schoolmaster sent them back to their father. After two or three years, Trubert eventually paid the fees and his sons were finally able to participate in communion.[37]

The poor were not exempt from paying the fees for first communion either. Marie Nicolle Baudier, widow of a *vigneron*, testified that in 1763 her nineteen-year-old son still had not done his first communion. He was normally employed by the *seigneur*, working in the vineyards, but Vernier told him that if he was unable to pay his fees then he would have to work for him instead, in the vineyards belonging to the curé's benefice. If her son refused to do this, Vernier told her, then he would track him down in the *seigneur's* fields and take him away to work in his fields.[38] But this was a mild threat, compared with what he told another poor couple, *vigneron* Thomas Jacquot and his wife Jeanne Duval. The couple had ten living children and seemed to have significant difficulty making ends meet; they were in no position to have to pay at least thirty *sous* for each of their children to take communion. Sure enough, sometime around 1751 two of their children were preparing for first communion but their parents had no way to pay their fees. Jacquot was told he had to pay eight and a half *livres* for the ceremony and for places in the church, even though they had no bread and had only their labour to feed their family. Jeanne Duval went to the curé and promised him that she would send her husband and son to work in the curé's vineyards for a week. But after the week was up, the curé told them that they had to work for another week as well to cover the fees. Jeanne returned to the curé to explain that the only resource their family had was the labour of Thomas and their oldest son and that if they were working for him for free then the family would not be able to eat. Vernier compromised, telling her that he would pay them half the usual rate. So, they worked for another week. Some time later, Jeanne sent her daughter to collect the money from the curé. Vernier refused to give it to her, even after she told him that they had no bread at their house. Vernier told her that she should tell her father to take his ten children and tie them to a feeding trough for ten weeks. At the end of that time, he would surely have saved enough to give them bread.[39]

When questioned about these incidents during his trial, Vernier fell back on his usual excuse quite often, insisting that his enemies were making up lies about him.[40] Accusations that he refused to give first communion to children who could not purchase a candle from him were exaggerated, he argued. The testimony of Marie Anne Gougelet, wife of the former schoolmaster in Mareuil-sur-Ay, corroborated some of what Vernier said – she claimed that she had heard the curé tell the children during the catechism class that if they could not pay him for a candle for first communion they should ask their parents for any candle, even one that was less expensive, thus implying that Vernier was perhaps not as strict about making the families pay the fees for the first communion ceremony as other witnesses indicated.[41]

A common thread runs through most of Vernier's other responses: he claimed that everything he had done was with the intent of making sure that the children in his parish were properly educated before they took first communion. His strictness about catechism and fees was his way of instituting reform in the parish. He told the court that he had not excluded certain children of the parish from first communion because their parents had refused to pay the required fees; rather, he had refused to admit them because of their conduct and their lack of care for their salvation. The parents' testimony, he claimed, just showed that they were trying to cover up the ignorance and lack of preparation of their children. For example, he testified that the son of Denis Pierre was a "bad subject" and a "libertine"; he was not admitted to first communion because he never came to catechism classes, not because Pierre would not pay the thirty *sous*. Similarly, Vernier said that the two sons of Pierre Trubert were kept from doing first communion because of a "debauched spirit" and their lack of inclination to instruct themselves sufficiently in the principles of their religion. He continued his insults of Trubert and his family by adding that if their father had sent his children to be educated elsewhere, it must have been because he knew they would get a better education outside of his home rather than in it.[42]

In response to the complaint that Vernier made the youth of the parish wait too long to do their first communion – so long, in fact, that some had actually been of an age to be called up by the militia without having taken communion – the curé continued to insist that he was only doing his job by refusing to admit those who were not sufficiently educated. He blamed their parents for not taking their religious education seriously enough. He conceded that because of his poor health he only held the first communion ceremony every two or three years, but he explained that in a small parish like his there was not really a need to hold the ceremony every year. If there were young people who did not do first communion until their late teens or even early twenties, it was not because of his negligence, but because of theirs. The young people had not shown any of the necessary dispositions or obtained enough instruction to be sufficiently prepared for the ritual. He insisted that he never deferred people if they could not pay the fees or if they refused to work in his vines; he deferred them only if he did not feel they were sufficiently well instructed in the catechism and in the duties and obligations of a Christian.[43]

Vernier also defended his practice of charging fees. First of all, he said, the reason he charged everyone thirty *sous* for a candle was so that he could give each child, rich or poor, the exact same candle. He did not want to exacerbate the differences between the rich and the poor by having the children carry different-sized candles, and he believed that before he had instituted this policy some children had put off taking first communion because they felt ashamed when unable to purchase the same candles as everyone else. This way, everyone paid the same amount and he distributed the candles equally. Then, he collected the remaining candle stubs after the ceremony and used them for the funerals of poor people and for the confraternity. He also used some of the money collected to pay fees to the schoolmaster, the chorister, and the altar boys and kept a very small fee for himself. Vernier insisted that he was not asking for anything out of

the ordinary, claiming that the curés in neighbouring parishes asked
for twice as much as the thirty *sous* he required. This may have been
true, although no evidence other than Vernier's word was presented.[44]

As for the bench fees, Vernier again had a reasonable explanation.
He told the court that he had noticed in his first few years as curé that
after the first communion ceremony was over, some of the children
did not continue to attend services regularly. This was indeed a common complaint throughout France during the eighteenth century.
Once children had learned their catechism, they quickly forgot it.
After the coming-of-age ritual was over, they felt they had no reason
to remember it, and perhaps in their youth they had no desire to
attend a lot of masses or other church services. This certainly would
have irked Vernier; his frustration over this issue may have been part
of the reason why he had refused certain young people as godparents,
as we have seen. So his way of trying to get the young people to continue their religious education and to participate in parish services
was to build a specific bench for them to sit on. That way he could
keep any eye on them for a year or two after they did their first communion. This was Vernier's approach in trying to orchestrate good
behaviour in the parish. He charged for places on the bench for two
reasons, he explained. First, if the seat was paid for then the individual was more likely to sit in it. Second, charging for benches in the
church was a long-standing practice of the *fabrique* – money from
families who paid for the right to use particular benches was often a
significant source of income. Vernier insisted that it was the *fabrique*
who profited from the bench fees and that people were charged on
the basis of their financial standing in the parish. He also said that it
was the churchwardens who set the fees, not him. And he certainly
had not required anyone to work in his vines to pay for their spot on
the bench, he added.[45]

In light of this testimony, Vernier's actions seem less alarming. He
may have been a little too strict when trying to reform the behaviour
of his parishioners, and that strictness may even have led him to say
and do things that seem unwarranted. The suggestion that Thomas
Jacquot tie his children to a feeding trough was particularly harsh, for
example. But perhaps Vernier really was just trying to do his job and
ended up hurting the pride of his parishioners in the process. Catechism class, processions, burials, and other public events provided
plenty of opportunity for conflict, and they often ended up serving as
spaces where tensions between parishioners and their curé were made

public. They might also be spaces that curés tried to use for reform purposes, with perhaps limited effect. Either way, they were central to notions of parish and religious identity for both curé and laity.

### A Place for God to Dwell – But People Visited a Lot Too

None of these spaces was as important as the church, however. The church building, whether grand and ornate or in need of repair (and most were the latter), was the heart of the community and the parish. *Officialité* records reveal that conflicts did happen in churches, and these conflicts, more than any other, produced scandals. A church was a sacred space without parallel – a place for God to dwell, both figuratively and literally, in the form of the consecrated Eucharist. Conflicts had to be kept to a minimum, and blood could not be shed inside a church or the building would have to be placed under interdict until church authorities could perform a purification ritual. Clergy envisioned churches as a place of peace and calm, where discipline and order reigned. Curés during the Catholic Reformation period were expected to police behaviour in the church more strictly than anywhere else and might even push a little too hard when it came to that policing. For example, two curés went so far as to try to dictate the types of head coverings and hairstyles worn by women during the mass and other services. When Claude Nicolas Boulanger tried to keep women with inappropriate hairstyles out of his church, his parishioners went over his head and complained to a diocesan official. It is not hard to imagine that this particular official might have sighed and rolled his eyes as he wrote out the letter telling Boulanger to leave the women and their hair in peace.[46]

Churches were also public spaces, where large crowds of men, women, and children met and interacted on a regular basis. Community meetings might take place just outside of the church or in the cemetery, to avoid polluting the church, but there were plenty of occasions during the mass and other services when churches were noticeably lacking in peace and calm. Court records reveal lots of little details that might not be central to the main dispute but provide a picture of what everyday life in the church was like. People from inside and outside of the parish were in and out of the church all the time, sometimes coming and going during services, including the mass. Altar boys, schoolmasters, churchwardens, and clerks were busy lighting candles, ringing bells, preparing ornaments, and running errands for curés and vicaires. There were regular, albeit minor, disputes over benches and other seating (or standing) areas. When there were no services taking place, there might be lines of people outside of the confessional(s), talking and gossiping while they waited. Church repairs had to take place on a regular basis, meaning the presence of workmen was always a possibility. The church was, in short, a busy place, especially on Sundays and feast days, but on working days as well.

Curés thus had to manage their expectations when it came to conditions in the church, allowing for some degree of disruption while holding the line against the most egregious problems. Sometimes, this led to public conflicts and scandals. At the same time, the laity had their own ideas about appropriate behaviour in the church, and they were quick to hold their curé accountable for any infractions he might commit. Curés were not trying to sacralize the space despite stubborn resistance from uncivilized peasants; both clergy and laity believed the church should be a sacred space, even if their ideas about what that meant could at times differ.

The people of Saint-Médard de Croix (Noyon) had definite ideas about what their church services should look like, and they complained to the court about several disruptive incidents, all the fault of their curé, Guillaume Bruno Loris.[47] In 1721 the curé was angry with the schoolmaster because he did not want to serve as the churchwarden for the parish. In retaliation, Loris decided he was going to try to prevent the schoolmaster from fulfilling the functions of his office. Schoolmasters regularly doubled as parish clerks and helped to chant the mass. When the schoolmaster, on the first Sunday in January that year, began to chant as he usually did, the curé came out of the sacristy and stopped him. Loris angrily chased the schoolmaster away from the lectern and then said a low mass (a high mass could only be done with an additional chanter). Witnesses noted that Loris was wearing the alb when he treated the schoolmaster so disrespectfully; they clearly believed this added to the scandal. A priest wearing liturgical vestments was not supposed to be angry, and an angry priest certainly was not supposed to say the mass. The next day, Epiphany, Loris did in fact forgo any mass in the church that day, without finding another priest to replace him, which caused a great scandal in Saint-Médard de Croix and in the surrounding parishes.

Loris demonstrated his disrespect for the clerical office and the church on at least three other occasions. One day when the parish was assembled for the mass he took the clapper from one of the bells (it had been removed and was in the sacristy) and hit a bench in the choir so hard that it broke. The curé's hand was injured when he hit the bench; another parishioner wrapped it up for him and he went ahead with the mass, much to the astonishment of the rest of the parishioners. Another Sunday the curé noted that three women were leaving the church, "for some business," testified witnesses. Loris stopped the service (he was just beginning the mass) and shouted at them, calling them witches. Then he told the people assembled that he was going to leave for half an hour. Still wearing the alb and stole, he left the church. When he came back, he spent an hour chastising his parishioners before finally saying the mass.

Finally, Loris seems to have reserved the worst treatment for a parishioner named Jacques Flament, one of the village notables. The Flament family had experienced difficulties with Loris during the fifteen years he was curé, and one day during a service on the feast of Saint Hubert the curé attacked Flament in the church. He grabbed him by the collar, pulled him from his seat so roughly that buttons popped off his shirt, and then dragged him to the sanctuary and hit him three or four times in the head. Loris did not finish the service, although he did later say the mass. Unfortunately, there is no surviving interrogation of Loris and no verdict in the case, so we do not know if he had good reason to treat his parishioners so violently. But it is clear that nothing, in the eyes of the parishioners who testified, would justify such behaviour taking place in the church. Parishioners expected their curés to demonstrate more decorum than that, especially in the presence of the Holy Sacrament.

Other cases provide a bit more detail about the actions of both priest and parishioner and highlight where conflicts in the church were likely to originate. One of these was, predictably, about the benches in the church. Not only did parishioners argue among themselves about where families of status should sit, but curés argued about it as well. Nicolas Hourblin once had a loud and public argument with the wife of the *seigneur* about the placement of her bench. She wanted it to be in a particular spot in the church, but that spot was already occupied by the lectern that the curé used during the mass. While the curé was doing the procession, the dame got her servants to move the lectern and relocate her bench. When Hourblin came back to celebrate the mass, he noticed what she had done and an argument ensued. He scuffled with the dame's servants but was able to return the lectern to its rightful place. However, at that point he felt he needed some time to "regain his senses." He took off his vestments and left the church. When he did not return, the congregation assembled in the cemetery to decide what they should do, since they did not want to miss the mass that day. Before they could make any decision, however, Hourblin returned; everyone went back in the church and he said the mass as usual.[48]

This incident was one of many that had set the parishioners at odds with their curé in Muizon; Hourblin was accused of multiple violent episodes along with drunkenness and an affair with a woman. But in the parish of Saint-Gilles (Reims), just one argument over a bench was enough to lead to a court case all by itself. In 1761 Charles Lardiere had been curé of Saint-Gilles for twenty-three years. He had evidently gotten along with his parishioners well until May of that year, when an argument over a bench broke out. François Louis, a parishioner, paid twenty *sous* to the churchwarden for the right to sit in a particular bench. When he found out about this, Lardiere approached Louis and told him that the churchwarden had not been authorized to lease this bench, since the person it belonged to was still living and in the parish. Louis believed the curé was wrong, because the next day his wife, Catherine Latour, sat in the bench at the mass. When the curé saw her there, he stopped the service and walked over to her, calling her a tramp and a slut; he dragged her off the bench and through the church, the length of seven benches, and she hit her head at least once. Then the curé did the mass, which, according to the eleven witnesses who gave their testimony about this incident, caused a scandal in the church.[49]

Another common trigger for conflicts in the church was the failure on the part of churchwardens, altar boys, or other parishioners to properly prepare the materials needed for the mass. For example, Gabriel Mottet once went to perform the mass at his church in Ruffey on a working day. He put on the appropriate vestments in the sacristy, but when he approached the altar he found that the lamp had not been lit. The clerk was a little late and was running to find a flame to light it, but Mottet did not want to wait. He took off his vestments and began to curse, saying that those who were there were "insolent buggers" who had no spirit of religion.[50] For Nicolas Quentin, the problem was candles. On 26 October 1726, the feast of the dedication for the parish of Vaudemange, Quentin and his parishioners got into an argument about which candles should be lit at which altars. The people did not like the arrangement Quentin settled on, so there was murmuring during the mass. He interrupted the chanters to warn the people to stop murmuring and to participate in the service with respect and tranquility, but that only seemed to increase the noise in the congregation.[51]

Candles were a problem for Jean Baptiste Lanneau as well. One feast day in 1766 he began the mass and found that no one had lit any candles or prepared any wine or water. This was probably the result of a dispute taking place between the curé and the parishioners – he did not like the churchwarden who had been chosen. Perhaps the frustrated churchwarden had purposely failed to do his job in order to make his feelings known to the curé. In any case, the parishioners told one story about what happened next, and the curé told another. According to the parishioners, the next Sunday the curé began the mass early, before the bell-ringers had even finished and before the churchwarden had lit the candles. When the curé saw this, he took off his vestments and went back to the presbytery, declaring that he would not say the mass that day, even though it was a day of obligation. The parishioners then argued among themselves about whether they should just go home or wait and see if he came back; after about thirty minutes he returned and started the mass. Lanneau argued in his interrogation that indeed he had taken off his vestments after the procession because there were no candles lit at the altar. But he said nothing about starting the mass early. He claimed that he asked the churchwardens to light the candles, but when no one did he was forced to return to the presbytery to get a lantern so he could light the candles himself. He added that it was only because of his own vigilance that the parishioners were able to attend the mass that day.[52]

Another incident involving Lanneau shows just how much these disputes involved notions of authority in the parish. Curés guarded their authority over their churches carefully: arguments that took place within churches were often more about challenges to that authority than anything else. The conflict about the candles was really about the relationship between the churchwardens and the curé, and who had a right to name those churchwardens – the curé or the parish as a whole. Lanneau showed how threatened he felt another Sunday, when the bell-ringers rang the bells for the mass before he had given them the order to do so. The curé expressed his anger at what the bell-ringers had done and then left the church for a half hour. When he came back he took the Holy Sacrament from its place in preparation for the benediction and then said in a loud and bitter tone, "Everyone wants to be the master in this parish but we will see who it will be in the end." In his interrogation Lanneau denied saying anything like that, but he also repeated to the court that the bells should not be rung until the curé gives the order.[53]

Perhaps the greatest example of conflicts over authority, however, is the case involving Matthieu Faivre. Of all the curés we have examined here, he was probably the strictest when it came to church rules – even more so than Vernier. In multiple instances, Faivre demonstrated that he would go to great lengths to enforce his ideas about behaviour, especially at church. There were three instances that took place in the church that show just how difficult Faivre could be and how his parishioners reacted to those difficulties. The first instance happened before the mass on the first day of the year, either 1738 or 1739. The curé did the aspersion of holy water and when he reached the back of the church he saw the teenaged Nicolas Petithuguenin kneeling by the door. Knowing that the young people of the parish usually tried to sit in the back of the church so that they were "more free," he decided to ask the boy to move closer to the front. According to witnesses, when the young man did not immediately comply, the curé seized him by the hair, hit him, and kicked him, and he would have continued this abuse had someone not intervened. This event caused a great deal of scandal, and parishioners were afraid that the same thing would happen to them – or at least, that is what they told the court. Faivre denied hitting Petithuguenin, saying he had only taken him by the arm to lead him away from the back of the church.[54]

The second incident involved another member of the clergy: Sieur Compagny, who was the director of the seminary in Besançon. The director's mother and sisters lived in Faivre's annex, Labergement. One Sunday the curé did his usual mass in Saint-Théodule, at the parish church. This was the mass of obligation for the parish and the annex, so parishioners from both villages should have attended. But that Sunday Faivre noticed low attendance at his mass. After some inquiries, he discovered that Sieur Compagny had said a mass in Labergement, followed by vespers and a catechism class. Faivre felt threatened by this, perhaps justifiably, so at a later service he angrily and publicly declared that he would not suffer anyone else to say a mass or do services in either of his churches. He admonished his parishioners for preferring a low mass said by Compagny to his parish mass and told them that anyone who had heard Compagny's mass instead of his had committed a mortal sin.[55]

Finally, Faivre also went so far as to try to lock the doors of the church to punish people for being late. At a Christmas midnight mass in 1745, the curé ordered Nicolas Joseph Bressand to close the door to the church right before he was going to begin the mass. Bressand testified that he was told to bolt the door as well, even though only a few people had arrived. After a few minutes, a crowd of about fifty people were knocking on the door, until a woman who was already inside unbolted and opened it. When people began to come in and Faivre heard the noise, he came out of the sacristy without finishing dressing and shouted that if he found out who had opened the door he would chase them out of the church. He even threatened to hit the guilty person with the large cross he used in processions. No one would tell him who had opened the door, so he went back to the sacristy to finish his preparations. He ordered the door to be closed and locked again, and he said the mass as usual, although he refused to give communion to any of the parishioners who presented themselves. He only gave communion on Christmas day the next morning, at the ten o'clock mass. Faivre told the court that he had ordered the church door closed, but not locked, because of the excessive cold and fog. He denied everything else, but enough people testified of the night's events that it seems clear Faivre was lying.[56] He had tried to enforce strict rules about the timing of a mass and his parishioners had pushed back, as they had on many other occasions.

Parishioners were also likely to resist if their curé delivered a sermon that they did not like. For the most part, sermons in rural parishes were probably routine and uninteresting; people were undoubtedly hoping they were short more than anything else. However, some curés might see sermons as an opportunity to bring about reform in their parishioners. If a pastor felt that a particular sin was especially problematic among his people, he might emphasize that sin and the need to reform in his sermons. Anyone who has sat through a particularly pointed or fiery sermon has probably looked around at the congregation and wondered just who the preacher was talking to – curés might even give a *prône* or sermon tailored to just one or a few individuals. French Catholics knew that a pastor was going to chastise them for their sins and shortcomings from time to time; the god of the Old Testament was an angry god, and curés were angry sometimes too. But curés had to handle this criticism in just the right way.

Since so many people were angry about the so-called sermon that Vernier gave on Ascension Day in 1763, when he scolded seven young parishioners for their activities after a procession, Vernier clearly had not doled out his criticism in the proper way. What exactly did he do wrong? The damage to the grain that the youths had caused, not to mention their disregard for the holiness of the day, was indeed problematic. When Vernier gave his testimony of the event, he claimed that before his sermon one of his parishioners had complained to him of the youths' activities. We have no way of knowing if Vernier was telling the truth, but in this instance, in all likelihood, he probably was; if the youths had caused any damages to the crops it is hard to believe there would have been no complaints. This sort of behaviour was anything but extraordinary, however, especially since it was an infraction involving youths.

The accused young people were all between the ages of twenty-one and thirty: Michel Antoine Cartier (twenty-one), Valentine Guimbert (twenty-two), Antoine Henry (twenty-four), Étienne Labbaye (thirty), Marie Jeanne La Marle (twenty-seven), Françoise Patron (twenty-three), and Geneviève Visse (twenty-four). Parish records indicate that all seven were also unmarried when the event took place. As in most parts of northern Europe, the average marriage age in France was usually in the mid- to late-twenties,[57] so any given community might include individuals who had considerable independence but who were not yet married. These young people often formed some of the most active and dynamic social groups in early modern parishes, despite their unmarried status. Six of these seven individuals married in either 1765 or 1766, less than two years after this incident took place.[58] Two of the seven married each other, in December 1765: Antoine Henry and Marie Jeanne La Marle. Geneviève Visse married a man from outside of the parish in July 1766. Three of the seven married on exactly the same day: 29 January 1765. On that day, Valentine Guimbert married Jean Thomas Poncelet, Étienne Labbaye married Catherine Guimbert (Valentine's sister), and Michel Cartier married Marie Jeanne Poirot. This would seem to indicate that they were part of the same social group and probably had been since childhood.

Young, unmarried individuals, in the early modern period as well as today, often test boundaries and in the process get into a bit of trouble. In the early modern period more than a few brides were pregnant when they got married – and this is just one easily measurable sign of the boundary-testing that took place among early modern youths. (For the record, none of the seven individuals got married as a result of pregnancy, as far as we know. If they were engaged in anything riskier than running through the fields with their friends, there is no evidence of it.) These individuals were also well-connected in the parish. They were not from the wealthiest families of Mareuil-sur-Ay (the Salmons, the Billecarts, the Joffrins, the Roberts) but they were not at the bottom of the social pyramid either. Several of them even had godparents who were from wealthy families: three of the women had godmothers from the Salmon family, for example. The Ascension Day Seven were from well-established, although not elite, families and therefore their feast-day excursions were probably not seen as overly threatening or worrisome. So in cases like this, the youths in question would probably have been scolded but their wrongdoings would have had few serious or lasting consequences. For young, unmarried adults, this type of behaviour would certainly not be unexpected or out of the ordinary.[59]

At the same time, if damages had indeed been done to the crops because of the actions of these individuals, some people in the parish were probably happy that Vernier had tried to hold the youths accountable. One witness, Agnes Jacquot, even testified that laughter had been heard during the curé's sermon; perhaps some residents of Mareuil-sur-Ay felt these rowdy young people had gotten what they deserved.[60] Few would have questioned that some sort of reproach was needed. If Vernier had approached the youths individually and admonished them, or better yet let the farmers involved handle the situation themselves, the incident probably would have passed by without much notice. What the parishioners who attended the sermon resented, however, was the public nature of Vernier's reprimand. By naming the individuals and their parents, Vernier had created a scandal of the highest order. This public scolding was a breach of trust between the laity and the curé. It was as if he had announced from the pulpit sins that had been confessed to him in the confessional. Curés were supposed to smooth over scandals, not exacerbate them with increased publicity.

When asked about the incident, Vernier did not attempt to deny that he had publicly admonished the youths. But he did try to defend his so-called sermon, insisting that it was his duty as a pastor to hold the young people accountable for their actions. He claimed that after the mass in Avenay on Ascension Day, his parishioners had scattered and only a few of them had walked back to Mareuil-sur-Ay with him and the other clergy. Later that day, he had heard complaints from a number of people about the disorderly conduct of the youth after the procession. Some had gone to cabarets, some had been seen dancing, and others had cut through the fields on their way home, causing damage to the grain. Vernier specifically named Marie Jeanne Bellot (wife of Denis Pierre, who was one of the curé's enemies) as one of the individuals who had personally complained to him about what had taken place in the fields.

Vernier indicated that because of his parishioners' complaints, and because of the public nature of the youths' infraction, he believed it was his duty to dole out public criticism. To justify the fact that he had pointed out specific people from the pulpit, he also told his interrogators that the complaint made about the youths' activities was already public. He admitted that he had scolded several people that day but insisted that he had done it in an appropriate manner without unnecessary harshness. He also said that he had never admonished any of his parishioners by name before or after this incident, and the reason he named names in this case was to encourage fathers and mothers to watch over the conduct of their children and to improve the conduct of those children by shaming them for what they had done. He was authorized by the precepts of Saint Paul and by the example of Jesus Christ to make these sorts of public reprimands for public crimes, he said. None of the named youths had done anything like this again, he added, suggesting that his actions had prevented further disruptions in the community. In other words, his actions were all about reform, discipline, and order. He concluded by insisting that his intention was not to insult anyone, but that if his zeal could be regarded as faulty then so be it.[61]

The fact that Vernier's error was not that he scolded the seven young people for what they had done but that he did it publicly from the pulpit is demonstrated further by evidence from additional court cases. Pierre Sellier was reprimanded for naming his parishioner Barthélemy Matel from the pulpit, calling him Pilate.[62] Hermand de Lafosse, curé of Cugney (Besançon), was known for lashing out at his parishioners in the church, calling them worthless rascals and scoundrels. Witnesses noted that de Lafosse did not name anyone specific in his sermons, but he did point out the worst offenders when they were leaving the church; parishioners felt that this was just as bad.[63] Claude Nicolas Boulanger also called his parishioners names, referring to them as miserable and unhappy, and he even wished that the malediction of God would fall upon them and their goods. During one of these sermons, he said there was a libertine in the parish and that his name began with an A and he lived below the village. So, claimed witnesses, everyone knew he was talking about Antoine Guyot.[64] Another time, Boulanger went to the pulpit and made a long speech about a lawyer in the parish, and everyone knew exactly whom he was talking about. The curé later recognized his mistake and apologized to the lawyer and everyone else in another sermon, but the apology was too little too late, and his case ended up before the *officialité* anyway.[65]

In other cases, parishioners did not like the material curés used in their sermons, feeling it to be inappropriate for the sacred space of the church. According to witnesses, Jacques Philbert François stated in one of his sermons that "there is no more common sin in the parish than the sin of impurity, and no one would know this better than a confessor like him."[66] This was too close to revealing the secrets of the confessional, and parishioners thus resented the subject of this sermon. The people of Saint-Théodule and Labergement did not appreciate the fact that Faivre used angry words from the pulpit, stopping just short of naming individuals. But even more egregious was his proclivity to issue maledictions on the people and their goods. Faivre told the court that he had only told the people that in general God does not allow those who offend Him to prosper and that maledictions will fall upon those who do not follow the rules of God and the church. He believed that people took it the wrong way and thought he was calling down the wrath of God upon them. Given Faivre's track record, it seems likely he was only making an excuse.[67]

In several other cases, curés were accused of using the public forum of the sermon or the *prône* to threaten or intimidate parishioners when they were involved in a dispute or lawsuit. As we have already seen, Vernier used the pulpit to try to coerce his parishioners to drop a complaint against him about his lack of a vicaire at the very beginning of his time as curé of Mareuil-sur-Ay. Similarly, Jean François Coyer stepped up to the pulpit on the second Sunday of Lent in 1762 and took a paper from his pocket as if he were going to do an exhortation. Instead, he read the accusations he was charged with and then said "many scandalous things." This sermon only added to the scandals Coyer had already caused, and many offended people left the service as a result of what he said.[68] Nicolas Hourblin, also during Lent, right after the mass, brought up his recent difficulties with his parishioners. He said that he could see two or three people in the parish who were a good shot and that it would be better for them to shoot him than to depose against him. He also said that he was like a lamb, ready to be devoured by a pack of wolves. Hourblin admitted in a confrontation that he had indeed said these things, because he would rather lose his life with honour than keep it with infamy.[69] Whether Hourblin gained infamy or not is up for debate, but he did lose his parish.

Churches and cemeteries were busy, public spaces, but they were also sacred spaces. The laity claimed a certain ownership over those spaces, since they spent so many important moments there. This was where they confessed their sins, consumed the body of Christ, prayed, sang, baptized their babies, and buried their dead. They had expectations about the nature of the space, and one of those expectations was that their curé should watch over it carefully and respectfully. Curés who got angry, either at their children during catechism class or with individuals whom they publicly named at the pulpit, were heavily criticized. At the same time, curés who tried to institute even minor reforms might find themselves locked in prolonged battles over their authority and their right to make changes in their own church. Parents might resent their attempts to raise standards of religious education, while churchwardens and other villagers found ways to subtly resist when curés intervened too heavily in affairs regarding benches, candles, and bell-ringing. Both curés and parishioners had specific ideas about the administration of sacred spaces, and those ideas could easily lead to conflicts. But those conflicts demonstrate how important rural religion was in the eighteenth century. If it had not been central to their ideas about community then these trivial matters might not have escalated into scandals at all.

# 5

# The Affairs of the Curés

It cannot be imagined that a man of fifty would take a bath with a thirty-year-old schoolmistress, in the presence of a thirty-five-year-old priest, unless he had lost his head.[1]

Nicolas Hyacinthe Vernier

Celibacy has proved a rather difficult challenge for Catholic priests and monks throughout the history of the Roman Catholic Church. Who can forget the stories of clergymen seducing both noble and peasant women found in Boccaccio's *Decameron* and its French counterpart, Marguerite de Navarre's *Heptameron*? Priests who broke their vows of celibacy were a recurring theme in medieval and early modern literature; if these stories are to be believed then it was routine for priests to seduce the women they confessed, assigning vulnerable women sex acts as penance, while savvy friars cuckolded unsuspecting husbands by using trickery to sleep with their wives. These stories were told with great exaggeration to satirize the multiple problems with the clergy and draw attention to the need for reform. In the eighteenth century, pornographic literature featuring clergymen was widespread and contributed to a movement to end clerical celibacy in France.[2]

But outside of these hyperbolic tales, real parish priests did engage in sexual relationships – about that there can be no doubt. Medieval and even some early modern curés regularly had common-law wives who bore them children; in this way, they were seen to have families just like anyone else in the parish. Ruth Mazo Karras consulted a number of different studies for various regions during the medieval period and found that for the most part, if a parish priest was well liked and did his job, his parishioners looked the other way if he had a concubine.[3] In the sixteenth century, visitation records from the German diocese of Speyer, examined by Marc Forster, show that more than half of the parish priests visited between 1583 and 1588 had a concubine. Parishioners did not seem to find this upsetting and rarely complained about it.[4]

Bishops and other clergymen did find this situation problematic, however; clerical celibacy was thus one of the early targets of the Catholic Reformation movement. A wave of decrees about celibacy had been issued in the eleventh and twelfth centuries, well before the Reformation period, although they were not uniformly enforced and many priests refused to comply with the church's orders. There were also still many inside and outside of the church who argued that because celibacy was so difficult, priests should be allowed to marry to avoid scandals. When Protestant churches began allowing and even encouraging priests and pastors to marry in the sixteenth century, the Catholic Church took a hard line on the issue to differentiate itself from the new churches. Rules about celibacy began to be enforced with greater regularity. Bishops told priests to give up their concubines or lose their benefices. Servants had to be either close relatives or above a certain age, usually forty or fifty, presumably because they believed priests would be less tempted by older women but also because post-menopausal women would not be able to have children.[5]

For the most part, these efforts by the church saw a great deal of success. Priests had the rules about interactions with women drilled into them throughout their time in seminaries and during synods and visitations.[6] The rules in handbooks like the *rituel* were clear and hard to ignore. By the end of the eighteenth century in France, visitation records show that curés' common-law wives had virtually disappeared. In 1775 the bishop of Nîmes listed several problems with parish priests, including hunting, unauthorized absences, and wearing non-clerical clothing when travelling. He said nothing about concubines, only that too many curés were asking for dispensations to have underage housekeepers, probably because it was much easier to find younger servants than older ones.[7] At the same time, if we focus on other issues besides priests' concubines, we find that there were still substantial problems with sexual indiscretions. The vast majority did not have common-law wives, but there were some who failed to remain sexually abstinent. Parish life provided plenty of opportunities for priests to seduce and take advantage of young girls and women. One of these opportunities, examined by Stephen Haliczer, was the confessional. Haliczer argues that because priests were no longer allowed concubines, they had to look else-where for sexual contact. One of the only places where emotionally intimate relationships with women were acceptable and even nec-essary was the confessional, leading to multiple attempts at seduc-tion during this sacrament. Some of these priests then ended up on trial before the Inquisition.[8]

Anne Bonzon has also shown that curés in the diocese of Beauvais still struggled with celibacy in the sixteenth and seventeenth cen-turies. She examined over 100 *officialité* cases, dated between 1530 and 1650, and found that problems of a sexual nature were reported in 62 per cent of the cases. These problems included soliciting women of the parish, keeping concubines, and visiting prostitutes.[9] James R. Farr also notes that problems with clerical sexuality persisted in Bur-gundy throughout the seventeenth century.[10] In the eighteenth cen-tury, these problems continued – certainly in the dioceses of Reims and Besançon, but probably all throughout France and the Catholic Church as a whole. Testimony from the *officialité* shows that curés found women who were willing to voluntarily engage in sexual rela-tionships with them, and in other cases they used their status and influence to seduce women who were less than willing. Perhaps unsurprisingly, at least a few appear to have committed rape, and oth-ers attempted it. Women, certainly familiar with unwanted sexual advances and sexual violence from the men in their lives, often found they had to fear these abuses from their curés as well.

This does not mean that every accusation of sexual impropriety made against a curé was legitimate. Parishioners knew exactly what would get the attention of the authorities when they wanted to make complaints about their curé. The court was not likely to take a case that was only about disputes over tithes, the timing of church ser-vices, or misuse of the funds of the *fabrique*, for example. These were all such routine problems that church authorities expected parish-ioners and curés to work them out on their own. But certain events could trigger a court case much more easily: violence in the church, a curé who completely ignored the religious education of the youth, or a priest whose negligence allowed people to die without the sacra-ments – these were much more serious problems. Perhaps the most serious of them all was a curé who had not remained celibate and had engaged in either consensual or non-consensual sex. Church authorities had placed so much emphasis on this aspect of the curés' character that frustrated or angry parishioners knew it would get those authorities' attention.[11] That meant witnesses were eager to report any hint of improper relationships in their complaints and in their testimonies.[12] Parishioners recounted rumours that they had heard about women and the curé, always adding the caveat that what they were saying was indeed rumour but reporting it nevertheless in the hopes that it would help their case. Sometimes, people may have gone so far as to fabricate entire relationships between women and curés. Knowing this makes the situation much more complex than it appears on the surface. Although there certainly were some curés whom we might describe today as predators, and others were simply sinners, most curés did in fact follow the rules. Curés thus ran the gamut in terms of their sexual behaviour, and parishioners were not only aware of this but tried to use it to their advantage.

Many of the women involved in these cases, whether they were victims or otherwise, were servants.[13] Curés regularly employed female servants for a variety of jobs, including domestic tasks like cooking, cleaning, and sewing, but also farm-related tasks like taking care of animals and working in the fields. Curés often owned land personally or as part of their benefice, and they needed farmers to work that land. During harvest season, just about everyone worked in the fields, and that included the curé's servants, both male and female. Some servants were employed full time and lived at the presbytery, while others lived in their own homes. One female servant might be designated as the housekeeper, although some curés had relatives available to take on that role. Some servants might stay for years; others lasted for only a few weeks. All of these servants had a much more intimate relationship with the curé than any other people in the parish.

The literature dealing with servants is primarily focused on urban households – and rightly so, since that is where the majority of servants in the early modern period were employed.[14] But curés' servants deserve attention too, since they were so commonplace in rural society. They had one major thing in common with servants in urban households: they were at risk for sexual abuse. In Geneva between 1650 and 1815, 60 per cent of rape victims who reported their abuse were servants, and 67 per cent of rape victims in cases heard by the Old Bailey in London in the late eighteenth century were servants as well.[15] Studies dealing with illegitimate pregnancies in urban areas show that the proportion of unwed mothers who were also servants could be as high as 90 per cent.[16] For rural areas, Fabrice Mauclair demonstrates that between 1697 and 1790, the courts in the rural *seigneurie* of La Vallière, northwest of Tours, registered 205 *déclarations de grossesse*; Mauclair notes that most of these women were servants.[17] Some of these pregnancies, whether they were in a rural or urban context, were the result of consensual relationships, but many were surely not. Although the percentage of priests who fathered children with their servants is probably quite small, court cases show that this situation did certainly happen. Just because a servant was employed by a rural priest rather than an urban householder did not mean she was free from fears of an unwanted pregnancy or rape. The forms of sexual abuse that are much more difficult to quantify – inappropriate language and innuendo, unwanted touching, and non-penetrative sexual assault – could take place in curés' households as well.

Servants were not the only targets of curés' advances, however. Women of any social status in rural society might find themselves involved in a sexual affair, unwanted or otherwise, with a curé. The following pages will look at three categories of curés who had inappropriate relationships with women, whether they were servants or not. The first category includes what we might call serial offenders: curés accused of multiple incidents involving inappropriate conduct with women, ranging from seduction to groping to rape. There are nine curés in this category; their activities are often the most upsetting to modern readers simply because of the abusive nature of some of the relationships and the descriptions of assault. At the same time, most of these serial offenders did not seem to be rapists. At least two of them only appeared to get in trouble with women when they had been drinking, and their activities were lewd and vulgar rather than criminal. Others simply struggled to remain celibate and eventually decided to enjoy the pleasures of the flesh as much as they could, usually with willing partners. These curés were also likely to use their position in the community to gain access to sexual favours. Their behaviour in these instances might not seem that much different than that of some laymen in rural society. In fact, some activities of lecherous curés were viewed as scandalous not necessarily because of their poor treatment of women, which was common in eighteenth-century society anyway, but because of the incongruity of those activities with the holy responsibilities they held. As with so many other criticisms of curés, it was when their activities affected church services and the sacraments that people were most upset.

The second category of curés includes those who engaged in relationships with one or two women who became just like concubines.
Their actions probably would not have received much attention in
the medieval period, but because Catholic Reformation sensibilities
had penetrated even rural villages by the eighteenth century, their failure to remain celibate was not only noted but criticized. The problems for the five curés in this category seem straightforward, but those
of the five curés in the third category were anything but. In these five
cases, as well as in Nicolas Hyacinthe Vernier's, it is not entirely clear
if the curés were actually guilty of the sexual crimes their parishioners
accused them of. The conflicting testimony makes it difficult to sort
out what happened, but the cases do help us to better understand the
relationship between parishioners – especially female parishioners –
and curés.

Historians face a myriad of difficulties when studying sexual relationships, whether consensual or coerced.[18] Sources are limited and
flawed in many ways. The cases I examine here were not, in most
instances, about rape in and of itself. With a couple of exceptions,
most of the women involved in sexual relationships with a curé did
not testify in these cases, nor were they the primary plaintiffs. The
cases are about the moral behaviour of clergymen, and the central
question is whether the curé should be deprived of his benefice rather
than punished for rape or assault. In that way, *officialité* records are
both useful and flawed – they may provide details about everyday life
(including sexual aspects) that are missing from other sources, but
some of those details may have been invented. They thus tell us
things that might have happened, in a way that is illuminating of the
culture surrounding sexual relationships, but without any clarity on
whether they actually did happen.

Rapes were, and still are, so chronically unreported that statisti-
cal analysis of sexual assault is often limited. For example, Anna
Clark found that between 1770 and 1800, only forty-three cases of
rape were tried by the Old Bailey court in London.[19] Surely there
were many, many additional women who were raped or sexually
assaulted in that thirty-year period. As Clark and others point out,
rape was underreported as there were many disincentives for victims to try to bring their rapists to court, including prohibitive
costs, lack of access to courts, a patriarchal and oppressive judicial
system, and a culture that shamed women for any sexual contact,
coerced or otherwise.[20] Because of this, it seems to me that no mat-

ter the limitations of the sources, including *officialité* records, any evidence that might be labelled anecdotal is still eminently valuable for the study of women's lives. Since so many incidents of sexual violence never made it into the courts at all, when evidence can be found in court records, even if it is secondary to the case itself, it deserves to be examined and analyzed. Much of the testimony elucidated below is secondhand or thirdhand, and some of the people involved may have been inventing facts to slander their curés. I certainly do not claim that the experiences related here are in any way representative of all French villages. But that does not mean they are not instructive in helping us understand both curés and their parishioners. At the very least, they demonstrate that sexual assault by a curé, as well as consensual sexual relationships between curés and their parishioners and servants, were not beyond the realm of possibility.

### *"The Curé Is Known Throughout the Country for Chasing Skirts":* Serial Offenders

The first two serial offenders were also serial drunks. Both Claude Joseph Richard, curé of Foucherans (Besançon), and Pierre Regnier, the curé of Les Grandes-Loges (Reims), were known for their problems with alcohol.[21] Their love of wine was also paired with a love of women. One winter night, sometime around midnight, Richard showed up drunk at the home of his parishioner Michel Verger. Finding Verger in bed with his wife, the curé asked him to move over and got into the bed between them. (Why Verger allowed this to happen was not explained.) Then Richard spoke to them, using obscenities, detailing "what happens between a man and his wife."[22] Richard was also known for engaging in other scandalous conversations and for touching women inappropriately when inebriated. Regnier had similar problems; his parishioners reported that he took "criminal liberties" with women by kissing them and caressing them. In one case he followed one of his parishioner's servants around her house, trying to get her to kiss him and asking her if he could see her bedroom.[23] Regnier also danced with girls at a wedding, and he appeared drunk on that occasion as well.

Parishioners' testimony makes it seem as though these curés were fine when they were sober, but when they were drunk they had to be watched carefully or they would behave inappropriately with

women.[24] Their indecent talk and attempted kisses were more annoy-
ing than threatening, but in other instances women had a great deal
more to fear from their curé. The case against Jean Baptiste Le Grand
tells a story that was all too common in the early modern period: the
curé had an affair with his servant, and she ended up pregnant. She
went to a nearby village to have the baby but came back several times
to see the curé, and sometimes she stayed at the presbytery for five or
six days at a time.[25] Furthermore, there was a lot of rumour about a
girl in the parish named Margueritte Colignon; villagers had noticed
that she was seen at the presbytery too often. Two young men, Pierre
Claude Rouy and Nicolas Rouy, waited for Margueritte at a time
when they suspected she would be on her way to the presbytery. They
confronted her in the church cemetery, slapped her a couple of times,
and warned her to stop visiting the curé's house. These events caused
a great scandal in the parish, and witnesses said that they did not want
to confess with such a curé. Others said that they did not even want
to attend the mass because of his behaviour.[26] Witnesses seemed to
believe that the incident in the cemetery showed how much the
peace of the community had been disturbed, and they blamed Le
Grand entirely.

In 1716 there were similar rumours going around the villages of
Gevigney and Mercey (Besançon): it was said that the curé, François
Jacqueney, was having an affair with Clere Vautherot, the wife of the
surgeon in Gevigney. They were known to visit each other's houses,
night and day, and the common talk was that he had used both
money and violence to try to get her to submit herself to him. He had
even tried to engage the community to buy the house next door to
hers so that he could use it instead of the current presbytery, even
though it was further away from the church. Many people also testified in the *information* that the surgeon himself had complained to
them that the curé was trying to take advantage of his wife.[27]

Some people in the village believed that Vautherot was a willing
participant in this affair, but her testimony told a much different, and
much more disturbing, story. She told the court that he had solicited
her many times but that she had always rejected him. He offered her
money and told her that he had already "enjoyed other women." She
tried to explain to him that she found only horror in his propositions,
asking him what he would say to her, as her confessor, if she came to
him and confessed to having an affair. He responded indignantly,

scolding her for trying to preach morals to him. Then he gave an excuse that was, as we will see, rather common: he told her that if she sinned with him, he would either absolve her himself or get another priest to do it. She still resisted. On two separate occasions he tried to force her with violence, but each time she was saved by the fact that there were other people around. The second time it was her husband who came to her rescue, when he heard her cries coming from his stable.[28] If the curé was willing to do this to one woman, there were probably more.

Another one of the serial offenders was Gabriel Joseph Blondeau, curé of Courcuire (Besançon). Although his violent behaviour and his drunkenness were the major focus of the case, Blondeau had more than his fair share of troubles with women. A lot of the testimony dealing with his various affairs is secondhand, but it still seems clear that either drunk or sober (but especially drunk) Blondeau was known for groping the women in his parish every chance he could get. Multiple people said that they had talked to women who had complained that the cure had touched them, grabbed them, or said "immodest things" to them. Firsthand accounts corroborate this testimony. One victim of Blondeau's sexual advances was Claudinette de Chasoy, age twenty. She testified that many times he had spoken to her using dirty words and that he had tried to touch her breast and put his hand under her skirts. She told the court that she always resisted his attempts to "do violence to her purity."[29] Another woman, Claude Rigaud, told the court that she was staying at her mother's house in Courcuire when late one night the curé violently opened the door. She and the other women who were there jumped out of their beds, still in their nightclothes, but realized quickly that he was drunk. At some point during the commotion the curé approached Claude and touched her breast; "Voilà," he said, "what pretty apples."[30]

Barbe Baudoin, a thirty-six-year-old woman of Courcuire, testified that Blondeau had assaulted her many times, especially after she became a widow. He had kissed her despite her resistance; even on the day that the authorities published a *monitoire*[31] asking for more information about his morals he had come to her house and kissed her, she said. One evening the curé had sent for her and when she refused to go to the presbytery he had come to her house, "with a design to attack her purity." She had hidden and escaped his attentions. Baudoin also testified that she had had many conversations with the curé's mother, who lived at the presbytery and was a witness to all the women he kept company with, at all hours of the night. Baudoin claimed that Blondeau's mother had admitted that it was up to her to "get rid" of him, but that she did not want to do it.[32]

The incident that had the most people talking, however, was about a girl named Jeanne Claude Constantin, who had engaged in a sexual relationship with Blondeau and was not shy about admitting it. She said that she had never "done bad" except with the curé, and that she had spent many nights at the presbytery. Concerned about what might happen to her, her family sent her to live in Avrigney, another village about five kilometres away, to learn sewing from Nicolas Journet and his wife, Simone Vincent. They both provided depositions and told the court that Jeanne Claude had been open with them about her relationship with her curé. She even told Vincent that she feared she was pregnant but then added that if she was, the curé had told her he would give her something to abort the baby. During this time, the curé would come to see her in Avrigney, and she went to see him in Courcuire. They met on the road, and one time a man discovered them in the bushes. She begged the passerby not to tell her family what he had seen, but he did anyway; her relatives decided to send her to a religious institution known as the Refuge in Besançon. At the time of the case she was still there, under the name Soeur Claude of the Refuge.[33]

It seems clear that in these three cases, Le Grand, Jacqueney, and Blondeau had engaged in some sort of sexual affair with at least one, and probably multiple, women. In the case of Jacques Philbert François, the curé may not have succeeded in persuading women to enter into a sexual relationship with him, but he certainly tried. One witness, the *laboureur* Louis Lolieu, portrayed François as a little naive when it came to both women and the duties of his estate. Lolieu said that François was perfectly capable of fulfilling his religious functions if he wanted to, but he was too quick to drink and engage in "dishonest discourse." François even told Lolieu that when he kissed women or went to visit them it was just for recreation and because he liked them. Lolieu took the liberty to say to François that a curé should not be so free with his parishioners, and especially with women. The curé responded that for people of his character, it was too difficult to be shut up all the time – he needed diversion in his life.[34] Apparently, François had completely given up on his vow of celibacy and had made it his mission to seduce any women he could find.

Lolieu did not say if he knew anything about any specific affairs, and he did not give the names of any women who might have been involved, but several women of the parish also testified and their descriptions of conversations with François show just how far he had strayed from the rules regarding clerical morals. One of the curé's targets was Marie Lefebvre, the wife of the parish clerk, Louis Sauclon. One summer day when Lefebvre's husband was out of town, the curé came to her house to tell her he had decided he no longer wanted Sauclon to serve as the clerk but that he had not fired him yet because he wanted to talk to her first. He then told Lefebvre that he liked her, and that if she gave in to his desires no one would know. She refused. His next tactic was to flirt, asking her if he was not handsome enough for her and boasting that he had been with other women prettier than her. When she still resisted, his flirtation turned to threats. He told her that other women recognized that this sort of thing was allowed for men of his character and had not turned him away. He even told her that affairs with women were permitted for men of the church, even though they were not allowed for secular men. She had just been badly instructed, he said – they could live well together! She continued to resist, and he told her that if she did not give in within two months' time then he would fire her husband. Evidently, she continued to resist, because François fired the clerk.[35]

Marie Anne Joly, the twenty-two-year-old wife of a merchant in the parish, told a similar story: François had made comparable statements and advances toward her. His initial pick-up line, if you want to call it that, was to tell Joly that he had had a dream about her, in which she had slept with him and given him great pleasure. When he woke and realized it was just a dream, he wished that it was true, and hoped that she would make it true. As with Marie Lefebvre, he said that no one would find out, that it was allowed for people like him, and that other women of the parish had already given in to him. This time, he also added that he had heard about a noble lady who had been chased from the Parisian court because she would not submit to the desires of an ecclesiastic, insinuating that he would try to chase her from the parish if she continued to refuse him.[36]

Neither of these women said that François had touched them, other than to fervently grasp their hands, but two others said that he had gone so far as to grope them. Marie Anne Noé testified that before she was married François would follow her around the village trying to get her alone. He gave her kisses and put his hand on her breast, assuring her that if she consented to his desires nothing would happen and that he would never abandon her. He made the same propositions to her in the confessional and at catechism, so her father forbade her from going back. Another woman gave even more disturbing testimony. She said that when she was visiting her son, a resident of the parish, the curé had come to eat with them, and after the meal he had said he wanted to tell her something about her son. They had gone into a room for privacy, and while there he had taken his penis out of his pants and forced her to touch it. She had resisted his advances, telling him that he should be ashamed of himself.[37]

Another curé tried tactics similar to those that François used. In the parish of Dun (Reims) in 1741, the curé Louis Charles David was a notorious womanizer. As one member of his parish put it, "the curé is known throughout the country for chasing skirts."[38] At least three servants left his service because they were pregnant, although it is unclear whether it was the curé or his valet who was responsible. One of the curé's servants – one who had not gotten pregnant – tried to ignore what was happening while she was in his service but clearly found it troubling. In her testimony she said that she often saw women enter his house, but since she "is not in charge of the curé's conduct, she didn't pay attention to what he did or didn't do." However, she continued, she felt that what the curé was doing was wrong, and she often spoke about it to her confessor, "with bitterness in her heart."[39]

David's shenanigans were patently obvious to Christine Regnart, a servant in the house across the street from the presbytery.[40] Regnart testified that on one summer Sunday evening after vespers, she saw from her window that the curé had returned home. He was soon followed by one of his "girls," as the witnesses called them, named Elisabeth Mauclaire. Peering out from her window, Regnart first saw Elisabeth in the street and then noticed the curé wave his hat, beckoning Elisabeth to join him in his garden. Elisabeth looked up and realized that Regnart had seen the curé's gesture, so she pretended she was looking for her aunt, whose house was on the same street. Elisabeth even called up to Regnart, asking if she knew where her aunt was. Regnart, fully aware of what was happening, just said, "Go on, he's waiting for you over there." But Elisabeth persisted in her ruse, waiting in her aunt's courtyard for a half hour while the curé peeked around the corner of his wall several times to see if she was still there. Eventually Regnart was called away by her mistress, so she was unable to tell the court whether Elisabeth kept her rendezvous with the curé or not.

On another occasion Regnart had even better evidence of their affair, however. One evening in the winter she saw Elisabeth in the street again, at about ten o'clock at night. Regnart was in her room and, hearing noise from the street, ran to the window to see Elisabeth throwing snowballs at the curé's window. Regnart then ran downstairs and outside to see what Elisabeth was doing, but during the time it took her to descend the stairs Elisabeth disappeared. Regnart went across the street and, because she saw that the gate to the curé's yard was not locked, went inside. Once there, she saw footprints in the snow that led to the back of the garden, where, she said, there was usually a ladder used to provide access to the other garden. The ladder was gone and the trail of footprints stopped, which made Christine think that Elisabeth had climbed the ladder and then taken it up with her into the curé's room.

Regnart herself was also one of the objects of David's affections, although she did not return his sentiments. One day she heard the curé calling out from one of his windows:

"Christine, Christine, I want to talk to you!"
"What do you want to say to me?" replied Regnart.
"I want to tell you something, come on, my heart, I beg you. You can come in through the garden, with a ladder, and no one will see you."

Regnart told the curé that if he wanted to tell her something then he could talk to her through the window but that she would not go to the garden because she did not want people to gossip about her. David asked her again, "Come over, my love, no one will see." But Regnart was just as persistent as her curé and stayed at her master's house. For the next two weeks, every time she passed by the window that had a view to the presbytery the curé begged her to come and see him. He proposed that she give some excuse to go to a garden owned by her master and that he would meet her there if she did not want to risk coming to the presbytery. She refused, saying that this proposition was inappropriate for a man of his character and that he would have to be content with his other girls. David responded and said that he had given up seeing them, and that anyway they were not that pretty and he liked her better. Regnart retorted that in that case she knew he was making fun of her, since she was not actually pretty. Pretty enough, she admitted, for a man who wanted to marry her according to the laws of God and the church, but since he was a curé and could not marry her then this sort of conversation was inappropriate.

Most scandalous of all was David's affair with a dame of the parish, who visited him at the presbytery when her husband was away and sent jealous and accusatory notes to David's other paramours. According to Marie Grandjean, the wife of one of the village notables, the affair had actually begun in her home.[41] She had agreed to allow the dame and David to meet at her house, believing that they had confidential things to discuss. It is likely that Grandjean thought she was avoiding scandal by giving them a secure place to hold their conversations, rather than the church or the presbytery. She believed that their interactions were entirely innocent, but when she was informed by her servant that the pair often went up to the attic together Grandjean began to pay better attention and noticed that indeed they did seem to spend a good amount of time there alone. She made a small peephole in the door to the attic, and then the next time they went in – well, she saw with her own eyes what she and her servant had suspected. As she put it, the curé took "criminal liberties" with the dame. Grandjean did not want to allow such "disorders" in her home, nor did she want to admit that she had been spying. So she just told them that people were starting to talk and she would rather they found another place to meet. But she knew that they saw each other elsewhere, Grandjean added. At the very end of her testimony, Grandjean noted that the day she saw the curé take criminal liberties with the dame, it was Holy Friday – just two days before Easter. Despite all his affairs and his poor reputation in the parish, the curé never missed saying the mass during the holy season.

Jean François Aubriot de Boncourt had a bad reputation for his relationships with women in his parish as well. In general, his parishioners said that he spoke "too freely" with women, leading to a lot of rumours. He made inappropriate comments about women, and so many women were seen coming and going from the presbytery that some parishioners had lost confidence in him as a pastor. He also went walking with women in public, out in the fields or in the woods. One man even testified that he had seen the curé, when visiting the town of Rethel, go swimming in the river with two friends, one male and one female. The witness said he had followed them to the riverbank, hiding behind trees so that he could see what was happening; he found the curé and his friends laughing and singing while splashing in the water. It seemed clear that they had been drinking as well.[42]

Aubriot de Boncourt was also suspected of fathering a baby with a servant; he made the usual excuses and said the baby was not his. But another incident perhaps demonstrates the way things operated for this curé. A miller and his wife lived on the outskirts of the parish, and one night during a great snowstorm a girl named Berthe knocked on their door at around two in the morning. They found her in a "pitiable state" and let her in to warm up. When she told them that she was on her way to see the curé in Sorbon, the miller's wife tried to dissuade her, saying that he had a bad reputation and that it would cause a scandal for her to be seen there at an indecent hour. The girl seemed unperturbed and said she knew how to get in to the presbytery without being seen. The miller's wife convinced her to send a message to the curé instead; upon receiving the message, he sent back a bottle of wine and six *livres*, presumably to make up for the trouble Berthe had caused for the miller and his wife. The next morning, he showed up and talked to Berthe, scolding her for coming out in such bad weather, but then he left her there for most of the day, much to the consternation of the miller and his wife, until a male servant finally arrived saying he had been instructed to take Berthe back to Rethel. The miller's wife knew this was just a ruse, however, and told the court that the servant actually took the girl to the presbytery.[43]

These incidents involving David and Aubriot de Boncourt are comical enough that their antics could easily have ended up in Boccaccio's tales. The actions of one of the other serial offenders though, Hermand de Lafosse, are less humourous. The women in his parish must have lived in constant fear of his advances. Jeanne Bournet testified that the curé tried to kiss her when she was working in his garden; she left before he could succeed. Jean Claude Clest told the court that when his daughter went to the curé to talk to him about what needed to be done for her upcoming marriage ceremony, he asked her to go into the sacristy, where he solicited her. She was scandalized, but resisted and left. Antoinette Vienot went to the presbytery with her little brother to ask the curé to hear his confession so that he could be confirmed. Instead of attending to her brother the curé grabbed Antoinette and made her sit on his lap; he took her hand and placed it, over his clothes, on his "shameful parts." Gabrielle Gérard told the court that de Lafosse had groped her several times, including once when she was pregnant and he was visiting her house. The curé told her that he would give her grain, or money, or whatever she wanted if she gave in to him, but she ran out of the house to escape him. Another time he brought her a bouquet of flowers. Afraid, she left the house before he could try anything and said, "Go to the devil with your bouquets." Women in Cugney were not even safe from the curé in their own homes.[44]

Curés like these were willing to use whatever methods they could to try to get what they wanted from women, whether those women were parishioners or servants. Flattery, blackmail, violence and promises of money, goods, or absolution in the confessional were all on display with these men. The women they came into contact with would certainly have had cause to fear them no matter the type of social or religious interaction they were engaged in. These nine men were probably not the only ones who created this fear in women either. Although they were certainly not representative of all clergy in Reims or Besançon, there were probably others who engaged in similar behaviours and just did not get caught or prosecuted. Furthermore, cases involving clerical sexuality were being tried more frequently by secular courts instead of the *officialité*.[45] The small number of cases in church courts may be just the tip of the iceberg.[46] Perhaps only the most serious cases against eighteenth-century curés gained the attention of the French courts, but that does not mean that curés had stopped having sex, consensual or otherwise.

No matter how representative these curés were, however, the responses of their parishioners show certain expectations. Women knew that curés, like other men, might threaten or assault them; they had to use the same tactics, successful or not, to avoid those assaults. Some even tried to use this to their advantage, hoping that they could reap material benefits from a sexual relationship with the curé without ruining their reputations or getting pregnant. We usually do not hear from these women, as they were unlikely to be willing and available to serve as witnesses in court cases. But the women who resisted, as well as some men in the parish who knew about these affairs or solicitations, clearly did have higher expectations for the curés.

Before the Catholic Reformation, these expectations simply did not exist. Curés had common-law wives and few people seemed to care. But by the eighteenth century, parishioners expected sexual abstinence from their curé, and when he failed, it was a scandal for the whole parish. We see this in women's responses to solicitations or assaults: many women, from the wives of village notables down to clerks' wives and servants, resisted not just because they were horrified by the attacks on their bodies but because they resented the attacks on their souls. Over and over they insisted that their curés had acted in ways that were incompatible with their holy estate. The Catholic Reformation had thus succeeded in creating an image of what a curé should look like, and parishioners complained to the authorities when the curé in their parish did not live up to that image.

### Bad Subjects: Curés and Concubines

Not only did parishioners complain when the curé assaulted or solicited them personally, but they also complained if the curé kept a mistress or engaged in a long-term relationship with a woman. Gabriel Mottet was accused of having an affair with a servant named Marie Gaudot. The case materials do not make it clear how long the affair went on, but even after she left the parish to get married Mottet would meet her in a nearby town, to the scandal of everyone in the parish as well as the town.[47] Jean Baptiste Le Marie had an affair with a servant as well; he admitted the affair and even said that he was so attached to her that he would rather die than ask her to leave. The servant, a woman named Marie Anne, was also known as a "bad subject" in the parish because of her drinking and debauched lifestyle. Once, when Le Marie was out of town, she had a man from a nearby parish come and stay with her. This caused such scandal that the parishioners engaged a soldier (a visiting relative of someone in the village) to deal with the situation. He went to the presbytery and told the man that the curé's house was not a place for a rogue like him. The soldier forced them both out and handed the keys to the presbytery over to the *syndic*, who kept them for the next two or three weeks until the curé returned.[48]

The servant of curé Guillaume Bruno Loris, Catherine Cotteret, became pregnant as a result of their affair. Sometime before she was due to deliver, the curé had her taken away to Douai in Flanders. She was gone for more than a year, which caused a great scandal because her father and other relatives had no idea where she had gone. The rumour in the parish was that she had the baby in Douai and gave the child the curé's name; he was baptized as Antoine Loris. She eventually returned and married in Beauvais, but she still came to visit Loris in his parish from time to time, adding to the scandal. Other parishioners found it problematic that Loris had carried on this affair at the time when his own father was living with him in the presbytery; the elder Loris had told his friends that the girl was a whore, and another relative indicated that it was the shame over the bastard child that had caused his death.[49]

Claude Louis Barban, curé of Servigney (Besançon), scandalized his parishioners by keeping a servant as his concubine and then maintaining a familiar relationship with her even after she married.[50] The servant, Jeanne Claude Rolet, was the daughter of Barban's housekeeper. Witnesses claimed there was no doubt that he was the father of her baby. One woman even testified that she had seen them in bed together.[51] Then, Rolet gave birth in the presbytery, and the surgeon came to help with the delivery.[52] Rolet eventually married Germain Carillon of Mondon, the annex of Servigney, and Barban continued to visit Rolet there. Multiple residents of Mondon testified that they had seen the curé going in and out of their house many times, especially on the days he came to perform services at the church in Mondon. One woman said that she saw Barban kiss Rolet,[53] and, even more strangely, he seemed to publicly acknowledge Rolet's child as his own: the curé told a young boy that if he wanted to marry his daughter when he grew up he would give him a thousand écus.[54] Once during a meal, perhaps after drinking a bit, Barban joked with other parishioners, saying he was sad that he had only produced daughters.[55] Witnesses were also scandalized that Rolet and her children (she had since had others with her husband) often visited the presbytery, where he played with them and had them eat at his table. Barban claimed that Rolet visited because her mother, and the children's grandmother, was his housekeeper, but parishioners still found it problematic.[56]

Barban acted much like a medieval curé by maintaining this illicit relationship, although a few generations earlier he probably would have kept Rolet as his concubine indefinitely, instead of marrying her off to Carillon. Some parishioners did not seem to have a problem with this relationship. Four witnesses in the case had only praise for Barban. The schoolmaster, who would have worked closely with the curé, said that he had nothing bad to say about Barban. Eleven of the sixty-two witnesses even said that they knew nothing about the complaint – nothing about Rolet, or about the "libertinism" that he was accused of. Perhaps these individuals felt that as long as Barban fulfilled his duties as a pastor he could do what he wanted with his personal life. Many others, however, were scandalized, and the court agreed with them. Barban not only lost his benefice, he was also fined and told he could never possess a benefice with care of souls again.[57]

Curés often chose servants for their concubines – or perhaps "chose" is not the right word. It was much more difficult to maintain a long-term relationship with someone other than a servant, since other women could not live at the presbytery. Claude Antoine Monnier, however, seems to have managed it. Monnier had lived in the presbytery even before he became the curé, because the previous owner of the benefice was his uncle. During this time, he began a relationship with a girl of the parish, Claude Louise Marquis. When his uncle was doing vespers and catechism, he would sneak off to see Marquis at her house. For awhile he had a position as a vicaire in another parish, but he would still come to see her whenever he visited his uncle. Once his uncle died and he was given the benefice, he became even bolder about his relationship. Witnesses reported seeing them together all over the parish. A woman testified that she had seen the curé touching Marquis inappropriately; she was scandalized and told Monnier that it would be better for him to say prayers than to do what he was doing. He retorted that it was none of her business. Monnier apparently solicited other women in the parish as well, and there was a great deal of murmuring because of all this; Monnier's actions had caused a serious scandal.[58]

Each of these five cases contains enough evidence that points to the fact that these curés were guilty of engaging in long-term affairs with women, flaunting the very clear rules set by the church about celibacy and interactions with women. As with any other case, there is certainly the possibility that witnesses lied or exaggerated details to ensure that the curé was removed from his position. Curés gave excuses for their conduct that might seem plausible, if it were not for the weight of the testimony of dozens of witnesses who countered those excuses. But even acknowledging the possible deceit of witnesses and parishioners, the evidence strongly suggests that they were guilty. The core of these five cases was always the curé's affairs, and any problems with the sacraments, alcoholism, or parish services were seen as secondary. In other cases, however, the evidence is not quite so clear. In these next cases, it is entirely possible that parishioners falsely accused their curés of inappropriate behaviour to get the attention of the authorities and have a better chance of replacing their curé.

## Rumours and Accusations

The case of Nicolas Dumontier of Roupy (Noyon) demonstrates how
parishioners might try to manipulate the court system with exaggerated or false accusations. Dumontier was accused of drunkenness and
neglecting his pastoral functions. His parishioners also suspected him
of fathering a child with one of his servants, a woman named
Françoise Payen, the daughter of one of Roupy's day labourers. Nine
witnesses testified in the case, and all but one of them, the village
clerk and schoolmaster, indicated that there were rumours about
Dumontier and Payen and that he was the father of her baby. However, Payen made a *déclaration de grossesse* (required by all unmarried
pregnant women in early modern France) and named a man from a
neighbouring parish as the father. After the nine witnesses testified in
the *information*, the court requested testimony from three other individuals, including Françoise Payen and her father, who both confirmed that the curé was not the father of her child. They also told the
court that there was nothing scandalous going on and that she lived
at her father's home rather than the curé's. Both she and her sister did
work for him, they said, but neither of them had ever spent even one
night at the presbytery.[59]

The *officialité* court in Noyon convicted Dumontier of three things:
employing a woman, age twenty-seven (and therefore below the prescribed age for servants) for a period of fifteen to sixteenth months;
being subject to wine and appearing drunk at services; and neglecting to teach the catechism on some Sundays and feast days. He was
told that after a period of six months at the seminary he could return
to his position in Roupy as long as he promised not to have any
young women at his house. Dumontier appealed the case to the court
in Reims, claiming that his parishioners were trying to slander him;
the court there decided that since Payen had not lived at the presbytery for any period of time she had never officially been his servant. They reduced his sentence to six weeks. We will never know if
the rumours about his activities were malicious or just the result of
his unwise association with a young, pregnant woman, but in any
case, Dumontier successfully convinced the court that they were just
rumours and he kept his job.[60]

In another case, it seems a little more obvious that parishioners had
invented an inappropriate relationship between a servant and their
curé to get the attention of the authorities. Jean François Fouchard,

curé of Grandvillars, was, as we have seen, accused of refusing to bury the father of a prominent individual in the region because the desired cemetery was not enclosed. Most of the testimony in the case dealt with that issue, but a few people also noted that there was a young woman living at the presbytery – the daughter of his housekeeper. People claimed they did not know how old she was, but they guessed somewhere between fourteen and eighteen. If she was over fourteen, it would have been against the rules for her to live there; however, none of the witnesses said they knew of, or heard any rumours about, any liaison between Fouchard and the servant's daughter. When Fouchard told the court that she was younger than fourteen, they let the matter drop and asked nothing more about it.[61]

In a similar case, parishioners who testified against Claude Nicolas Boulanger of Auxon-Dessous (Besançon) also invented an affair to slander their curé. In a letter that the inhabitants of the village sent to the archbishop they complained that Boulanger had wronged them in several ways.[62] First, he had undertaken unfair lawsuits against his parishioners. Second, he had let a child die without baptism because he had not wanted to get out of bed. Third, he had insulted them from the pulpit. Fourth, he had treated schoolmasters so badly that they had quit and left the parish. Fifth, he had used land from the cemetery to enlarge the courtyard of the presbytery. Sixth, he had refused to do an extra service that the parish had requested and paid for. While these things were surely troubling to the villagers, nothing on this list indicates that Boulanger had engaged in any illicit affairs.

Yet when the *officialité* began to investigate the situation in Auxon-Dessous about a year and a half later, after an argument about the sale of some oak trees belonging to the parish, witnesses testified that an unmarried woman named Margueritte Parrancy, age around thirty, was frequenting the presbytery so much that everyone had started to call her "monsieur le vicaire." Eight of the twelve witnesses who gave depositions named Parrancy and said that she was frequently seen at the presbytery, and they all repeated her nickname. Two of these individuals said that they had heard people call Parrancy "monsieur le vicaire," but they did not think that there was anything suspect about their relationship. One witness said that they believed she was *fort sage*, or very well behaved.[63] At the very end of the interrogation, Boulanger was asked about Parrancy, and he said that she had a very good reputation and only came to the presbytery for domestic service and had never slept there. Even though his relationship with her was innocent, he said, as soon as he had heard about the rumours he stopped her from coming to the presbytery. The court seemed satisfied with this explanation and did not ask anything further.[64]

These three cases (Dumontier, Fouchard, and Boulanger) cast quite a bit of doubt on the reliability of witness testimony when it comes to curés' sexual behaviour. They may have been guilty of being poor pastors, but that does not mean they had committed any sexual crimes or even sins. In another case, however, the curé involved, Pierre Mercier of Vigneux (Laon), was convicted by the court and forced to give up his parish so he may have been guilty.[65] At the same time, Mercier's attempted defence shows that false accusations of affairs with curés were commonplace. Curés had to pay close attention to their public activities, especially around women, or they might face rumours that were difficult, or nearly impossible, to counter. Once a rumour began, no matter whether it was true, exaggerated, or completely unfounded, the curé might lose the trust of his parishioners and find himself out of a job.

Mercier admitted to having three different servants who were all too young. Even though they had only stayed at the presbytery for a short time, the fact that he had employed them at all automatically made Mercier look guilty. Furthermore, he had received an order from the diocesan authorities to let the first of these servants go, so the fact that he still hired two more young women makes him look even more guilty. One twenty-four-year-old woman, Jeanne Marie Cornet, was his servant for four months. Mercier claims that he let her go because she was lazy and continually indisposed. After she left Mercier's employment, she worked for a couple of months with someone else and then ended up staying with a woman in another parish, Madame Dupenty, who supposedly took her in out of charity because she was, unfortunately, pregnant.

Madame Dupenty then approached Mercier and told him that Cornet was planning on naming him as the father of her child unless he gave her 150 *livres*. He maintained his innocence, saying that he would not give her anything because he was not the father and because he was not obliged to pay for "the follies of others." Madame Dupenty persisted, telling him that if he did not give her the money then she would name him as the father and it would cause scandal no matter if it was true or not. Or, she might decide to abort the baby. Dupenty said it was just as if he was facing a thief in the woods – he would hand over his purse to save his life, would he not? Mercier eventually decided that he would give her half the amount she had requested. But Cornet was not satisfied with seventy-five *livres*; she went to the *procureur fiscal* in Vigneux, Louis Warnam, and told him that she had been promised 150 *livres* or she would make the declaration against Mercier. Warnam warned Mercier about this but the curé just got angry and said that the girl was a whore who had stolen grain and linens from him and that he would not give her anything else. So, Cornet declared Mercier to be the father of her child, and soon everyone in the parish and in the surrounding villages knew it. She gave birth to the child soon thereafter, but it did not survive more than a few days.

During his interrogation, Mercier denied that he was the father of the child. He said that while Cornet had been in his service he had suspected that something was not right with her and that he kept her only because he could not find anyone else. After she left he found out that she had stolen from him and that she had been frequenting young men of the parish. He insisted that he had given her money only in the hope that she would not abort the baby and because Madame Dupenty had been so persistent. The case really came down to Cornet – either she was lying about the father of her baby or she was not. It is possible that Mercier was the father, and it is equally possible that Cornet was a desperate young woman who tried to blackmail her former curé and master to get herself out of a sticky situation. The court may have decided that the damage had been done either way and that Mercier could no longer be effective as a curé. They had no choice but to require him to leave Vigneux for good.

One of the most difficult cases to untangle is that of Nicolas Vauquelin, curé of Saint-Pierre de Crépy (Laon). Less than three years after arriving in the parish, Vauquelin received an order from the bishop requesting that he spend three months at the seminary and begin to reform his behaviour.[66] The order says that Vauquelin was guilty of the following infractions: changing the rites and usages of the parish on his own authority; criticizing his parishioners and members of the religious orders from the pulpit; being absent from the parish and causing people to die without the sacraments; and not getting along with the curé of Notre Dame de Crépy, the other curé in the town. Thus, we know that Vauquelin was difficult from the very beginning of his time in his parish – much like Vernier. He upset the usual workings of the parish and the parishioners complained, leading to the bishop's order. The bishop's reprimands did not work for long, however; seven years later, in 1736, things had gotten so bad in Saint-Pierre de Crépy that the *officialité* began an investigation.

In the 1736 *information*, witnesses testified that Vauquelin had not reformed his conduct after his stay at the seminary. He still did not get along with the other curé, he still did not say the mass correctly, and he had all kinds of problems in the confessional, including confessing everyone, even women and girls, in the sacristy instead of in the confessional. He mishandled the funds of the parish and started unnecessary lawsuits. He even carried around a saber whenever he was out in the streets. Parishioners reported that they had lost their confidence in him, and some refused to do their Easter communion while he was still their curé. In addition to all of this testimony, there were multiple accusations that the curé had been soliciting and assaulting women in the parish and in the town.

These accusations involved ten different women, five of whom had been servants for Madame de Foucault, an elderly dame of the parish with whom Vauquelin associated frequently. Marie Louise Rossignol was one of these servants, and she testified that when Vauquelin visited he would follow her around and try to seduce her. Three or four times he exposed himself in front of her and "made his seed fall on the ground."[67] A woman of the parish, Marie Madelaine Flour, testified that one day she went to the presbytery to receive a payment for some cheeses she had sold to Vauquelin. While she was there Vauquelin flirted with her and asked if she would kiss him. At first she thought he was just teasing, but then he exposed himself to her. She pulled out a knife and told him that she would stab him in the gut if he tried anything, and then she left.[68]

Other women, servants and otherwise, gave similar stories. But careful examination of the testimony and Vauquelin's interrogation leads to some important questions (see table 5.1). First, two of the women who were allegedly assaulted did not testify in the case, and there is only vague secondhand evidence about what may have happened to them. Three other women contradicted the rumours that had been going on about them in their testimony and either denied that Vauquelin had tried to seduce them or said nothing about it during their depositions. This included Anne Madeleine Magnier, who told the court Vauquelin had never propositioned her and that what people were saying about her was the result of rumours started by her

Table 5.1  Possible assault victims in the case against Vauquelin (1736)

| Witness | Relationship/Occupation | Summary of testimony |
|---|---|---|
| Marie Louise Rossignol | A former servant for Madame de Foucault; current wife of Pierre Baudier | Rossignol gave testimony that Vauquelin tried to seduce her; Pierre Pottier gave second hand testimony. The court did not ask Vauquelin about this event in his interrogation. |
| Marie Michelle Lemaire | A servant for Madame de Foucault | Lemaire testified that Vauquelin tried to seduce her. Vauquelin denied it. Antoinette Belle-soeur, Pierre Flour, Madelaine Cochart, and Marie Louise Cordevant gave secondhand testimony. |
| Antoinette Charpentier | A servant for Madame de Foucault | Antoinette Charpentier testified that Vauquelin tried to seduce her when she was making a bed. Vauquelin claimed she was trying to seduce him. Antoinette Bellesoeur and Marie Louise Cordevant gave secondhand testimony. |
| Marie Jeanne Prudhomme | Former servant for Madame de Foucault; current wife of Nicolas Voisin | Vauquelin was asked in the interrogation if he seduced her; he denied it. She said in her testimony that she had only heard rumours and knew nothing about Vauquelin's relation-ships with women firsthand. |
| Margueritte | Former servant for Madame de Foucault | Antoinette Bellesoeur gave secondhand testimony, and Vauquelin denied during the inter-rogation that he seduced her. Margueritte herself did not testify. |
| Anne Madeleine Magnier | First husband was Jean Courtonne; second husband Louis Viellart | Antoinette Bellesoeur and Michel Cordevant gave secondhand testimony, saying that Jean Courtonne complained to them that Vauquelin had tried to seduce his wife. Magnier herself testified that her husband had only said that out of "derision" for the curé and that he had not tried to seduce her. |
| Marie Jeanne Lefevre | Former servant for Madame de Foucault; wife of Nicolas Lefevre, clerk of the parish | Antoinette Bellesoeur gave secondhand testimony, and Vauquelin was asked if he had tried to seduce her. He denied it. When Lefevre testified, she said nothing about being seduced. |
| Charlotte Varloteau | Former servant of Madame de Montigny; wife of the clerk of Saint Nicolas aux Bois | In the interrogation, Vauquelin was asked if he tried to seduce her; he denied it. Varloteau did not testify, and there was no secondhand testimony about any incident. |
| Marie Madelaine Flour | Wife of Nicolas Camus | Flour testified that Vauquelin tried to kiss her and she threatened him with a knife. He was not asked about this in the interrogation, and there was no secondhand testimony. |
| Suzanne Huille | | There were multiple rumours that Vauquelin assaulted her; Vauquelin went to great lengths to try to prove that Huille was making the story up. |

first husband (who had since died).[69] These contradictions and denials make it look as though the rumours may have been just that – rumours, rather than actual events. Another woman, servant Antoinette Charpentier, testified that Vauquelin had tried to assault her when she was making her mistress's bed. When the court asked Vauquelin about this, he claimed that it was the other way around. He told the court that he had walked into Madame de Foucault's house to check on things after noticing that all the doors were open. He heard a noise coming from the dame's bedroom; thinking she was sick in bed he opened the bedcurtains and found Charpentier in an "indecent posture," laughing at her trick.[70] Perhaps Charpentier, and other women, were simply trying to ruin the curé's reputation.

The story of the tenth woman, Suzanne Huille, is the most difficult to understand. Many people testified that they had heard rumours that Vauquelin had assaulted Huille at the presbytery and in other locations. Some of these witnesses claimed that they had heard the story from Huille herself, and Huille gave a long deposition as well.[71] According to her testimony, one day in May 1735 she went to the presbytery to find out if Vauquelin wanted to sell her some hay. He then grabbed her roughly by the arm and shoulders and forced her into his bedroom. He exposed himself to her and tried to rape her, but she resisted so much that "he could not achieve his unhappy ends to dishonour her." It is possible that Huille did not want to admit that she had actually been raped since the act of penetration, even by force, could damage a woman's honour.[72] But in any case, she claimed that after he spilled his semen on the ground he relaxed a bit and gave her the chance to get out of the house. She told everything to her friend Antoinette Bellesoeur, and the rumours began to spread. Soon, influential people of the town began coming to her and asking her to retract what she had said to stop the rumours.[73]

A meeting between Huille and Vauquelin was then arranged. According to Huille, the curé told her that she should just say that she was joking around with Bellesoeur but was overheard by some young men of the parish who spread the story through the whole town as if it were fact. Under increasing pressure from the curé and others, Huille retracted. The curé wrote up a document outlining her retraction, and he got at least sixty people to witness and sign it. But Vauquelin's attacks on Huille did not end there. About a week later, she was at the home of Pierre Pottier working with her friend Margueritte Pottier, his daughter, when Vauquelin suddenly appeared. When Pierre was working in another part of the house he approached Huille and told her that because of her he could now do anything he wanted to the women of the parish without fear – no one would believe anything anymore since she had retracted her accusation. Then he again groped her, in front of Margueritte, discharging his semen into his hand and smearing it onto her face. Huille testified that this was horrible to both her and Margueritte, and they both cried for a long time afterward.

Vauquelin had a very different story to tell. Besides the denials he gave to the court in the interrogation, he also wrote a long letter to the authorities.[74] He began by saying that the town of Crépy used to have a church where Huguenots were allowed to preach. The people of the town were all Catholics, but Protestants from all over the region would come to this church to hear their pastors, bringing trade and business to the town. When the site was destroyed and the preaching stopped, so did the business. According to Vauquelin, the lost income made many people bitter and gave them nothing to do but trouble their curés. Because he tried to bring reform to the parish, he said, they turned against him and were looking for ways to get rid of him. But because he did his duties as a pastor and did not drink or gamble, they had to make up lies about him.

Many of the problems stemmed from some of the young women in the parish, claimed Vauquelin. Women like Margueritte Pottier and Antoinette Bellesoeur held gatherings in the evenings called *veillées*, at which there were scandalous debaucheries. These social affairs were common all over France, and curés were almost always suspicious about them, especially if men and women attended together.[75] In this case, Vauquelin tried to stop the *veillées* in his parish, telling the young women who attended regularly that they were breaking the laws of the kingdom by disrupting public order, as well as the laws of God. He said he spoke to them individually and in public, from the pulpit, telling them to consider their reputations and to pay attention to their honour. He told the parish that the *veillées* would bring down the wrath of God on the whole town and that "the demon would take the four corners of the building like he had done with the oldest son of Job and that all who were complicit in this iniquity would be enveloped in the same ruin."[76] His warnings began to keep many people away from the *veillées*, so the young women came up with a plot to get revenge on their curé.

According to Vauquelin, these young women enlisted the help of Suzanne Huille.[77] He described her as a bad subject who was only hired by the most desperate farmers during the harvest, for a very small wage. Although she was related to three-quarters of the people in Crépy, few wanted to have much to do with her. To slander him, the young women of the parish persuaded her to claim that the curé had assaulted her. After a few months her conscience pricked her, and she came to the curé to ask for forgiveness. To make sure that the parish believed him, he got sixty people to witness her retraction and then assumed that the matter was closed, until it was all dragged up again during the court case.

Vauquelin certainly exaggerated his innocence in his letter. The bishop's order from 1729, plus the pages of witness testimony about his problems during services and with the finances of the parish, demonstrate that he had caused multiple problems in Crépy – but perhaps these problems were the result of his excessive zeal and lack of tact or political savvy rather than any moral failing. The fact that Vauquelin had not been reprimanded in 1729 for anything to do with sexual misconduct or interactions with women is telling. It is hard to believe that a man who "spilled his seed" as much as Vauquelin was supposed to have done would have begun only in 1735 with Suzanne Huille, eight years after he had been granted the benefice. Is it possible that Vauquelin did grope and assault all or even just a few of these women? Yes. But is it also possible that a few women, like Antoinette Bellesoeur, took it upon themselves to start rumours about Vauquelin's sexual exploits because they did not like the fact that he had criticized their behaviour? Yes. Given the fact that some of the rumours were clearly invented and that so many of them seemed to come from Bellesoeur, this seems more likely. The outcome of the case suggests that the church authorities were unsure about Vauquelin's character as well. The initial case, conducted in the *officialité* court of Laon, convicted Vauquelin and sentenced him to a year's retreat at the seminary. He was told he could never possess another benefice with care of souls. But he appealed the case to Reims and was given a modified sentence that allowed him to exchange his benefice for another outside of the diocese of Laon. As with Mercier, it seems that no matter whether Vauquelin was guilty or innocent, his reputation had been destroyed.

*Vernier's Women*

The information found in these cases dealing with curés' sexual affairs can perhaps help us to see Vernier's situation a bit more clearly. Some of the most disturbing testimony about his conduct involved his relationships with women, and to the modern mind this may be the most upsetting thing about the fact that Vernier was not removed from his parish despite the substantial allegations against him, including seducing servants, rape, and chasing his pregnant servant from the diocese. But upon further examination, and in the context of other noteworthy cases, Vernier's responses to these allegations seem more believable. Perhaps his parishioners exaggerated or fabricated the incidents they described in their depositions. Remember also that the court discarded much of the testimony that came from his servants, as well as his neighbours Denis Pierre and Marie Jeanne Bellot. While surely not everything these witnesses said were lies, we still have to take their testimony with a grain of salt.

Vernier was accused of engaging in sexual relationships with a so-called cousin. During his interrogation Vernier claimed that the reputation of this cousin was beyond reproach. He evidently had not known her well, but a relative of theirs, an abbess in Metz, had recommended that she come and live with him to help out with his household after his sister Reine's death. She stayed in Mareuil-sur-Ay, in the presbytery, for about two years, and she and his other, younger, sister had been much consolation to him after Reine's death, he claimed. He gave the court her surname (Vernier) and indicated that her late father was a *seigneur* in Lorraine. When asked if he had kissed her and touched her inappropriately, he told the court that he always behaved with modesty and decency and only gave her innocent kisses if he left for the countryside and then again upon his return. It is certainly possible that Vernier's servants had seen these kisses and, either intentionally or unintentionally, misinterpreted them. He also said that he had indeed given her a gold watch – not as a payment for her sexual favours, as one of his servants had insinuated, but as a gift for her willingness to join his household and help him recover his health after the death of his sister.[78] All of these responses seem believable, even if there is no corroborating testimony.

As for the accusations that he seduced his servants (besides Marie Madeleine Appert), Vernier simply denied that anything untoward had ever happened. When the court asked him if he had treated a servant with violence and then raped her, telling her that he knew better than her, he responded "that there is nothing in this whole interview that is more false."[79] Again and again, when asked about specific incidents, he said that they had never happened. He suggested at one point that he might have been seen in a situation with a servant that seemed intimate, but it was only because sometimes he had to have wounds on his legs treated and corns removed, and he needed the help of whoever was in his service to do this.[80]

The Appert affair necessitated a more in-depth investigation. Vernier answered more than twenty questions about his relationship with Appert.[81] According to his version of events, Appert herself was to blame for all of her troubles. He claimed that she drank too much and was disrespectful to him and to his sister and cousin. He had slapped her on at least one occasion because of her misbehaviour, but that was the only time he had laid a hand on her, in any fashion. If anyone had seen them together, it was simply because she was his servant and he regularly required the help of his servants in delicate matters. Vernier denied ever spending the night with Appert and said he had no idea why her mother thought she saw a cord stretching from his room to the servants' room. He explained Margueritte Jacquot's testimony by saying that the older servant often went to bed early, leaving Appert to tend to his needs and those of his sisters, so of course Appert did not go to bed until later. He also said he knew that sometimes Appert snuck out of the house during the day to go and visit a friend and that it was possible that she had done so at night as well, without him knowing. Vernier also tried to malign Appert's mother's character as well, claiming that the servant usually tried to avoid her mother because the older woman was always trying to take her wages. He maintained that her mother was just trying to extort money from him, and that was why she had been spreading false rumours.

Furthermore, Vernier continued to deny that Appert was ever pregnant. He insisted that the surgeon, Fortemps, had never said anything to him about a pregnancy, and he had not heard any of the rumours. When asked if he knew what they were saying about her in Athis, he simply said that he knew absolutely nothing about the thoughts and remarks that could have been made in Athis about Appert, implying that he was above any sort of village gossip. And, he added, she certainly had not been taken away by Le Clerc in the middle of the night. In fact, Le Clerc also testified in the *information* but said nothing about this. Vernier claimed that he fired Appert for drunkenness and theft on the Monday after Pentecost. She left on Tuesday, and at that time he had no idea where she went. When Gougelet came to ask about her daughter, he told her the truth – that he did not know anything. He explained to her that he had employed many servants in his two decades as a curé, and he rarely followed their activities after they left his service. Then one day she arrived with a letter explaining that Appert was working on a farm near Laon. Vernier said he did not know whether this letter was authentic or not. It was later brought to his attention that by September 1765, she had indeed ended up in Paris in a hospital, where she died. Vernier produced a certificate signed by one of the nuns working there, testifying to the fact that Appert had entered the hospital on 19 September 1765 and died on the 23rd but that she was not pregnant when she died.

If the plaintiffs had had the opportunity to sum up their complaint about the Appert affair, it might have gone something like this. Marie Madeleine Appert was a young, innocent servant who was exploited by her master and manipulated into thinking that she could engage in a sexual relationship with him without any consequences. When she became pregnant, she regretted her actions and, realizing that the curé was not going to help her, fell into despair. Vernier then contrived to get rid of her by having her carried off in the middle of the night. While deceiving the girl's family and the members of his parish, he hid her away until she and his unborn child died in a Paris hospital. The surgeon, locally known and respected, knew that she had been pregnant, and any certificates Vernier produced that argued the contrary were fabricated. His long history of moral lapses with other servants only made it more likely that what had happened to Appert was entirely his fault.

On the other hand, Vernier argued that Appert was simply a dishonest and foolish servant whom he had fired for failing to do her job properly and for treating him and other members of his household with disrespect. The girl's mother, a difficult subject to say the least, had fuelled public rumours and gossip about the situation that were untrue and the worst kind of slander. Appert met a bad end not because of him, but because of her own foolishness. If his servants and the surgeon gave evidence against him, it was because they believed the false rumours and slander and had been duped by his enemies into providing false testimony.

Either scenario is a believable one, making the historian's job that much more difficult. Fortunately, some of Vernier's other relationships with women can provide more information and perhaps a different perspective. In addition to corrupting his servants, Vernier was accused of inappropriate relationships with the schoolmistresses of the parish. However, any irregularities in his relationship with the schoolmistresses, compared with either the other charges against him or the abuses committed by other curés, seem rather tame and, once he was able to tell his side of the story, even a little bit humourous.

In the eighteenth century, the Soeurs de l'Enfant Jésus was a religious order that provided education for girls in rural parishes. The order sent out their members in pairs to villages in the countryside, and the communities would provide a house for them to live and teach in, as well as enough of an income to keep them fed and clothed and to keep their home heated. Mareuil-sur-Ay was one of only thirty-eight villages out of the nearly 700 that made up the diocese of Reims to have a school established for girls,[82] and the institution of the school seems to have been due to the efforts of Vernier's predecessor, Antoine Corbier. There were two sisters when Vernier arrived in 1747, but the troubles began around 1765, when two new schoolmistresses arrived. They were both young and pretty; the youngest one, Soeur Jean, was described as "an exquisite beauty, still in the flower of her youth."[83] Both of the women, however, developed a close relationship with Vernier.

Seventeen witnesses complained about an inappropriate relationship between Vernier and the schoolmistresses, noting that the women visited the presbytery too frequently and were often seen leaving his house at indecent hours. Several people said that the schoolmistresses were poor teachers as a result of their evening activities at the curé's home – they were so tired that they sometimes fell asleep during school, leaving the older girls to take over for them. Parishioners wondered what it was that the sisters were doing that made them so sleepy during the day. Furthermore, they noted that it was against the rules of the order of the Soeurs de l'Enfant Jésus to allow schoolmistresses to stay more than one year in any particular village. This rule was in place to prevent the teaching sisters from forming any attachments to a parish or its inhabitants. But the sisters who arrived in Mareuil-sur-Ay in 1765 had stayed for four full years, until August 1769. The parishioners insisted that it was because of Vernier's intrigues that Soeur Jean and her companion had not been transferred, while Vernier claimed it was the head of their order and the wife of the *seigneur* who had wanted them to stay.[84] But in any case, the four years they were there caused a great deal of consternation in the parish.

Initially, the sisters could hide their comings and goings between their house and the presbytery because the two houses were adjacent to each other and shared a garden wall. And, as several witnesses pointed out, there were ladders on both sides of the wall so that either the schoolmistresses or Vernier could come and go as they pleased. Three of Vernier's servants testified that they had seen these ladders and knew what they were used for. The vicaire also noted that he had seen the ladders but insisted that he never saw anyone use them and that he had no idea why they were there.[85]

Sometime in 1766, the activities of the school sisters became more noticeable to the parish, however, because in that year Vernier moved to a different house. The new presbytery was no longer adjacent to the schoolmistresses' home, and the village began to notice just how often the teaching sisters were visiting the curé. Servant Pierre Philippot testified that the schoolmistresses had a key to the new presbytery. Marie Nicolle Baudier, as a neighbour of the schoolmistresses, testified that she had a "perfect knowledge" that they visited the curé's house every day, and sometimes twice a day. Often, she added, they stayed until nine, ten, or even eleven in the evening. Nicolle De L'Epine testified that while she was a servant for the curé the schoolmistresses often stayed very late in the evening. Sometimes the curé told her to go to bed even though the teachers were still there, so she was unsure just how late it was when they finally went home. Their visits also occurred early in the morning; François Durand testified that one winter he saw one of the teaching sisters (the prettiest one) come out of the presbytery at six in the morning. She had a head covering on – the kind that women wore at night – and slippers on her feet.[86]

A whole host of people must have known about the schoolmistresses' visits to the presbytery, because they were caught rather publicly at least twice. In January 1768 the two women left the presbytery at eleven o'clock at night but when they got home they discovered that the lock on their door was not functioning, leaving them stuck out on the street. Many people were witnesses to their consternation when they found they were locked out of their house in the middle of the night. They had to return to the curé's, where they stayed until the next morning when a locksmith was called to break open the lock. A few months after this incident, some of the villagers felt sufficiently bothered by the relationship between the schoolmistresses and the curé that they decided to try to catch the schoolmistresses in the act. One night in May 1768, several villagers stationed themselves in the road near the presbytery to find out just what time the teachers went home that evening. Six people claimed they saw the teachers leaving at ten o'clock. Sadly, the spies seem to have caught them on an early night – the plaintiffs' complaint made a point of saying that this was about an hour earlier than their usual habit.

Just exactly what were the schoolmistresses doing at the curé's house for all of these evenings? Three other witnesses indicated that there was some sort of sexual component to their relationship – at least between the curé and Soeur Jean. Marie Jeanne Bellot testified that one day she was looking for the curé and was told that he was in his garden. When she went to look for him there, she was shocked to find that he was lying on a mattress with the young and pretty Soeur Jean. She told the court that she was embarrassed and did not want to see any more of what was happening, so she left immediately. Even worse, the pair was once discovered by one of her children: the twelve-year-old boy went looking for the curé and found him under a makeshift shelter in a corner of the garden with Soeur Jean, stretched out on a mattress. He testified that he saw them kissing "many times." The plaintiffs in the case noted that this young boy "would never forget this image, engraved upon his spirit."[87]

Claudette Gérard must have had a vivid memory too, of what she saw taking place between Soeur Jean, the curé, and the vicaire one summer's day. She testified that she and a friend (who had since died, and thus could not testify) were on their way to the mill and their path took them near the edge of the curé's property, on the banks of the river. The curé had set up some sort of bath there by attaching a sheet, almost like a hammock, to four posts in the shallow water. A person (or persons, as the case may be) could sit on the sheet and thus bathe comfortably in the river. Gérard saw Vernier sitting in the bath, covered only with a sheet. Then she noticed that the vicaire was there as well, standing near the bath and helping someone else out of it.

Gérard said that their view was obstructed and that they could only see the hands of the person the vicaire was helping, but when the individual spoke, saying, "Watch out, you're going to let me fall!" Gérard and her companion recognized the voice of none other than Soeur Jean.[88]

When the court asked Vernier if he had ever taken a bath in the river with the schoolmistress, he responded: "It cannot be imagined that a man of fifty would take a bath with a thirty-year-old schoolmistress, in the presence of a thirty-five-year-old priest, unless he had lost his head." [89] He further explained that at the old presbytery there had indeed been a type of bath, made out of sheets suspended from poles and placed over the river but that he had always bathed in it alone and had only exposed his legs. The bath was entirely private, he said, and could only be reached by a ladder; no one passing by the site would have been able to see or hear anything. Therefore, the accusation that he had once bathed there with the vicaire and Soeur Jean, as Claudette Gérard had testified, was entirely false and slanderous.

Vernier vehemently denied that there was anything suspect about his relationship with the schoolmistresses. He told the court that he would defy any truthful person to testify that he had made more than a dozen visits to the teachers' house in four years. Because he was their superior in the village, as well as their confessor, he was obliged to visit them a few times, but he had tried to avoid going there simply to prevent people from talking and slandering him. He was happy to admit that they visited the presbytery rather often, however, but he insisted that their visits were purely innocent and entirely justified. At times they needed his counsel – again, since he was their superior and confessor. If there were any problems involving the parents of their students (and there were lots of problems in such a difficult parish), it was only natural that they should come to him for help and advice, because he knew the parishioners best. Furthermore, since the rules of their order prevented them from visiting anywhere else in the parish, their only social activity had to take place in the presbytery, usually with his sister and cousin.

Vernier also complained that the village did not pay the schoolmistresses adequately, so they barely had enough to live on. Out of his concern for their welfare, he said, he helped them out as often as he could. That meant they ate many meals at the presbytery. He also pro-

vided the wood they used to heat their home and school, and he sold
them grain at half price. If they were seen at his home at odd hours,
it was because they used his oven to bake their bread or because they
had come over for milk or some other little necessity. They did not
have a key to the presbytery, but the latch on the door could be
opened from the outside so they could come and go as they pleased.
No one had ever used the ladders to access either of their yards
because the walls were too high and the ladders too short. As to the
accusation that he had been seen kissing and caressing Soeur Jean,
Vernier simply denied it and again insisted that his parishioners were
trying to slander him. Although this excuse could easily have been
false, the court had no evidence other than secondhand testimony
that Vernier was lying.

Since so much of the testimony came from witnesses the court
considered suspect, they seemed to have had no choice but to give
Vernier the benefit of the doubt. Claudette Gérard was the only person who testified about seeing Soeur Jean in the bath by the river
and her testimony was rejected. The only other witnesses who suggested that Vernier and Soeur Jean had a sexual relationship were
Marie Jeanne Bellot and her son. The court rejected Bellot's accusations outright, and they probably unofficially dismissed her son's testimony about this as well, because he was so young when he supposedly saw the curé and the schoolmistress kissing in the garden. It
should also be noted that it was Bellot's daughter Antoinette Elizabeth Pierre who testified that as a child she had overheard Vernier's
sister tell the curé that he ought to be able to live without a woman.
It is also significant that Étienne Dufrene, the locksmith who had
been called to let the schoolmistresses back into their house after
they had been forced to spend the night at the presbytery, said nothing about this event. He talked about the confusion on the day of the
Fête-Dieu procession, and the argument between Marie Jeanne Joffrin and Vernier over the altar decorations, but he did not mention
the schoolmistresses at all.[90]

The rural women of eighteenth-century France, of any social station
and background, had to be on their guard against sexual advances
from men, and in some cases that included their curé. Perhaps not
Vernier, but certainly others. Court records show that some curés –
and we will never know exactly how many – used the influence they
had as priests and as village notables to seduce women, both with their
consent and without it. Their actions could result in pregnancies, bro-

ken and strained relationships, and parish scandals. Parishioners lost confidence in a priest who had affairs with servants or seduced their wives and daughters, and in some instances they refused to receive the sacraments from him or attend his masses, creating division in the community. Claire Cage has recently demonstrated the existence of significant opposition to the principle of celibacy in the eighteenth century, and perhaps some rural villagers were part of that opposition.[91] But no matter whether they believed priests should be celibate or married, no one seemed to think that allowing priests to give free rein to their sexual desires was the solution.

In fact, expectations for curés went beyond just staying away from servants and the women of the parish. Eighteenth-century curés were expected to behave in ways that showed their dedication to their holy estate. They were men apart and were held to higher standards than lay people. One of the most important ways that they were to be men apart was to maintain a state of celibacy, certainly, but they also had to avoid any conversations, activities, or relationships that might give their parishioners the slightest cause for concern. Their language was to be free from sexual innuendo, their servants had to have a reputation for decency and be above a certain age, and their interactions with women had to be limited to avoid suspicion. If curés broke these unwritten rules too often, they might find themselves in the middle of an investigation and a court case, with their jobs and reputations on the line. The laity themselves saw it as their duty and their right to hold curés to these high standards: they were the ones who interacted with the curés the most and had the means to enforce them. Neither bishops nor court officials could police every curé in their diocese with any sort of regularity, but parishioners could.

Curés' sexual behaviour was thus another matter for negotiation in rural parishes. It was a bargaining chip held by both male and female parishioners – a way to influence curés to do what they wanted. Knowing what diocesan authorities would look for in complaints about curés, parishioners reported and exaggerated rumours about curés' affairs when it suited their purposes. What Vernier viewed as kindness toward the schoolmistresses and perhaps some degree of friendship, his parishioners portrayed as scandalous and even criminal. Curés who had underage servants or who were a little too familiar in their everyday interactions with women might be depicted as debauched and unfaithful to their holy estate. Any curé who found himself at odds with his parishioners over the sacraments, tithes, or even cemeteries and bell-ringing might discover that his intimate activities, innocent or otherwise, were on display for the parish and the diocese to see and judge. The relationship between priest and parishioner was thus central to the peace and unity of the parish as a whole. Scandals – even invented scandals – had to be addressed and corrected in order for the community to thrive.

# 6

# Disturbing the Peace

> If I use injurious terms, it is no different from how these brutal men treat their horses. No one can complain that I use violence against them, like other curés of the diocese.[1]
>
> Jean Baptiste Lanneau, curé of Louvercy and Mourmelon-le-Petit (Reims)

Early in 1721, Jean Baptiste Prevot of Seraucourt went to see his curé at the presbytery. When he arrived, he found that another local curé, Jacques Philbert François of Artemps (Noyon), was visiting. The three men chatted socially for a bit, and Prevot asked François how things were going with his parishioners, since he was in the middle of a lawsuit against the village. Although the subject of the lawsuit was not specified, it was evidently contentious because François told Prevot that his parishioners were rascals and that there were four or five of them he would like to see hanged. Prevot was shocked at this sentiment and told him that it was "extraordinary" for a pastor to seek to destroy his flock and that he should live in peace with his parishioners. François responded that he was not the one who wanted any trouble, but rather it was his parishioners who were trying to get rid of him. He added that he had no intention of giving up his parish and wanted to stay just to make them angry.[2] The curé of Seraucourt also had a low opinion of François; although we do not know if he said anything during this conversation, on another occasion he gave a *prône* in his parish in which he said that if people were saying about him just the hundredth part of the things they were saying about François, then he would leave his parish out of fear for his own salvation and that of his parishioners.[3]

Curé François was, then, known in his parish and in the surrounding region for disturbing the peace. He did not "live well" with his parishioners, for a variety of reasons. One of the ways that curés were supposed to be separate from the laity was that they had to be outside of and above the usual arguments and disputes that took place between villagers. In fact, they were to do everything in their power to resolve disputes, dispel tensions, and rebuild family and community relationships. As Prevot said, a pastor should live at peace with his flock. If a curé did not do this and instead created disputes and enmity through his conduct or his involvement in parish or village affairs, then parishioners felt the integrity of the community was at stake. If the curé could not be counted on to make peace in the parish, then who could? Curés and their behaviour were central to the identity of the parish itself.

In his study of eighteenth-century records of the *sénéchaussée* court in southwest France, Julius Ruff notes that 2.1 per cent of the people accused of physical violence in his sample, and 10.2 per cent of those accused of verbal violence, were clergymen. This means that clergy were overrepresented in these cases, since they made up less than 1 per cent of the population. However, he notes, almost half of these cases involved conflicts not with lay people, but with other clergy. Therefore, "these proceedings had little effect on the lives of ordinary laymen of the region."[4] It is thus crucial to examine *officialité* records, where the vast majority of the defendants were clergy, to understand more fully the role of clergy within rural parishes. The court systems, although they did overlap in some areas, primarily dealt with separate issues. To examine religious issues, *officialité* records are key. They demonstrate that clerical actions, including those that were violent or abusive, did in fact affect the people in rural villages.

There were several significant ways, outside of their religious duties, that curés could disturb the peace of the parish. The first, which we dealt with in the previous chapter, was by having affairs with women. This chapter will examine four others: conduct unbecoming a priest, alcohol, violence, and creating enmity in the parish. This last category is the most complicated and the most significant. Ironically, because the curé was so integral to the everyday life of parish, he could not keep himself separate from village disputes and affairs. There was so much overlap between the religious and the temporal (especially when it came to tithes and other church property) that curés could easily make mistakes and end up in the same position as François – in danger of losing their benefice. This is often where Nicolas Hyacinthe Vernier went wrong as well; although he appar-

ently did not suffer from problems related to alcohol, he was violent
at times and his public behaviour earned him a great deal of enmity
from his parishioners. His missteps in the social and economic
aspects of Mareuil-sur-Ay's village life created the context for the case
against him. Whether it was intentional or not, he disturbed the
peace of the village and his parishioners felt they had to take matters
into their own hands.

## Conduct Unbecoming a Priest

In the eighteenth century the official pronouncements and statutes
made by church authorities, as well as the records of the diocesan synods, show that bishops and other clergymen were concerned that
their curés were not separate enough from the laity. They wanted
parish priests to act like priests, not peasants. Because attitudes are difficult to police, they fell back on things that were easily observable –
the things that curés did and the way that they dressed. Hence the
existence of multiple decrees about how curés should wear their hair
and the types of clothes that were appropriate for ecclesiastics. Curés
were also supposed to avoid the pastimes that were popular in rural
villages, like gambling, dancing, and hunting.[5]

For example, in the orders published after a synod held in Reims in
1669, priests were told that they must be "a visible example and a perfect model for all others, because their vocation is to preach publicly
and to imprint piety." Therefore, they were never supposed to be seen
in public without the tonsure and the appropriate cassock.[6] This rule
was repeated in 1788; at this synod priests were told to keep their hair
short and that sleeveless cassocks were forbidden. At the same synod,
curés were warned against having dirty clothing, hiring servants who
were below the age of thirty, attending wedding celebrations (unless
the invitations came from "people of quality" who could not be
refused), eating meals with the laity, singing, participating in or
watching public games, hunting with firearms, or being involved
in business.[7]

As might be expected, some curés had difficulties with these things.
However, the lack of significant complaints from the laity about curés
who broke these rules probably indicates that even if bishops cared
about how curés wore their hair, parishioners did not. Failures in
these areas would certainly not be the only reason for a court case,
and parishioners only mentioned them if they were especially egre-

gious. For example, Nicolas Hourblin was accused of playing games
with his parishioners in public places, even on feast days and Sundays. He was seen playing with both men and women, and witnesses
said that if someone rang the bells for vespers while he was playing
he refused to quit, telling everyone that since he was the curé they
would not start the service without him and he could keep playing
for as long as he liked.[8] Surely there were many, many curés who took
part in similar activities in rural parishes; Hourblin was only singled
out because he played with women present and because it interfered
with parish services. If other curés played games but in a less public
venue, and still did services and sacraments on time, it was unlikely
that anyone would complain.

Hourblin was also accused of wearing secular clothes instead of the
soutane, but the more important issue was his involvement in secular
activities. People noted that they saw him driving a cart loaded with
dung, hay, or other things and that this sort of activity was inappropriate for a man of the clergy.[9] Jacques Philbert François was also criticized for his clothing choices – or rather, his lack of clothing. Witnesses told the court that he had been seen many times walking in the
streets of the village wearing a robe and a nightcap before services on
feast days and Sundays. The parish clerk also related a more embar-
rassing incident. The clerk testified that he saw the curé in the church
with his "shameful part" visible and protruding from his clothing.
The clerk told François that he should make himself decent, but
François just said, "Oh, is it out? It doesn't embarrass me. I would go
out in the streets like this!"[10] Clearly, the curé's clothing choices were
just one sign of a larger problem with his conduct. But if a curé was
a bit lazy about wearing clerical clothing, most parishioners probably
did not notice. As we have seen in previous chapters, parishioners
were more concerned when their curé did something inappropriate
while wearing the holy vestments than they were if he wore secular
clothing when going about his day-to-day affairs in the village.

The regulations about hunting were a bit different. While rules
about dress, dancing, and gaming were in place to separate the clergy
from the peasants, rules about hunting were meant to separate them
from the nobility. Hunting was primarily a noble pastime and viewed
as inappropriate for clergy. But overall, complaints about curés going
hunting were minor, and they were also tied to church services.
Although some witnesses gave offhand comments about seeing their
curé with a gun or out with dogs, the only serious offender seemed to

be Nicolas Quentin, accused of hunting "daily" with a gun, a dog, and friends. His activities were interfering with church services as well, since parishioners believed that Quentin rushed through the mass so that he could have more time to hunt. They also claimed that he did not teach catechism or do any preaching during Lent and Advent, preferring to be out in the countryside instead.[11]

By the eighteenth century, most curés knew better than to be caught in public in a state of undress. Most refrained from gambling or hunting as well, or at least they made sure that these sorts of activities did not get in the way of their pastoral duties. Either that or their parishioners did not mind when they participated in them and thus refrained from reporting them. Interestingly enough, Vernier was not accused of anything that would give the authorities cause to believe that he did not separate himself, physically and culturally, from his parishioners. A couple of witnesses thought it was odd that he had a dog that he dressed up like a jester (he told the court that it was his housekeeper who was responsible) but other than that he was not accused of any conduct unbecoming of a priest.

### The Drunk Priest of Savigny, and Other Problems with Alcohol

Not only did Vernier generally behave appropriately for his estate, he also seems to have avoided difficulties with alcohol. During his interrogation Vernier was asked if it was because he indulged in too much wine that he had mistreated his servants and said vespers later than the prescribed hour. Vernier responded, indignantly, that he "defies any soul that breathes to say truthfully that he has ever taken a glass of wine beyond the limits of temperance."[12] Only one witness testified that Vernier had any sort of problem with alcohol, so Vernier was probably telling the truth. Either he did not drink to excess or he managed to hide the effects when he did drink. Whatever problems Vernier caused for his parishioners, they were not the result of alcohol.

Nevertheless, it was regularly problematic for other clergymen. Alcohol was ubiquitous in early modern France. One historian estimates that at the end of the eighteenth century each French person, including men, women, and children, drank 105 litres of wine per year.[13] As long as the price was low enough, everyone preferred wine to water or just about any other drink.[14] Wine was seen as healthy, not only because of the fact that it was often difficult to find clean water

sources, but because within the Galenic medical system it was
believed that wine would restore balance to the humours.[15] Drinking
was also a way for men to demonstrate their manliness and virility.[16]
The consumption of too much alcohol was seen as problematic, however, in that it could easily lead to disorder. The French government,
at a variety of levels, tried to reduce the amount of difficulties stem-
ming from drinking and drunkenness by passing laws and ordinances
regulating cabarets and other drinking establishments. An edict of
1536 made drunkenness a crime, but this law was virtually impossible to enforce, and authorities concentrated on limiting the hours
that cabarets could sell alcohol. Serving was supposed to end early in
the evening, and alcohol could never be sold during the hours set
aside for the Sunday mass. Moralists joined their voices to those of
royal and municipal authorities, and a discourse that depicted alcohol
as the source of all kinds of moral problems was common by the eighteenth century, despite the fact that it was still consumed on a daily
basis by nearly the entire population.[17]

The clergy were not only among the moralists promulgating this
temperance discourse – they were also one of its targets. The image of
the drunk priest was common and priests who appeared drunk in
public were condemned and mocked. A. Lynn Martin suggests four
reasons that help to explain why moralists and others paid so much
attention to clerical drinking. First, priests had a sacramental function
in society, and drinking and drunkenness might interfere with their
proper performance of those sacraments. Second, priests were called
upon to preach against the sin of gluttony, and since drunkenness was
a prime example of that sin, it was viewed as hypocritical if they did
not practice what they preached. Third, the long-standing association
of alcohol with sexual activity meant that people might assume a
drunk priest was a priest who had failed to keep his vow of celibacy.
Finally, moralists advocated the view that represented the tavern as an
antichurch and the tavern keeper as an antipriest – curés could not
very well be seen in such ungodly circumstances.[18] As a result of the
need for priests and curés to be set apart from their fellow Christians,
then, they were held to higher standards when it came to drinking
and drunkenness, as with so many other aspects of their lives.

This high standard was problematic for curés – and not just
because of any difficulties with being temperate in their alcohol consumption. Alcohol played a vital social role in everyday life, and curés

must have found it hard to engage with their parishioners without alcohol or visits to the cabaret. Historians have convincingly demonstrated that not only was alcohol an important social lubricant, but the tavern was also one of the most important sites for social interactions.[19] These historians have argued that the image of the disorderly and debauched tavern was largely a creation of the elites in their efforts to separate themselves socially and economically from peasants and workers; while violence did certainly occur in taverns, overall the drinking culture had a positive effect on social relationships. Sharing a drink was common for people from all classes of society, and it more often led to friendship or business deals than drunken brawls. Alcohol was an important feature of community and religious celebrations as well. If this was the case, then where did that leave curés? Forbidden from participating in these social rituals, both by the dominant cultural discourse and by the rules of the church, they were not supposed to use alcohol to create, cement, repair, or celebrate social and community relationships. No wonder so many curés had problems with alcohol – it would have been very difficult for them to avoid it.

One of these unfortunate curés was Jean Drouin, of Savigny (Reims).[20] By all accounts he had been an alcoholic for his entire seven- or eight-year tenure as curé. The *information* for his 1740 case consists of one incident after another, describing the problems Drouin caused when he was drunk. One couple, Nicolas Hamé and Marie Danton, recounted an evening that the curé spent at their home, along with other guests. The party ate and drank until finally everyone except the curé left. According to Danton (who had given birth to a baby a few days before and was anxious for Drouin to leave), he kept asking for more wine. Hamé tried to tell him that he had had enough, but he insisted, and Hamé felt he could not deny him since he was the curé. Drouin stayed until around midnight and then said he did not want to leave and would just sleep there. Hamé told him there was no bed for him and that he should go back to the presbytery. The curé rose from his chair but immediately fell to the floor; Hamé helped him back up. He took a few steps and fell again. Hamé finally got him out of the house, but when the couple looked outside the curé had fallen onto a pile of manure and was making no move to get up. Hamé wanted to leave him there but his wife feared that some accident would happen if he spent the night on the manure; she persuaded him to wake their male servant and the two men dragged the curé back to the presbytery.[21]

Unfortunately, Drouin's problems with alcohol were well known throughout the region – even in Reims, more than twenty kilometres away. The court heard depositions from seven residents of Reims, and all of them testified about Drouin's behaviour in the cabarets after he had been drinking. One woman said that once she saw him staggering drunkenly in the street, with a crowd of children following him and chanting about the drunk priest of Savigny. But nothing else compared to the ordeal that the curé put Guillaume Gaillart through.[22] A merchant and resident of Savigny, Gaillart travelled with the curé to Reims about a year before the trial took place. The two men planned to lodge together at an inn, but they ate their evening meal separately at other establishments. When Gaillart returned to the inn around nine in the evening the proprietors refused to let him in, saying that since he was with "that drunk curé" they did not want to lodge him. Unbeknownst to Gaillart, Drouin had already returned from his supper, so drunk that the innkeepers had thrown him out. Gaillart insisted that he had no idea where the curé was, but still he was refused entry.

Since Gaillart was unable to convince the innkeepers that Drouin was not with him, he decided to go find another inn, but when he turned around to walk away he found the curé lying in the gutter, dead drunk, his wig and skullcap scattered around him. Gaillart picked Drouin up (out of charity, he explained) and with much difficulty got him on his feet. They went to another street to find another inn, but the proprietors there did not want to take Drouin either. Gaillart, desperate to find a place to sleep for the night, just kept telling them, shouting through the closed door, that the curé was not with him. This time he was lying, but he persisted and managed to get inside. When the door opened a crack, he took his chance and quickly shoved Drouin through. The innkeeper, now resigned to his fate, helped to get Drouin into a bed. They stripped him of his muddy and wet clothes, leaving them to dry on the kitchen oven. The curé stayed in bed for most of the next day.

In his interrogation Drouin gave feeble excuses for his actions. For example, he said that when Gaillart found him he had simply slipped and fallen into the gutter and was so stunned he could not get up. The innkeeper, seeing his muddy clothes, had only assumed he was drunk. He also tried to lay some of the blame on Gaillart by insisting that the reason the first inn turned them away was because the merchant had an unpaid debt there.[23] But by the end of the interrogation, Drouin seemed to have given up on his excuses. He admitted that his clerical colleagues, his friends, his parishioners, and his superiors had all counselled him to be more temperate in his drinking, but as of yet he had been unable to succeed. He promised to try again and expressed to the court his hope that God would help him.[24] Drouin was removed from his position; after spending a month in the seminary the diocesan officials decided to give him one more chance, but since he had caused so much scandal in Savigny they sent him to a new parish for a fresh start.[25]

Pierre Regnier, curé of Les Grandes-Loges (Reims), also suffered from alcoholism. He was well known in the village and in the surrounding area for getting drunk and becoming angry and violent, especially if anyone tried to refuse him more wine. The owner of the cabaret in nearby Sillery testified that Regnier had been drunk in his establishment three times, insulting people and swearing at them. One of these times he had arrived at the cabaret already drunk, with his clothes wet and muddy. He had even asked the *cabaretier* if he could borrow some clothes to change into. A merchant who was also at the cabaret found Regnier's behaviour repugnant and told him that a person like him was not worthy to say the mass. This angered Regnier, who exclaimed *sacre dieu* several times and threatened to find three or four men in Les Grandes-Loges who would break the merchant's arms and legs. The *cabaretier* managed to get Regnier out the door and avoid any violence; he told the court that he begged the curé not to come back.[26]

The *cabaretier* of Les Grandes-Loges, Nicolas Vallet, knew better than anyone what happened when Regnier got drunk. He testified that he had seen the curé drunk many times. One day Regnier had been drinking excessively and came to Vallet's establishment to drink more, even though it was against diocesan rules for curés to drink at the cabarets in their own villages.[27] Vallet saw the curé approaching his cabaret and decided to hide so that he could avoid giving him anything else to drink. He told his servant not to serve the curé or talk to him, but of course there was little chance that she could just ignore him. Regnier asked her where her master was, and when she refused to tell him he got angry and called her a whore. Then he left, but Val-

let was angry with the way Regnier had treated his servant so he met
him in the street to tell him off. Regnier cursed at him and threatened
to kick him in the groin.[28]

Like Drouin, Regnier eventually admitted to the court that he had
a problem. He was asked if he knew that his drunkenness, swearing,
and threats had scandalized his parish and those around it, and if he
was regarded by the people as a drunk. In response, he said that in
truth he had noticed that the parishioners approached the sacraments
less often than they did in the first years he was the curé, although he
did not know if he was the cause. When asked why he ignored the
advice of his superiors to stop drinking, he said that he had attempted to follow their counsel but had not succeeded, because of "human
frailty."[29] Regnier was removed from his functions and did a retreat at
the seminary for six months; the records do not indicate if he was
eventually allowed to return to his parish or not.

Alcoholic curés like Drouin and Regnier would obviously be chal-
lenging for many reasons, but if too much wine kept the curé from
performing the mass or the sacraments properly it was especially
problematic. Since everyone in early modern France drank wine,
parishioners certainly did not expect their curés to avoid alcohol altogether. Alcohol in and of itself was not seen as inherently evil or sin-
ful, but if curés' actions when they drank affected the peace of the
parish then it became a problem.[30] The laity wanted priests with
enough self-control to know when to stop and to avoid being in a
state that would preclude them from fulfilling their functions. For
example, parishioners noted that one day Jacques Philbert François
was on his way to the church to baptize a child when he fell in the
cemetery; witnesses then realized that he was so drunk he could barely stand when he performed the baptism.[31] But that was nothing
compared with what happened in 1713, on the first Sunday of Lent.

That morning, the parishioners and churchwardens got the church
ready for the mass and rang the bells announcing it, just as they
always did. But then they realized that the curé had not yet returned
home from the nearby parish of Saint-Quentin. Since parishioners
were required to attend the mass on Sundays, everyone was wondering what they were going to do when someone outside the church
called out that something was happening on the road – in the distance, it appeared as if someone had fallen into the river. Parishioner
Claude Dubois ran to help and discovered it was the curé who was
flailing about in the river, along with his horse. Dubois got the curé

and the horse out of the water and helped him get back to the presbytery. Others helped him change out of his wet clothes, but when
they saw how drunk he was they urged him to find someone else to
say the mass to avoid a scandal. François insisted on doing it himself,
though, and with his parishioners' help he dressed in the appropriate
vestments and started the service. He dropped the paten twice during
the service and had to lean on the altar to stay upright. At one point
he just stopped in the middle of what he was doing; parishioners
reported that he appeared to have no idea what he was supposed to
do next. After being prompted by the churchwarden he was able to
finish the service but dropped the paten again when he returned to
the sacristy.

When the court questioned him, François insisted that he had not
been drunk on this occasion. He said his horse had balked when
crossing a bridge and thrown him into the river. (He did not explain
why his horse was also found in the river.) He also told the court
that he regularly suffered from certain indispositions and dizzy
spells, which made him stumble or have trouble remembering
words. He said he dropped the paten because his hands were cold
and that these were mistakes that anyone could have made in similar circumstances.[32] Another curé, Jean Baptiste Le Marie, made similar excuses when the court asked him about his drunkenness; he
blamed his problems with alcohol on "attacks of apoplexy and
lethargy" that made it look like he was drunk.[33] Parishioners accused
him of coming to vespers drunk and sleeping through the whole service (presumably it was performed by a vicaire or schoolmaster).
Several also testified that during the mass they feared his drunken
state would lead him to drop the holy sacrament, thus polluting the
body of Christ.[34]

The parishioners of Volon (Besançon) reported that their curé,
Antoine Michel, performed services and rituals when drunk. Once
when doing a mass he stopped the service and said out loud to the
schoolmaster, who was assisting, that he did not know where he was.
Although he was able to continue, everyone saw that he was drunk;
at one point he leaned on the altar for seven or eight minutes, burp-
ing as if he might vomit.[35] Another time he needed the schoolmaster's help when he came to administer the viaticum to Pierre Amyot
and appeared to be drunk; the schoolmaster had to help him stay on
his feet and prompt him when he forgot what to do. This scandal happened in the presence of about thirty people, who had come to be

with Amyot on his deathbed.[36] One witness testified that he and others had seen the curé drunk or sleeping in the confessional, and his administration of the sacrament of penance was so irregular that they sometimes wondered if they had actually received it.[37]

Stories like these could be multiplied *ad nauseam*. Fifteen of the curés in my sample were accused of some sort of problem with alcohol, if not outright alcoholism. Because curés were supposed to present a certain image to their parishioners and to the people of the surrounding villages, it was seen as part of their duty to practise greater self-control than the laity when it came to wine. They also needed to be ready to perform the sacraments at any time and thus had to keep their faculties intact. When they did not, they were viewed as disrupting the peace of the parish. This happened when curés became violent with their parishioners as well.

### Angry Curés: Violence in the Parish

Violence, just like alcohol, was a regular part of early modern life and played an important regulatory role at all levels of society.[38] Masters beat their servants, parents hit their children, and arguments at the cabaret or even the cemetery could easily lead to blows. Curés, like most adults in early modern society, would have seen acts of violence as acceptable ways to police behaviour.[39] Although a certain amount of violence from their curés would have been accepted, if it was excessive then parishioners would complain. The definition of excessive could vary widely depending on the circumstances, but increasingly, as curés were being held to higher standards of conduct, those who used any sort of physical violence or even expressed a great deal of anger might be criticized.[40] Again, the curé was supposed to help smooth over the kinds of situations that produced violence in the rural parish – he was not supposed to create those situations himself.

Instead of protecting the weak and the innocent, as a good curé was supposed to do, Vernier seemed to prey upon the most vulnerable members of the village: beggars, children, and the elderly. Three people gave testimony about an incident that had occurred on a Sunday sometime around 1761 or 1762. Vernier was in the street outside of the presbytery preparing a *repoisoir* (an altar used during processions) about an hour before mass when a beggar came to the house to ask for alms. Vernier did not see him until the man had already knocked on the door and been turned away empty-handed; the beggar returned to the street complaining that the woman who answered the door (either a servant or Vernier's sister) had refused to give him anything. Vernier heard the man's complaints and then proceeded to beat him with a stick. Jeanne Duval witnessed the beating and said the curé acted with barbarism and fury and kept hitting him until the stick broke; then he began kicking him instead. Duval went to the beggar's aid and implored Vernier to stop beating him. The curé did eventually stop, but he then dragged him over to the cabaret to be locked up until the officers of justice could be summoned.[41] The cabaret was evidently not the most secure of prisons and the beggar escaped after a couple of hours. Another beggar did not fare as well: Vernier himself reported that he tied up another vagabond in his courtyard and had him picked up by officers of the maréchaussée in Épernay.[42]

Vernier treated his own parishioners poorly as well. François Durand testified that he had seen the curé hit a woman in the head three times as he chased her from the church. The woman in question was a widow who had died by the time of the case and could not provide her own testimony; Durand told the court that Vernier had called her names and shouted that he had no time to deal with her. Pierre Blondeau testified of the abuse he had received at the hands of the curé when he was an altar boy at the age of nine, reporting that one day he was in the sacristy and the curé smacked him with his breviary so hard that his nose bled for five hours afterwards. He said he never knew why the curé hit him. Children must have expected to be hit when they misbehaved, but this level of violence was certainly excessive. In another incident, Marie Nicolle Jacquot testified that when her brother was about twelve or thirteen, he was outside the presbytery making fun of a girl who had brought a letter to the curé. Vernier chased the boy down and hit him so violently that he ended up in bed for two or three months.[43]

Other witnesses testified further of the abuse Vernier inflicted on children during catechism class. Margueritte Jacquot claimed that she went into the church during the time usually set aside for catechism and found Vernier in the sanctuary beating a young boy with kicks and punches. Marie Nicolle Baudier told the court that during catechism class she saw the curé beating a teenage boy so violently that several other children fled from the church in tears. Marie Jeanne Jacquot (Visse) testified that one year on the feast of Saint Nicolas, her children joined the other children in the village to ask the curé if he would say a mass for them, as this was the tradition in the parish. They brought money to pay him, but he refused to say the mass; the children made do with going to Mutigny to hear the mass instead. The next Sunday they went to catechism and the curé made them kneel under the crucifix, saying that they had disobeyed him by going to Mutigny. He was going to have the schoolmaster whip them in the sacristy but Jacquot came into the church at that time and stopped him. She told Vernier that the children did not deserve to be punished, since they had only gone to Mutigny because he was derelict in his duties. The curé became very angry and shouted at them all to get out of the church. But the affair was not over; the next day the curé came to the village school and pulled one of Jacquot's sons out of class to give him a beating. She testified that he was in bed for four days, and they had to have him bled because he was having fits.[44]

Another incident involved three young girls who were members of the confraternity of Saint Hilaire, charged with doing a collection one year. The girls testified that on the day before the feast of Saint Hilaire, they went to the church to ring the noon bell. According to the established tradition in the village, the girls would ring the bell and then give the curé the alms they had collected in the name of the saint. But Vernier was annoyed by the bell-ringing and sent a boy up into the belfry to tell them to stop and come back down into the church. They did, and the curé left his confessional to reprimand them for ringing the bells. One of the girls, angry at the scolding, told him that was fine, but since they were not allowed to ring the bells then they would not give him the alms they had collected. This made Vernier angry, so he grabbed her by the arm to throw her out of the church; he then hit her hard enough to dislodge her head covering. Exposing a woman's hair was a serious enough offence, but then he kicked her and she fell over a row of benches, making her skirts fly up and "expose her nudity" to everyone in the church.[45]

Vernier was also caught several times mistreating his servants and other workers. Once, one of his workers was using a cart to bring a load of hay to the presbytery. The man rode on top of the hay instead of walking beside the cart, so Vernier hit him several times with a stick and then fired him. Jean Lamarle reported that he could see into Vernier's courtyard when he was standing on the stairs in his house, and from that vantage point he saw the curé kick one of his servants in the stomach so violently that she began bleeding from the nose. Nicolle De L'Epine testified that she worked for the curé for fourteen months but left because he hit her. Margueritte Jacquot told the court that in 1763 she was a servant for Vernier, and that year he told her she was required to work on the feast of Saint Hilaire. She refused, saying that in fifty years no one in the parish had worked on Saint Hilaire's day, so the curé fired her. When she went to the presbytery to retrieve her trunk and her things, Vernier called her names and refused to let her in to get them. She stood her ground, asking for her trunk and the shoes that were in the stable. In response, Vernier took the shoes and threw them over the garden wall into the neighbour's courtyard. Then he called Jacquot a harlot and told her to get out. Jacquot again refused to leave, telling Vernier that he was the one who had a harlot in his home (probably referring to the cousin who was living in the presbytery at that time) and that she would not leave until she got her trunk. Jacquot's daughter Marie Anne Robert was with her, and she joined in the fray as well. Vernier began complaining about the dissipation and drunkenness of the parishioners in the village and said that the next year he might not even say the mass at all on Saint Hilaire's day. Marie Anne told him that was fine; someone else would say the mass. Incensed, Vernier slapped her and then choked her so forcefully that she told the court she thought she might die right then and there.[46]

Vernier's responses to questions about these incidents during his interrogation are quite revealing. In a few cases he denied that the act of violence had taken place. For example, he claimed that he had never hit Pierre Blondeau or made his nose bleed.[47] But other times he admitted what he had done – not because he was sorry but because he felt he was justified in using violence against misbehaving children, servants, or beggars. When the court asked him about the two vagabonds whom he had beaten when they had shown up at his door, he explained that in both cases the beggars themselves were at fault. One of them was drunk and said nasty things to his sister, so he felt justified in subduing the man and turning him over to the authorities. The other was someone who had been causing problems in the village and who had even threatened to set fire to several buildings. So, since he had masons and carpenters working at his house that day he got them to tie the rascal up until the authorities could retrieve him.[48]

Vernier also felt justified in his treatment of his servants. He admitted that he called his servant Nicolle De L'Epine names and hit her but said it was because she had said insolent things to him. He also admitted that he had spoken harshly to Robert, and that when she and her daughter had made accusatory statements to him his patience had run out; he had then slapped the daughter and taken her by the neck to push her out of the presbytery. He also insisted that the feast day in question was the feast of the translation of Saint Hilaire, rather than the feast of Saint Hilaire itself, and it had been declared a working day by the diocesan authorities, so he was within his rights to ask her to work. The servant who had been transporting hay in a cart had not been beaten because he sat on top of the hay but because he had been driving so close to the river that he could have fallen in and lost the hay altogether.[49]

As for the girls he supposedly mistreated in the church when they rang the bells, Vernier again insisted that he had been correct to punish them. He explained that he was in the confessional with a woman who was advanced in age and a little deaf. He had no problem with the fact that the girls rang the bells – only that they did it for so long and with so much more noise than usual that he could not hear what his penitent was saying to him. Their overenthusiastic bell ringing was keeping him from fulfilling the functions of his ministry, he said, so he felt obliged to ask them to stop. He admitted that he had hit one of the girls but said that it was only with the palm of his hand on the side of her head, which made her head covering come off. He denied ever throwing her over a bench and said she was never indecently exposed. Vernier gave a similar response when asked about his violent treatment of the young people who attended his catechism classes, telling the court that the poor morals of some of the young people, or their lack of attention to his instructions, had put him in the position of giving them some penance, "as is done in all parishes."[50]

Other curés gave similar excuses for incidents in which they were accused of using violence: they believed what they had done was justified because of their position and because of their need to keep order in the parish. For example, witnesses said that curé Aubriot de Boncourt found a man named Jean Baptiste Fay in the cemetery during vespers. Although Fay claimed to be unwell the curé hit him, threw him down on the ground, and kicked him in the head and stomach. Aubriot de Boncourt denied this violent behaviour but explained that he often had problems with parishioners going out to the cemetery instead of attending services. He felt it was his duty to try to get Fay to go back into the church, but when Fay had responded insolently to his entreaties the curé had taken him by the arm and led him back inside.[51] The curé felt justified in using some sort of violence to enforce the rules of the diocese, and he felt confident that the court would agree with him.

Matthieu Faivre gave a similar justification for an incident that took place in his church during catechism class. Faivre approached one of the children and hit him in the face with a book, making his nose bleed; the child ran out of the church with his hat over his face. The boy's father testified that he found his son in the cemetery after vespers, with his face and clothes bloody. Faivre claimed that the boy had been playing around during catechism and he had indeed hit him, but not hard enough to draw blood.[52] Faivre was also seen hitting and kicking a valet because he had rung the last bell for vespers without the curé's permission; in another instance he hit a miller of the village because he was grinding grain on a feast day.[53] Jean François Person, of Buzancy (Reims), was also accused of hitting his parishioners in the church. In one instance it was one of the altar boys who was serving at mass; the blow made his nose bleed. In another instance he hit both the schoolmaster and his son with his breviary, again shedding blood. When the court asked him if he hit people in the church "because they did not want to submit to his will," he responded negatively and said that he only "corrected" those who made noise or were irreverent.[54]

During his interrogation, the court asked Jean Baptiste Lanneau if he "speaks to his parishioners with gentleness." Lanneau responded, "If I use injurious terms, it is no different from how these brutal men treat their horses. No one can complain that I use violence against them, like other curés of the diocese." The court then asked him to name any such curés; he responded that he had nothing to say about that.[55] Clearly, parishioners would not have been shocked when their curés used physical force to reprimand unruly children, servants, or even adults. Only when that force crossed the line and became excessive were they likely to complain. The curés cited above may have crossed that line, or parishioners may have been exaggerating to draw attention to their curé's other flaws. In a few cases, however, some curés regularly committed violent acts against their parishioners, seriously disrupting the peace of the parish.

One of these curés was Gabriel Joseph Blondeau. In general, Blondeau was known as a violent person. Depositions are full of sto-

ries of how he hit people, drawing blood many times. Anne Vail-
laudet testified that he had hit and kicked her father so badly that he
was unwell for more than three weeks.[56] Hilaire Jannin told the court
that at an evening meal Blondeau had thrown a glass of wine in his
face and then punched him – for no reason at all, said Jannin.[57] The
fact that he had been seen at the window of the presbytery shooting
at animals, including birds in the cemetery and some pigs roaming
the streets, was also worrisome to the people of Courcuire. But most
upsetting was his violent treatment of his mother and sister, who
lived with him at the presbytery. Once he hit his sister after a disagreement over a glass of wine; his mother was obliged to run for
help. When she came back to the presbytery with other parishioners,
he flew into a rage, telling his mother that he would rather see the
devil than see her. In front of many witnesses, he took their clothes
and personal items and threw them out in the street, deliberately
damaging some of the items in the process. He refused to let his
mother and sister back into the house; they were temporarily taken
in by other members of the parish.[58]

Pierre Mercier of Vigneux was also known for having a temper and
for getting so carried away in his anger that he easily became violent.
Pierre Nettelet, a *laboureur* of Vigneux, told the court that he and the
curé had had a disagreement, and Nettelet had accused him of taking
something that belonged to him. Mercier had become angry and said
he was going to go home and get his gun so that they could go into
the woods and settle it with a duel. Nothing ever happened, but Nettelet also testified that on another occasion he had seen the curé arguing with someone else in the parish. Nettelet had tried to help them
settle their dispute but had only succeeded in turning Mercier against
him again. The only thing that had stopped Mercier from hitting
him, said Nettelet, was the fact that he was so much bigger than the
curé. Jacques Durbecq also said that he and the curé had gotten into
an argument about a financial issue; the curé had accused him of
being in league with his servant to steal from him. They had both
become angry and Mercier had grabbed a gun, but before anything
happened other individuals who were present had stopped him and
taken the gun away. Other parishioners testified that their disagreements with the curé also became quite heated, and that he often
threatened further violence with either a gun or a saber.[59] When
asked if he had hatred and enmity for his parishioners, Mercier said
no. When asked if his parishioners hated him, he said that he could

not say what was in their hearts but that there could be some among them who had hatred for him.[60]

There was certainly mutual hatred and enmity between Antoine Michel and his parishioners – or at least his violent actions would suggest it. Humbert Montarlot testifed that the curé had wounded him in the head about six or seven years previously; he had taken Michel to court and had been awarded a sum of money. However, Michel had refused to pay it and Montarlot gave up trying to get the money because he was afraid of what the curé would do in retaliation. Didier Gauly also won a lawsuit against the curé, and after the sentence the curé threatened to "break his head" many times and once came after him with a stick. Nicolas Thibouret told the court that Michel had fought with and then hit both his father and his mother; his mother had been quite unwell as a result. Nicolas Gurgey testified that his father worked as a *vigneron* for the curé for three years; at the end of that time the curé still owed him twelve *livres* in wages but refused to pay it. The *vigneron's* wife asked for the money but got only blows in return.[61]

Michel's many instances of violence – and there were more than just these examples – gave him a very poor reputation with his parishioners. While a curé who hit children at catechism or physically disciplined an unruly servant could easily be forgiven, those who used violence excessively or inappropriately could be accused of disrupting the peace of the parish. If a curé's violent actions prevented him from performing his religious functions effectively, or if they earned him a bad reputation, he could easily lose the respect of his parishioners. Curés had to be men apart – separate, and using greater self-control, than other men. They also had to avoid creating enmity in their parishes, for the same reasons.

### "He is So Opposed to the Spirit of Charity": Curés Creating Enmity

Curés were always public figures, with a great amount of social influence. When they used that influence in ways that the community saw as positive, they were praised and revered. When they used it in ways that created enmity in the parish, they were heavily criticized. Curés were probably called upon to settle disputes between their parishioners on a regular basis. One example of this comes not from a court case but from the journal of a schoolmaster in the village of Silly-en-

Multien, today located in the department of the Oise. Pierre Louis
Nicolas Delahaye was hired by the village in 1771, and he wrote an
account of his time as schoolmaster that spanned over twenty years,
until 1792.[62] During that time Delahaye worked with two curés – one
good, and one not so good.

The difficult curé was Claude Henry Marie Fauvelet, and Delahaye
first hinted that this curé did not get along well with the residents of
Silly-en-Multien when he explained the circumstances surrounding a
pay raise he secured in 1779. In March of that year, the Charity of
Silly-en-Multien (an institution separate from the *fabrique* and organized along the lines of a confraternity, but with considerable funds
to spend for the good of the parish) agreed to give the schoolmaster
an additional thirty *livres* a year if he taught the poor children of the
parish without charging their parents any fees. Delahaye had already
been doing this anyway, but the administrators of the Charity presumably felt he should be compensated for it. The curé opposed this
salary increase, but the Charity gave it to Delahaye anyway. The
schoolmaster did not explain why the curé was opposed to his raise,
but he suggests that it had something to do with Fauvelet's housekeeper, an influential and charismatic woman known as La Reine –
the Queen. Delahaye and his wife had chosen La Reine as the godmother for their son five years earlier, but their relationship had
apparently soured since then.[63]

Although there are no hints that the relationship between the
curé and La Reine was sexual, the parish did seem to be bothered by
how much influence she had over the curé, and other incidents
indicate that Fauvelet and his parishioners were not getting along.
Delahaye recorded that in May 1779 Fauvelet refused to give communion to a parishioner, despite the fact that he had done his Easter confession with the vicaire. During the services for Pentecost that
year Fauvelet shouted at village notable and future mayor of Silly-
en-Multien, Charles Carriat, from the pulpit, treating him like "a
naughty child or a common rascal." That month he also refused to
hold the traditional Fête-Dieu procession. In June when Delahaye
was ringing the bells for the curé's feast day, Fauvelet came and
stopped him, explaining that "he did not want any festivities while
he was at war." Then, in January 1781, the curé made out his will: La
Reine, and a man referred to only as Sieur Georges, were the primary beneficiaries of about 1,600 *livres*.[64] When the curé was on his
deathbed just a few days later La Reine and Sieur Georges were seen

by Delahaye (who described himself as piously praying with the vicaire at the curé's bedside) rifling through his cupboards, taking clothing and other items. They left as soon as Fauvelet took his last breath. The authorities were brought in by Fauvelet's family, who had to sort out the will and try to get anything back from La Reine that they could.

Delahaye was always appropriately deferential toward Fauvelet in his account; after all, he wanted to make sure that his readers would view him as a man of good reputation with a grasp on his social position in the village.[65] But by reading between the lines it becomes clear that the schoolmaster had little respect for Fauvelet. This is especially obvious in the way that he wrote about Fauvelet's successor, Jean Marie Bourget. Delahaye never had a negative word to say about the new curé. The schoolmaster regularly noted in his account that he spent time socially with Bourget, and he also recorded the services they performed together in the parish. He explained, happily, that parish services were finally getting back to normal; for example, in March 1781, just days after the new curé's arrival, he wrote that they had celebrated vespers in the parish, for the first time in a long time. Delahaye does not indicate that the two had any serious disagreements in the ten years they worked together as colleagues, and he wrote often of the respect that he had for Bourget. He cared very much about what the curé thought of him as well; Delahaye was extremely upset when someone in the parish (described as a monster vomited from hell) slandered him in front of the curé, and he only calmed down once other witnesses to the event assured him that both they and the curé were on his side.[66]

One of the incidents that Delahaye wrote about at length involved a dispute with another parishioner, and the way that the curé solved that dispute. One year, Delahaye, who as schoolmaster chose the altar boys for the year, did not select the son of one of Silly-en-Multien's *laboureurs* for the responsibility and thus earned the man's wrath. The *laboureur*, Jean François Hervaux, decided to get revenge on Delahaye by trying to deprive him of income he made from selling pigeon droppings (which he collected from the bell tower in the church as part of his job as schoolmaster). The two men argued at length over the matter and eventually went to the curé to sort things out. With Bourget's help, they were able to come to an agreement about Hervaux's son, and the matter of the pigeon droppings was forgotten.[67] Both men respected the curé and so accepted him in his role as arbiter

over the issue, and the matter was settled peacefully, without violence
or a lawsuit.[68]

Curés were thus expected to smooth over disputes in their villages,
not create them. Causing enmity among the parishioners was one of
the quickest ways to draw the ire of the village. For example, a
*laboureur* who testified in the case against Jean Baptiste Lanneau said
that the curé was "so opposed to the spirit of charity that when there
were two brothers who were quarrelling, instead of trying to bring
them back to union and concord which should reign in families, he
engaged one of the brothers to bring a complaint against the other in
the courts, because the curé hated that brother for signing the document against him about the election of churchwardens."[69] This caused
a great scandal in the village and in neighbouring villages as well.
Lanneau, by not accepting the churchwardens chosen by the people,
had already disrupted the peace of the parish, and then when he
urged the two brothers to start a lawsuit against each other, he created additional enmity. This was a far cry from making sure that peace
and order reigned in the parish, as a good curé was supposed to do.

Creating enmity in the village could happen in a variety of ways, all
revolving around parish life, traditions, and, especially, all kinds of
property. Three curés – Coyer, Hourblin, and Sellier – all created
problems when they pastured their animals in the church cemetery.
Despite the fact that curés were charged by their superiors to maintain the sanctity of the cemetery in the same way as they did the
church, some curés were guilty of causing pollution themselves. Witnesses reported that Pierre Sellier let his two cows, an ass, and sometimes even his flock of sheep into the cemetery to graze. One man testified that Sellier had hired him to plow part of the cemetery and
plant alfalfa there, specifically for the animals. Another parishioner
was scandalized when one day during services the ass nearly wan-
dered into the church – it allegedly stuck its head inside the door but
then thankfully turned around and went back into the cemetery.[70]
Hourblin was also accused of pasturing his animals in the cemetery
and of feeding his birds there. Parishioners grumbled that as a result
the cemetery was always covered with animal and bird droppings, creating a mess for people who wanted to kneel beside the graves. When
people complained to the curé he just told them that the cemetery
was his garden to do with as he pleased.[71]

Another curé did more than just pasture his animals in the cemetery. Claude Nicolas Boulanger dug up a section of the cemetery to enlarge the courtyard of the adjacent presbytery. He did this without the permission of the parishioners or any of his superiors, and he even moved the remains of the dead. The villagers complained to the authorities, who issued a decree ordering him to re-establish the cemetery as it was, but after two years he still had not complied. At that point Boulanger made things worse by give a speech during his *prône* in which he criticized a parishioner named Ougier for not allowing the curé his rights and for causing strife in the community. Boulanger told everyone that this man had threatened him that he would be reported to the secular authorities if he cut down a tree, as he claimed he had a right to do, and sold the wood for the use of the *fabrique*. He went so far as to say that Ougier should be chased from the parish. Witnesses were scandalized by the speech, not only because they did not believe that Boulanger was going to give the profits of the tree to the *fabrique*, but also because his actions were an "abuse of his ministry" that had caused a "public injury." It was this event that was the catalyst for the *officialité* case against Boulanger.[72]

Boulanger also upset the peace of the parish by causing difficulties with the schoolmasters, another common complaint from villagers. Reportedly there had been seven or eight schoolmasters in the village during the eleven years that Boulanger was curé. He mistreated them so much that either they quit or he fired them. In one case, he refused to say a mass because he did not want to work with one particular schoolmaster, even after the schoolmaster in question threw himself to his knees in the sacristy and begged him not to cause a scandal in the church.[73] Guillaume Bruno Loris also refused to work with a schoolmaster that his parishioners had chosen; when the churchwardens insisted, he called them names during his *prône* and said that they were "devils from hell."[74] On the other end of the spectrum, François Jacqueney was criticized for insisting on keeping a schoolmaster who lived a dissipated life and was subject to wine. Parishioners reported that Jacqueney had not wanted to rectify the situation despite being asked to do so by the inhabitants and a decree from the bishop during a pastoral visit.[75]

Pierre Mercier managed to create enmity between himself and his parishioners by profiting from pigeon droppings. In Silly-en-Multien, schoolmaster Delahaye had the responsibility for cleaning up the pigeon droppings in the church's bell tower, and then he had the right to sell those droppings to the farmers (who used them for fertilizer) and keep the profits.[76] But in Vigneux, Mercier was keeping those profits for himself. In fact, despite the orders he had received from his superiors to repair the holes in the church tower that were allowing the pigeons entrance, Mercier let the number of pigeons multiply so much that there were more of them in the church than there were in the dovecotes of the *seigneurs*.[77] He was also criticized for making the young people of the parish collect the droppings for him, during church services no less.[78]

In many of these examples, curés were criticized when they refused to follow the orders of their superiors. Sometimes these orders were the result of parishioners' complaints, and so it would make sense that villagers would be upset when their curé failed to follow them. In one particularly egregious case, Pierre Sellier was ordered to do a retreat at the diocesan seminary for three months, after a visiting bishop found multiple problems with his behaviour. When bishops gave an order like this, it was expected that the curé would pay another priest, out of his own pocket, to say the mass and provide services and sacraments for the parish while he was gone. The bishop waited for Sellier to make the necessary arrangements and then go to the seminary; when the curé still had not complied after two months he declared Sellier *interdit*. This meant he was not allowed to say masses, conduct services, or perform any sacraments. Despite this order from the bishop, Sellier continued to say masses and even tried to prevent the priest whom the bishop had sent in as a substitute from performing any masses in the church. For these errors, Sellier was taken into custody and put into the diocesan prison.[79]

In another case, the curé's failure to follow authorities' instructions was less serious but still troubling for those authorities and for the parishioners. One Sunday in the parish church of Ruffey (Besançon), a local *abbé* was given time to read a *monitoire* as part of the service at the mass. *Monitoires* were requests for information made by a court – in this case, a local criminal court wanted information about something that had happened involving two individuals of the parish. The *monitoire* required anyone with relevant information about the events to come forward and offer their deposition. The curé, Mottet, allowed the *abbé* to read the *monitoire* but then went to the pulpit after the *abbé* had finished and began to talk about it. After insulting the *abbé*, saying that he seemed to be in "a worse humour than usual," he declared that certain people in the parish, including relatives of the two people in question and servants, were not obliged to depose.[80] This was in direct opposition to the usual practice, and it caused a great deal of consternation among the parishioners. The customary penalty for failing to depose after a *monitoire* was excommunication, and people were not sure which authority they should obey.[81] Mottet's actions thus seriously disrupted the peace of the parish, creating enmity between him and his parishioners.

Other incidents demonstrate that curés might create enmity not with the entire parish, but with just one or two parishioners. Even this was problematic, however; curés needed to get along with everyone. François Maury was known in his parish for meddling in people's affairs and causing divisions within families. Parishioners reported that his conduct had "alienated the spirit of a great number of these parishioners, and this keeps him from doing anything good in the parish."[82] Gabriel Joseph Blondeau was accused of making up inappropriate songs about some of the young girls in his parish and distributing copies of those songs to people in other villages.[83] He also accused the two servants (one male and one female) of Pierre Menestrier, one of the village notables of Courcuire, of stealing two of his chickens. He confronted them at Menestrier's house, and the female servant responded to his accusations by saying that she and her master were not the type to steal chickens, and anyway they already had enough. So Blondeau kicked her in the thigh, which prompted the male servant to try to restrain him and tell him that this conduct was unacceptable for a curé. The argument, witnessed by multiple villagers, ended with the male servant and the curé chasing each other in and out of Menestrier's house, until several villagers stepped in and broke up the fight.[84] The whole affair was the result of already existing enmity between the curé and Menestrier, and the incident surely did nothing to help dissipate that enmity. Disagreements like these, when they involved the curé, affected the entire parish.

In another incident, curé Jean François Coyer made his long-standing enmity with Lambert Payon public by assaulting his character and treating him poorly in church. First, he spread a rumour that Payon, who had been out of town for a long period of time, had gone bankrupt and left the village. Everyone was then quite astonished when he returned and gave no indication of any financial trouble.

Other witnesses testified that Payon and the curé were once visiting
the home of another parishioner when the curé insulted him, calling
him names and threatening to hit him with a stick.[85] But perhaps the
greatest insult came in the church, during the mass. As usual, the curé
walked through the church before the mass, sprinkling the congregation with holy water using a special brush-like tool. When he got to
where Payon was sitting, he sprayed the holy water so vigorously that
witnesses reported Payon had to wipe his face with his handkerchief
and that his clothes were all wet. When the curé returned to the sacristy, he told the clerical assistants that he had "watered Payon well."
Coyer claimed that he was using a new brush and he had not realized
how much water it would hold, but this seems a feeble excuse.[86] Once
again, the enmity between the curé and just one parishioner caused
problems for the whole parish.

Perhaps the most difficult curé (besides Vernier, of course) was
Nicolas Vauquelin. We have already seen that Vauquelin was accused
of multiple assaults against women in his parish. But if the truth of
those accusations is in doubt, his other activities surely demonstrate
that he was the cause of much of the enmity in his parish. This enmity may even have been the reason why some individuals were willing
to either lie or exaggerate to the court about his interactions with
women. Vauquelin and the notables of the town, along with the
churchwardens, were in a state of constant disagreement over money
and the distribution of the funds of the *fabrique*. Parishioners reported that the curé had made himself "master of the goods of the *fabrique*" and spent funds without even asking for the advice or consent
of the parish.[87] He also confiscated all of the titles and papers of the
*fabrique*, taking them out of their usual lockbox in the church and
moving them to the presbytery where only he had access to them.
Witnesses complained further that he distributed the money meant
for the poor according to his own whims, and without asking for anyone to assist him in the distribution. One witness implied that he
might have given some of this money to people who were not poor
at all – he just wanted to bribe them to take his side in one of his
many court cases.[88]

Vauquelin also created problems because of his attitude toward the
poor in the parish. This attitude was usually on display when he was
required to perform burial services for poor people. Witnesses reported that these services were short and hurried, performed without any

ornament. Some said that he did the service so quickly they barely had time to get the body in the ground. For the poor he wore only a surplice, while for people who were well-off he wore a cape, used silver ornaments, and engaged the help of additional clerical assistants. When asked about this, Vauquelin admitted that he did different services on the basis of the financial and social status of the deceased person. He said that it was not fair that people who "ate all their goods" and never gave anything to the church should have the same privileges as those who had saved some money for pious foundations and for decorating the church.[89] He did not hesitate to treat the rich better than the poor and scandalized everyone in the process.

All of these incidents in which curés created enmity in the parish were certainly problematic, and they gained the attention of the authorities. But spraying someone with holy water or pasturing animals in the cemetery were not the most serious of offences. Instead, the real root of the most significant difficulties between priest and parishioner was, unsurprisingly, money. Lawsuits between curés and their parishioners – over tithes, fees, the *fabrique*, and many other financial issues – were absolutely routine. In fact, they were so common that for the most part they did not cause scandal. In many ways, curés were also businessmen out of necessity. Many of them had income from various pieces of property that had come to them as part of their benefice, and this required them to be involved in financial and agricultural matters that could easily lead to disagreements.[90] So just the existence of a conflict over finances or even a lawsuit did not automatically equate to scandal in the parish. Only the most litigious curés, or the most egregious behaviour involving financial disputes, created enmity with their parishioners.

For example, in addition to fathering a child with his servant, Claude Louis Barban was accused of continually engaging in lawsuits with his parishioners for over fifteen years; one witness noted that there had been three lawsuits since the beginning of 1747, when the *officialité* case against Barban began. Barban was also accused of telling his parishioners that he wanted to "ruin them all."[91] Parishioners in Les Mazures, Sécheval, and Anchamps (Reims) also complained that their curé, Jean François Coyer, would jump at any chance to start a lawsuit. When asked about this, Coyer said that he had only started lawsuits to acquire the money that was owed to him as part of his benefice, to get back money he had loaned, or because people had refused to pay him the appropriate fees for services. His parishioners told the court that he had indeed started many lawsuits over these things – and lost most of them.[92]

But no one seemed more self-interested when it came to money than Vernier. The curé of Mareuil-sur-Ay seemed willing to try to take advantage of his parishioners in any way possible, including by confiscating any money brought into the church from confraternities and collections. These donations were typically used by the *fabrique*, or by the confraternities themselves, for feast day celebrations, alms, ornaments for the church, or altar decorations. But Vernier did everything he could to appropriate that money for his own purposes. He tried to bully Nicolas Michaut into giving him money from the collection for Sainte Radegonde, but as warden of the confraternity Michaut refused. He tried similar tactics with the daughter of Antoine Liebbe, who had collected the small sum of just twenty-four *sous* for the confraternity; when she refused to give the money up he said to her, "*Voila*, the girl who is using her 24 *sous* to make a rope for her neck, and she would take a *louis* to finish it off." Another time, Vernier managed to insult Marie Jeanne Jacquot (Visse), her daughters, and the warden of the confraternity of the Virgin. Jacquot's daughters had been charged with doing a collection, and they brought it to the warden. But they asked if they could keep six *livres* of the money for about a week to help out their parents with some expenses. The warden agreed. Although confraternities usually were not in the business of loaning money to young girls, it probably was not entirely unprecedented, since in the early modern period borrowing money for the short term was a routine practice among all classes of society; in some instances the curé himself was the source of these loans.[93] Vernier was unhappy, however, with the arrangement the girls had made with the warden; at the next catechism class he insulted the girls in the church and told everyone that their mother had stolen from the Virgin to dress herself.[94]

Vernier used more significant threats with Christine Berthe Durand. As the prefect of the confraternity of Sainte Radegonde, she was in charge of the collections. On the morning of her wedding in January 1764, Vernier sent for her and told her that she could no longer be the prefect of the confraternity and that she had to give him the money that she had collected or he would not perform her mar-

riage ceremony that day. Believing that Vernier would make good on
this threat, she handed over the twelve *livres* that she had collected.
She finished her testimony by saying that she did not know what the
curé did with the money, but she was sure that it was not used to decorate the altar of Sainte Radegonde, because Vernier abolished the
confraternity soon thereafter.[95]

Vernier's dishonest methods were also regularly on display when it
came to the collection of tithes.[96] Everyone in rural France had to pay
tithes on various commodities that included grain, wine, lambs, and
even vegetables. Tithes were essentially a tax, and most people tried to
get out of paying as many taxes as they could; this meant there were
tremendous opportunities for conflict over tithes. And, of course, the
amount of tithe collected depended on the overall health of the harvest; in lean years everyone became a bit more desperate for their
share. Conflicts were also common in areas of France where the curé
was the tithe owner and thus had the right to collect certain tithes as
part of his benefice. A curé who was kind and charitable during services or in the confessional might behave more like an angry busi-
nessman when it came to tithe collection. It was difficult for curés to
stay out of village affairs when their livelihood depended on tithes.
Vernier, as might be expected, was not about to let his parishioners get
away with paying anything less than exactly what they owed.

Sometimes, this meant simple bullying. *Vigneron* Jean Varnier testified that he had been assigned to help collect tithes with Vernier one
year and said he found that Vernier was "very rigid" and rude toward
the parishioners during the collection. Helain Coinon testified that
one year when he was assisting Vernier with tithe collection the curé
made a widow pay him eleven pints of wine instead of the three he
was owed. That same year Vernier forced Coinon himself to pay fifty
*sous* in cash instead of the five pints of wine that he owed for the tithe,
even though that year wine was only worth three *sous* per pint. Other
times, Vernier bent the rules on tithe collection to get what he wanted. Jean Lamarle testified that one year he was serving as one of the
two assistants to the curé for tithe collection, and when they went to
a field belonging to Jean Salmon they found that it had not yet been
harvested. According to the rules on tithe collection, this meant that
they were supposed to wait before they collected anything, but
Vernier told Lamarle that he should harvest their portion anyway.

Lamarle refused, but the other assistant followed the curé's orders. This resulted in a lawsuit against Vernier, which he eventually lost, said Lamarle.[97]

In another incident, it was the farmer who was in the wrong, and so Vernier used this as an excuse to collect an exorbitant fine. During the harvest in 1760, workers employed by François Méa harvested the portion of the field designated for tithes and then failed to wait for the curé to collect the grain before harvesting the rest of the field. They were supposed to wait for twenty-four hours, but since they left the correct amount in the field, they thought it would not matter. Vernier disagreed, and he asked Méa for the sum of thirty *livres* in cash in place of the grain. Méa knew that the tithe for this small field was not worth anywhere near that amount and protested until the curé finally agreed to take nine *livres* plus the grain that had been set aside for him. That same year, Vernier ended up in a dispute with Jean Blondeau, a farmer for the abbess of Avenay. Blondeau was charged with collecting tithes on her land, which included a field belonging to Vernier's benefice. When Blondeau and his assistants were preparing to collect the tithe, Vernier suddenly appeared and grabbed the sheaves from their hands, scattering the grain in the fields. He believed he did not owe a tithe on that field and thus physically prevented Blondeau from collecting it. Blondeau went to the abbess and told her what Vernier had done, but she said she would rather not get involved. Rather than start a lawsuit, Blondeau decided to leave the matter alone and just let the curé keep the grain. From that time on, he paid the tithe out of his own profits, even though it cost him eight *livres* each year.[98]

Vernier was also known for failing to pay his debts or chronically underpaying servants and others who worked for him. The surgeon Nicolas Fortemps of Avenay testified that Vernier owed him forty *écus* for medical visits and medicine. Leonard Noel, a mason, told the court that he had worked for the curé for a significant period of time and although they had agreed on a price of sixty *livres* for his services ahead of time, Vernier refused to pay. Noel took the case to the court in Épernay and the curé was initially sentenced to pay but then appealed the decision; Noel said that because he was the father of nine living children and "without fortune" he was not in a position to pursue the case further and just took the loss.[99] Many workers complained that Vernier had refused to pay them their full wages; when the court asked him if he had forced "many unhappy day labourers" to start lawsuits against him for their wages, he simply responded "no." When the court pressed further and asked if he was in the middle of lawsuits over financial matters with nine different individuals, Vernier responded that his "conscience does not trouble him about his financial dealings with anyone." He also noted that he respected their right to pursue justice as they saw fit.[100]

As we have seen, one of Vernier's frequent responses during his interrogation was that he was being slandered by his "enemies." Although it sounds like an easy excuse to fabricate, it may have been true, in some cases. Vernier did have enemies, and when you look at the record of his financial dealings with his parishioners it is easy to see why. Because of his violent conduct and his meddling in financial affairs, he had earned the enmity of his parishioners and disturbed the peace of the parish. That enmity may have led his parishioners to form a plot against him, using his problematic actions, and perhaps inventing others, as the basis for a long and heated court case. Vernier did not see much of anything wrong with how he had behaved, going so far as to say that his conscience was untroubled when it came to his financial dealings. He was simply defending his rights as a curé and as a tithe owner, and as a private citizen as well. If he had not been a curé, his actions would probably have been less shocking. He might still have had "enemies," but his conduct would have been more easily justifiable. Rural people of all economic and social standings were more than willing to fight, physically or in the courts, for their rights – Vernier was no different.

Unfortunately for Vernier, curés were supposed to be different. Curés had to be separate from their parishioners. They were held to higher standards than the laity and were asked to deal with their parishioners charitably even if it did not make sense financially. At the same time, what exactly that separation looked like for parishioners was not always what church authorities intended. Bishops wanted curés who did not act like peasants. Their ideal curé was one who dressed appropriately, refrained from gambling, hunting, or dancing, and stayed out of the cabarets. Parishioners cared about these things too, but only if participating in these activities hindered their curé from performing services or sacraments. They did not mind so much if their curé had some of the same vices that they did. They did mind, however, if their curé did not keep the peace in the parish, either by failing to smooth over parishioners' disputes or by creating those disputes in the first place. In this way, parishioners' expectations for their curés were just as high as, if not higher than, the bishops? The role they expected their curés to play, as demonstrated by the times they took their curés to court, shows how central the curé was to the eighteenth-century parish.

# Conclusion

In a 1993 article, Andrew Barnes wrote the following about eighteenth-century curés: "Seminary-trained priests had a significant amount of time on their hands but not much they could do with it. In the second half of the eighteenth century, the lower secular clergy became a political force in France. One cannot help wondering whether these priests would have become so politically active if they had had more to do."[1] Barnes' views are not uncommon among scholars; religion in the eighteenth century is often characterized as stale, stagnant, uninspiring, and irrelevant. The once-vibrant reform culture of the sixteenth and seventeenth centuries had fizzled out, while the real revolt against the church that came with the Revolution had not yet begun. So, the eighteenth century ends up being viewed as a religious void, a time when the structure and framework of the church was still intact, but nothing really happened and priests had nothing to do.

Although it is beyond the scope of this book to speculate about why curés became more politically active in the latter half of the eighteenth century, I believe we can safely put away the assumption that it was because they did not have enough to do. The lives of most curés were anything but empty. Most performed services daily, and they were constantly called upon to administer the sacraments at the church and in the homes of their parishioners. They visited the sick, heard confessions, distributed alms, supervised schoolmasters and churchwardens, led processions, and often ran their own households and properties. Secular and personal activities overlapped with religious functions; curés socialized with colleagues and with parishioners, hosted meals and visitors, and travelled to nearby parishes to substitute for other priests or to take care of personal and family business. Parishioners and vagabonds knocked on their doors asking for charity, to borrow money, or for the opportunity for work. Some came just to ask the curé to settle their disputes, so that they would not have to take their problems to the courts. What Antoine Follain calls *petite politique* – the nomination of parish officials, the collection of taxes, lists of men fit for military service, community building projects, labour services – all might demand the curé's attention and expertise.[2] Curés were involved in multiple, varied, and essential activities in the village world, and they were, in fact, central to that world.

The centrality of the curé was guaranteed not merely because church authorities wanted it that way; curés were not simply "agents of the Catholic Reformation."[3] Religious community was built around the curé because the laity wanted it that way as well. Parishioners wanted curés who resided faithfully in their parishes so that they could be called upon to administer the sacraments at any time of the day or night. Sacraments and services, performed by the curé, thus symbolized the unity of the parish. A parish without sacraments, whether because of the fault of the curé or not, was a parish in scandal, public disgrace, and spiritual peril. Parishioners also wanted curés with high standards: men who were charitable, celibate, peaceful, accommodating, and able to exercise restraint and self-control.

It is thus clear that Catholic Reformation sensibilities had indeed penetrated even rural areas. Lay Catholics attended the mass and participated in the sacraments regularly, sometimes even more often than they were required to do. They knew what was expected of them, and even more importantly, they knew what was expected of their curés. One incident that took place in the parish of Savigny (Reims) demonstrates this well. We know from the previous chapter that the curé of the parish, Jean Drouin, was a hopeless drunk. After hearing his parishioner's description of him lying in the gutter with his wig on the ground next to him, we really do not need any more evidence about that. But there is one more incident involving Drouin that tells us as much about lay religious sensibilities as it does about the curé's alcoholism. One day Marie Jeanne Mittelette, wife of Savigny's miller, saw Drouin on the road near her house. He appeared to be drunk, and she watched as he collapsed at the edge of a pond. Luckily, she noted, he fell to the left instead of to the right, or he would have fallen into the pond and drowned. Mittelette and her male servant went to help him up and brought him to her house. Even though he was her curé, she began to reproach him for the state he was in. She "couldn't stop herself" from telling him that she would rather he did not stay for any length of time at her house, because any people who came to the mill might see him and think that she had been the one who got him drunk. She said his drinking was not appropriate for his character, warning him that it would lead his parishioners to distrust him. The parishioners are scandalized by your bad example, she said.

Drouin rebuked Mittelette for speaking to him in this way and insisted that he was not drunk; he claimed that even at that very moment he was in a state to do his functions. She responded that she was not in need of his ministry right then but that when she was disposed to give her confession she would not do it with him. Mittelette begged him to leave her house and then went out to the mill, saying that her children were frightened to see their curé in such a state and that she hoped when she returned he would be gone. Luckily for Mittelette, he did leave. Unfortunately for the wife of Guillaume Gaillart, he stopped at her house next, where she put him to bed after he vomited in her kitchen.[4]

Drouin's conduct was wretched, but what is interesting about this testimony is the fact that Mittelette knew he was not acting like a curé should and did not hesitate to tell him so. She was not in any sort of position of authority in the parish (she was a woman, after all), and yet when she felt her conscience prick her she spoke up and condemned her curé – the man who was her confessor, the man who performed the miracle of the mass, the man who baptized her babies and buried her relatives. In front of her children she shamed him for his drunkenness and told him to get out of her house. Although a reforming bishop of the seventeenth century might have been horrified to find a curé like Drouin in his diocese, he ought to have been rather pleased with Mittelette's response. Evidently orthodox Catholic ideas about clerical and lay behaviour had been successfully introduced into rural parishes by the eighteenth century.

Nevertheless, there was still reforming work to be done, and that work rested squarely on the shoulders of curés – at least those curés who were better behaved than Drouin. The needs and desires of the parishioners, combined with the pronouncements and requirements of the bishops and other diocesan authorities, created an interesting mix of pressures for curés. Far from being intellectually and socially removed from their parishioners, they were sandwiched in between the elite men they took orders from and the people they interacted with daily – people who sometimes gave their own orders. This had an interesting effect on the reform process. Reform was not over in the eighteenth century, by any means. Although most lay Catholics did participate in the sacraments and attend the mass, the church was still trying to change some of their activities. And, as these court cases make abundantly clear, the church was still trying to reform clerical behaviour too.

But there were limits to that work, precisely because of the position that curés found themselves in. Often they were caught between a rock and a hard place, juggling the expectations of multiple groups. Curés preached the importance of confession, hoping they could use the confessional to reform morals, but then found that they were so overwhelmed with long lines and interpersonal struggles that they could not use the confessional as effectively as they might have wished. Parishioners had their own ideas about baptisms, processions, holiday services, catechism class, and even the cemetery, and accommodating those ideas might mean contradicting the regulations of the church. Any curé who equated reform with complete control over his parishioners' lives might find himself in trouble. This is probably one of the ways in which Nicolas Hyacinthe Vernier went wrong – when he tried to control the confessional, for example. Faivre also faced difficulties when he tried to get his parishioners to take communion in the parish church instead of the annex church, and that battle for control created a multitude of difficulties. If curés or bishops went too far, they often lost ground. There were limits to reform, which were due to both the requirements set by the church and the parishioners' interpretation of those requirements.

What of Vernier, in the end? Was he guilty or not? The verdict that restored Vernier to his functions in Mareuil-sur-Ay came in 1772. In early 1774 he was still the curé, and when he filled out a questionnaire for the bishop he reported that all but a dozen or so of his parishioners were not especially difficult to manage. Then on 20 May 1775, Vernier was named a cathedral canon in Metz, a benefice he was still holding when the Revolution broke out a decade and a half later.[5] Although there are no records to prove it, it seems likely that the diocesan officials in Reims recognized that Vernier could no longer do any good in Mareuil-sur-Ay. Because he had won his case, they could not deprive him of his parish, but there must have been some backroom deal that got him a position as a canon. Although I have not examined this question in any depth, it seems the leaders of the Catholic Church were already resorting to relocating difficult priests rather than removing them from service altogether, albeit for different reasons than they did in the modern period.[6] Additional sources would be needed to determine if this truly was a pattern in the eighteenth century, or if that pattern had an influence on the policing of clerical misdeeds in the modern period, but it seems clear from the testimony in Vernier's case that diocesan leaders in Reims would have had good reasons for moving Vernier out of his parish and into a position without care of souls. There his talents, if indeed he had any, could be put to better use. It can be hoped that he had more luck getting along with his colleagues there than he did with his parishioners and that the people of Mareuil-sur-Ay found their new curé more to their liking. Maybe their court case against him had not been a complete waste of time after all.

In her book *A House in Gross Disorder* Cynthia Herrup examines the case of an English earl accused of rape and sodomy. Herrup's story ends in much the same way as mine does: we are left not knowing if either man, earl or curé, was truly guilty of any crime. There are no documents that will definitively prove that Vernier impregnated an unfortunate servant and raped another. We cannot know if the witnesses in the case against him were lying. After trying to understand his case for the past several years, I suspect that Vernier was a difficult and sometimes exacting priest who made enemies of his parishioners by behaving rather uncharitably and with extreme rigidity on certain issues, whether that meant in the confessional, in the church, or in financial matters. He did not respect some of the compromises that had been made between the laity and the clergy over the long period of Catholic reform, so when he named names from the pulpit, demanded greater attention to catechism, and tried to battle the cabaret his parishioners rebelled against him. His attempts to control the behaviour of his parishioners went too far, and he made things worse for himself by not realizing just how careful he had to be when it came to his servants and the schoolmistresses. He did not act with charity in financial matters and made enemies as a result. I suspect that many of the accusations against him regarding sexual misconduct were false, although I find I am less certain about that than I am about other things.

In any case, as Herrup argues, the verdict in the case is not what really matters.[7] Vernier's case and others like it are instructive for the information they provide about cultural and religious sensibilities.

These cases are a window into the rural world – a world that is often
ignored or allowed to remain obscured. Millions of French men and
women lived in villages like Mareuil-sur-Ay in the eighteenth century, where their social interactions and family relationships were inextricably tied to the parish community. What they truly believed about
the doctrines of Catholicism cannot be uncovered; certainly, some of
the laity were more practitioners of Catholicism than believers. But
regardless of their belief, religion was still the framework that they
organized their lives around, and at the centre of the frame was the
curé. Despite the scandals caused by irresponsible or criminal curés,
they were still the symbolic heart of the parish. Proactive parishioners
did everything they could to ensure that they had curés who suited
their needs: men who behaved like curés but who were also flexible,
charitable, and compassionate. The ways that they interacted with
those curés created and sustained the village community in the eighteenth century just as much as they had in the twelfth or the fifteenth
or the seventeenth centuries. The nature of the interactions, arguments, and compromises that took place between clergy and laity
might have changed over the centuries, but they were no less vital to
rural society.

# Notes

## INTRODUCTION

1 Archives départementales de la Marne (hereafter AD Marne), 2 G 1947,
   *information*, 20 April–13 May 1770, 29; AD Marne, 2 G 1947, *interrogatoire*, 16–23 April 1771, 8.

2 For an example of this type of narrative within the field of religious history, see the series published by Ashgate, *Catholic Christendom,
   1300–1700*. The series editor, Thomas F. Mayer (until 2016, when the
   series was acquired by Brill), notes in an introduction to each volume
   that by 1700 the place of religion in everyday life had transformed completely. He also indicates that the clergy had lost much of its local
   authority by then. Muir, *Ritual in Early Modern Europe*, examines the
   many uses and meanings of ritual in early modern Europe but then also
   insists that religious rituals had lost their meaning by the eighteenth
   century.

3 For two influential examples of the secularization model, see Vovelle,
   *Piété baroque et déchristianisation*, and Gauchet, *Le Désenchantement du
   monde*. Clark, "Secularization and Modernization," surveys a great deal of
   recent research that calls the secularization model into question.

4 McManners, *Church and Society*, 1:188–98.

5 Davis examines this in detail in her *Fiction in the Archives*. See also Gowing, *Domestic Dangers*, 41–8.

6 Hardwick, "Between State and Street," 126; Walshaw, *A Show of Hands*,
   60–1. For more on rural courts, see Crubaugh, *Balancing the Scales of Justice*; Hayhoe, *Enlightened Feudalism*; Mauclair, *La justice au village*;
   Schneider, *The King's Bench*.

7  Hardwick, *Family Business*, 14; Ruff, *Crime, Justice and Public Order*,
   unpaginated introduction.

8  As Hardwick argues in her examination of witnesses in suits for marital
   separation, "Local courts provided commonplace and effective intersti-
   tial political forums." See her "Between State and Street," 105. For more
   on historians' use of court records, see Muir and Ruggiero, eds., *History
   from Crime*. Two helpful works dealing with English court records are
   Gowing, *Domestic Dangers*, and Herrup, *A House in Gross Disorder*.

9  Some authors, like Bouchard, *Le village immobile*, have emphasized the
   lack of dynamism in French village societies, but this argument has
   been heavily criticized and most authors instead emphasize a great deal
   of change in the rural world during the early modern period, including
   the eighteenth century. See Follain, *Le village sous l'Ancien Régime*; Le
   Goff, *Vannes and its Region*; Vardi, *The Land and the Loom*.

10 Historians have used the *cahiers de doléances* to examine rural populations' exposure to the innovations of the eighteenth century. See
   Grateau, *Les Cahiers de doléances*, and Markoff, *The Abolition of
   Feudalism*, who both emphasize the willingness of rural peoples to
   adopt new ideas and use them for their own purposes.

11 Châtellier, *The Religion of the Poor*, 185, argues that far from being on
   the road to secularism, the eighteenth century was a "decisive period" in
   rural religion, when missions had gained fresh impetus. Goujard, *Un
   catholicisme bien tempéré*, argues that there was a certain amount of lai-
   cization, rather than secularization, in the eighteenth century, while religious life and structures remained integral to village life.

12 See especially Babeau, *Le village sous l'ancien régime*; Dewald, *Pont-St-
   Pierre*; Follain, *Le village sous l'Ancien Régime*; Goubert, *The French
   Peasantry*; Higonnet, *Pont-de-Montvert*; Gutton, *La sociabilité villageoise*;
   Jessenne, *Pouvoir au village*; Le Goff, *Vannes and its Region*; Maillard,
   *Paysans de Touraine*; Root, *Peasants and King in Burgundy*; Vardi, *The Land
   and the Loom*.

13 Bergin, *Church, Society and Religious Change*, 28, 223–5. Dixon, in his
   introduction to *The Reformation and Rural Society*, also notes that rural
   parishes in the Reformation period have not received enough attention
   in the literature and stresses the difficulty of lack of sources. He believes
   a better picture of religion in rural parishes can be produced through
   creative use of the sources that do exist.

14 Le Bras, *L'église et le village*, 33. See also Christian, *Local Religion in
   Sixteenth-Century Spain*. For the medieval period, see Arnold, *Belief and
   Unbelief in Medieval Europe*, chapter 4.

15 Bossy, "The Social History of Confession." His "The Mass as a Social Institution" also contains elements of this argument. See also Hepworth and Turner, *Confession*. For critiques of this position, see Briggs, *Communities of Belief*, 277–338, and Lualdi, "A Body of Beliefs and Believers."

16 Barnes, "Social Transformation," 141.

17 See also Lajaumont, *"Un pas de deux,"* who makes a similar argument about the Limousin region. Barnes, "Social Transformation," 145–6, also emphasizes the importance of the priest as the arbiter of religious ritual even though he downplays the role of the priest in other arenas.

18 Muir, *Ritual in Early Modern Europe*, 3–6, describes several different uses for religious rituals. See also Scribner, *Popular Culture and Popular Movements*, 1–16.

19 The most prominent farmers in early modern France – those who rented and farmed the largest tracts of land – were known as the *laboureurs*. Among the extensive literature on social distinctions in rural areas see especially Moriceau, *Les fermiers de l'Île-de-France*. See also Gutton, *La sociabilité villageoise*; Jessenne, *Pouvoir au village*; Lefebvre, *Les paysans du Nord*; Goubert, *Beauvais et le Beauvaisis*; Follain, *Le village sous l'Ancien Régime*; Jacquart, *La crise rurale*.

20 Hayden and Greenshields analyze the decrees made by French bishops in their *Six Hundred Years of Reform*; chapter 4 deals with the seventeenth century, when the greatest number of statutes were issued. They have also studied pastoral visits, which were at their highest level during this period as well.

21 See also de Boer, *The Conquest of the Soul*, chapter 6, who provides information about the limits of reform in early modern Italy.

22 Other historians who highlight this process of conflict and compromise include Barnes, *The Social Dimension of Piety*; Carroll, *Veiled Threats*; Fehleison, *Boundaries of Faith*; Flynn, *Sacred Charity*; Forster, *Catholic Revival* and *The Counter-Reformation in the Villages*; Harline, *The Burdens of Sister Margaret*; Hsia, *Social Discipline*; Luria, *Territories of Grace*; Vernus, *Le presbytère et la chaumière*. Dewald, *Pont-St-Pierre*, and Robisheaux, *Rural Society and the Search for Order*, make similar arguments about village life, although they do not concentrate specifically on religion.

23 Van Kley, "Christianity as Casualty," surveys much of this literature.

24 These historians include Aston, *Religion and Revolution in France*; Desan, *Reclaiming the Sacred*; Maire, *De la cause de Dieu*; Shusterman, *The French Revolution*; Tackett, *Religion, Revolution, and Regional Culture*; and Van Kley, *The Religious Origins of the French Revolution*.

25 French, *The People of the Parish*, 208. See also Kselman's introduction to

his edited collection, *Belief in History*, 8, where he argues that religious experience is worthy of study in its own right and not simply as a vehicle for examining other social, economic, or political factors.

26　This point is made abundantly clear by the overall tone, focus, and argument of the two-volume, magisterial work on the eighteenth-century church: McManners, *Church and Society*.

27　The record of this case can be found in AD Marne, 2 G 1947.

28　For more on the historical value of the stories of obscure people, see Kaplan, *Cunegonde's Kidnapping*, 233–4.

29　The outlines of the debate over popular culture were set primarily by Robert Muchembled and Peter Burke. The introduction to the third edition of Burke's study, *Popular Culture in Early Modern Europe*, provides an excellent synopsis of the debate overall. Muchembled, *Popular Culture and Elite Culture in France*, argues that an independent popular culture was deliberately suppressed by elites in the seventeenth and eighteenth centuries. Burke sees more overlap between popular and elite culture than Muchembled and does not argue for a decline of popular culture at the end of the early modern period. Most historians at present are likely to side more with Burke rather than Muchembled, arguing for more interaction between popular and elite culture. See also Garnot, *Le peuple au siècle des Lumières*, who provides convincing evidence that the attempts described by Muchembled to repress popular culture were largely unsuccessful.

### CHAPTER ONE

1　AD Marne, 2 G 1947, *information*, 20 April–13 May 1770, 41 *recto*. All translations are my own unless otherwise specified.

2　According to diocesan visits to Mareuil-sur-Ay, the parish was composed of 160 households and 500 communicants in 1672. In 1683, there were 480 communicants. In 1712, there were only 460 communicants, and by 1774 the number had dropped to 400. The earliest census available is for 1793, when Mareuil-sur-Ay was listed with 659 inhabitants. All of these villages were in the administrative unit (*doyenné*) of Épernay; visitation records giving details about the number of communicants are found in AD Marne, 2 G 286–7; census details can be found at http://cassini.ehess.fr.

3　McManners, *Church and Society*, 1:365–8.

4　Vernier provided this information in 1774 in a diocesan questionnaire.

AD Marne, 2 G 287. Of the 514 curés who answered a questionnaire in 1774, 451 had been ordained in the diocese of Reims. Only nineteen curés were serving in their home parish. Julia, "Le clergé paroissial," 200, 216.

5  On seminaries, see Degert, *Histoire des séminaires français*. For more on clerical education, see Tackett, *Priest and Parish*, 72–95.

6  Julia, "Le clergé paroissial," 215, indicates that most priests served for about twelve years, in one or more positions, before becoming a curé.

7  Lesprand, *Le clergé de la Moselle*, 2:295, indicates that Vernier was born on 8 May 1719. In 1774 when he filled out the diocesan questionnaire, Vernier listed his age as 54.

8  The *procureur fiscal* served as a defender of the rights of the *seigneur*, as well as those of village communities. They dealt with criminal and fiscal issues and helped to maintain good order and discipline. See Crubaugh, *Balancing the Scales of Justice*, 12; Renauldon, *Dictionnaire des fiefs*, 169–70; Mauclair, *La justice au village*, 89.

9  For more on vicaires, see Tackett, *Priest and Parish*, 98–101.

10  The exception to this is Brittany, where the parish priest was called a *recteur* and his assistants were called *curés*. Le Goff, *Vannes and its Region*, 244.

11  Bergin, *Church, Society and Religious Change*, 219. Some areas of France did not have as many vicaires as others. For example, Tackett notes that it was rare for priests serving in the diocese of Gap to have a vicaire. See his *Priest and Parish*, 37. In Reims, there were 131 vicaires and 514 curés. Julia, "Le clergé paroissial," 200. Wenzel, *Curés des Lumières*, 20, shows a similar percentage (25 per cent) for the diocese of Dijon on the eve of the Revolution. For Besançon, Vernus, *Le presbytère et la chaumière*, 24, 26, demonstrates the existence of a higher number of vicaires, indicating that in 1789 the diocese of Besançon had 840 curés and 384 vicaires. Playoust-Chaussis, *La vie religieuse*, 139, reports a similar percentage for the diocese of Boulogne: 107 vicaires for 220 parishes in 1790.

12  The new vicaire performed a baptism on that day and signed the record in the parish register. AD Marne, 2 E 405/2, Baptêmes, mariages, sépultures 1715–49.

13  AD Marne, 2 G 1947, *memoire*, August 1770, 5.

14  McManners, *Church and Society*, 1:389–90; Vernus, *Le presbytère et la chaumière*, 21.

15  Curés received their income in two ways – directly from tithes and

land, or a fixed salary paid by an ecclesiastical leader or someone else who had the right to collect tithes along with the responsibility to pay the curé. The fixed salary, or *portion congrue*, was set at 300 *livres* per year until 1768, when it was raised to 500 *livres*. Just before the Revolution, in 1786, it was raised again, to 700 *livres*. About one-third of all French curés received the *portion congrue*; thus the 900 *livres* that Mareuil-sur-Ay's curé reported in 1683 was three times more than many curés received in a year. The income from the tithes and lands was more than enough to support a vicaire as well as a curé. See McManners, *Church and Society*, 1:330, 335, 344; Tackett, *Priest and Parish*, 124.

16  AD Marne, 2 G 1947, *information*, 20 April–13 May 1770, 41–2, 161–3, 441–3. The witnesses were Jean Poirot, Paul Nicolas Blondeau, and Marie Magdelaine Calixte Cazin.

17  On the functions of village assemblies, and how they changed over time during the early modern period, see Follain, *Le village sous l'Ancien Régime*, 215–43. See also Gutton, *La sociabilité villageoise*, 69–83.

18  The *parlement* was the highest French court of appeal. It should not be confused with the English parliament, or representative assembly.

19  AD Marne, 2 G 1947, *information*, 20 April–13 May 1770, 163.

20  AD Marne, 2 G 1947, undated complaint, no page numbers.

21  The documents of the 1770 case indicate that these complaints and others were made to various authorities, but unfortunately records of them have not survived.

22  For a brief treatment of similar examples in Germany, see Forster, *Catholic Revival*, 196–206.

23  Kaplan, *Divided by Faith*, 78–9. Karras, *Unmarriages*, 160, examines the use of the term scandal in medieval court records and argues that the public nature of an infraction was what made it particularly scandalous, although the term was used differently in different contexts.

24  AD Marne, 2 G 1941, *information*, 14 September 1755, 3–4.

25  AD Marne, 2 G 1950, *information*, 30–31 July 1776, 12.

26  AD Doubs, G 824, *information*, 3 June 1741, 46. Michel was curé of Volon (Besançon).

27  AD Marne, 2 G 1947, *information*, 20 April–13 May 1770, 466 *verso*.

28  Le Tellier, *Rituel de la province de Reims*, 125.

29  Talleyrand-Périgord, "Synode de Reims," 4:800–1. The archbishop indicated that vespers should never be held right after mass, because that would leave too much free time for people in the afternoon. The best way to keep people from spending their Sundays in cabarets or other

diversions, he insisted, was to keep them busy with religious services spaced throughout the day.

30  AD Marne, 2 G 1947, *information*, 20 April–13 May 1770, 46, 433, 108–9.

31  AD Marne, 2 G 1947, *information*, 20 April–13 May 1770, 469–70.

32  Le Tellier, *Rituel de la province de Reims*, 247–61. For more on the *prône*, see Lualdi, "A Body of Beliefs and Believers," 134–51.

33  Vicaires owed their positions to the curés and were thus unlikely to criticize their superiors for fear of losing their jobs. See Tackett, *Priest and Parish*, 100–1.

34  AD Marne, 2 G 1947, *information*, 20 April–13 May 1770, 466–7.

35  On feast days of obligation, Catholics were required to attend mass and could not work. The number of feast days varied from diocese to diocese. Shusterman has calculated an average of thirty-three weekdays per year that were devoted to religious holidays in the early seventeenth century, but in some dioceses there were well over forty or fewer than thirty. The average number dropped to eighteen by 1780, again with significant regional variations. Shusterman, *Religion and the Politics of Time*, 19–20, 68.

36  AD Marne, 2 G 1947, *information*, 20 April–13 May 1770, 4–7.

37  AD Marne, 2 G 1947, *information*, 20 April–13 May 1770, 287–8. There were three women in Mareuil-sur-Ay named Marie Jeanne Jacquot; all three testified in the *information*. The mother of Geneviève Visse was the wife of Jean Baptiste Visse.

38  Bergin, *Church, Society, and Religious Change*, 267.

39  AD Marne, 2 G 1947, *information*, 20 April–13 May 1770, 233–4. The witness who mentioned this incident was Marie Louise Jacquot.

40  AD Marne, 2 G 1947, *interrogatoire*, 16–23 April 1771, 4–5.

41  The literature on confraternities is extensive; see especially: Barnes, *The Social Dimension of Piety*, chapter 3; Black and Gravestock, eds., *Early Modern Confraternities*; Donnelly and Maher, eds., *Confraternities and Catholic Reform*; Goujard, *Un catholicisme bien tempéré*, part 1, chapter 5, part 2, chapter 8; Lajaumont, *"Un pas de deux,"* chapter 7; Flynn, *Sacred Charity*, chapter 1; Agulhon, *Pénitents et francs-maçons*. Although Schneider, *Public Life in Toulouse*, chapter 7, examines the urban confraternities of Toulouse, his comments are still instructive.

42  AD Marne, 2 G 1947, *information*, 20 April–13 May 1770, 510–12.

43  AD Marne, 2 G 1947, *information*, 20 April–13 May 1770, 224–5.

44  See Carter, *Creating Catholics*, for my recent treatment of catechetical education in France in the seventeenth and eighteenth centuries.

45  AD Marne, 2 G 1947, *information*, 20 April–13 May 1770, 195.

46  AD Marne, 2 G 1947, *information*, 20 April–13 May 1770, 596–600.

47  AD Marne, 2 G 1947, *information*, 20 April–13 May 1770, 526–7.

48  AD Marne, 2 G 1947, *information*, 20 April–13 May 1770, 218, 220–1.

49  AD Marne, 2 G 1947, *information*, 20 April–13 May 1770, 145. The
    phrase in French was written as *si son pere baisoit bien sa mere*. The verb
    *baiser* appears to have meant "to kiss" in the eighteenth century, while
    today it has much more vulgar connotations and is often translated as
    "to fuck." The way that the curé used the word was clearly inappropriate
    in this case, since Marguerite Coinon had been scandalized by it.

50  AD Marne, 2 G 1947, *information*, 20 April–13 May 1770, 123, 259–60.

51  AD Marne, 2 G 1947, *information*, 20 April–13 May 1770, 17 *verso*.

52  AD Marne, 2 G 1947, *information*, 20 April–13 May 1770, 28.

53  Bergin, *Church, Society and Religious Change*, 254–7.

54  Le Tellier, *Rituel de la province de Reims*, 7.

55  AD Marne, 2 G 1947, *information*, 20 April–13 May 1770, 49; AD Marne,
    2 E 405/3, Baptêmes, mariages, sépultures 1750–69.

56  AD Marne, 2 G 1947, *information*, 20 April–13 May 1770, 335–6.

57  AD Marne, 2 E 405/3, Baptêmes, mariages, sépultures 1750–69.

58  AD Marne, 2 G 1947, *information*, 20 April–13 May 1770, 319–21.

59  AD Marne, 2 G 1947, *information*, 20 April–13 May 1770, 580–2.

60  AD Marne, 2 G 1947, *information*, 20 April–13 May 1770, 89–90.

61  AD Marne, 2 G 1947, *information*, 20 April–13 May 1770, 11–12.

62  AD Marne, 2 G 1947, *information*, 20 April–13 May 1770, 310–11.

63  Bishops often had a number of diocesan administrators, known as vic-
    ars-general, who helped them in the day-to-day workings of the diocese.
    In Reims, a large archdiocese, the vicars-general were usually bishops,
    and they certainly would have had the right to issue *billets*.

64  AD Marne, 2 G 1947, *information*, 20 April–13 May 1770, 356–60.

65  AD Marne, 2 G 1947, *information*, 20 April–13 May 1770, 531–3.

66  AD Marne, 2 G 1947, *information*, 20 April–13 May 1770, 346–50.

67  For a more extensive treatment of priests as healers, see Bernos, *Les sacre-
    ments dans la France*, 73–80, and Thayer, "Judge and Doctor."

68  AD Marne, 2 G 1947, *information*, 20 April–13 May 1770, 68–71.

69  AD Marne, 2 G 1947, *information*, 20 April–13 May 1770, 229–32. On the
    sexual language used to insult women, see Gowing, *Domestic Dangers*,
    chapter 3.

70  AD Marne, 2 G 1947, *information*, 20 April–13 May 1770, 339–40, 247–9.

71  AD Marne, 2 G 1947, *information*, 20 April–13 May 1770, 463–4; undated
    complaint, no page numbers.

72  AD Marne, 2 G 1947, *information*, 20 April–13 May 1770, 449–53.

73  AD Marne, 2 G 1947, *information*, 20 April–13 May 1770, 110–11.

74  AD Marne, 2 G 1947, *memoire*, August 1770, 43.

75  AD Marne, 2 G 1947, *memoire*, August 1770, 11.

76  AD Marne, 2 G 1947, *information*, 20 April–13 May 1770, 318.

77  AD Marne, 2 G 1947, *information*, 20 April–13 May 1770, 3–4; AD Marne, 2 E 405/2, Baptêmes, mariages, sépultures 1715–49.

78  AD Marne, 2 G 1947, *information*, 20 April–13 May 1770, 269–71; AD Marne, 2 E 405/3, Baptêmes, mariages, sépultures 1750–69.

79  AD Marne, 2 G 1947, *information*, 20 April–13 May 1770, 221–2; undated complaint, no page numbers.

80  The *syndic* served as a representative for the people of the village, and, with the *seigneur*, was their go-between with state institutions. His duties differed from region to region, or even from village to village, but included things like presiding over assemblies, representing the community in lawsuits, dealing with community finances and tax issues, and taking charge of efforts to combat epidemics and fires. In this instance, there was probably a lawsuit over tithes or other financial matters that involved the village and the curé. For more on the *syndic*, see Babeau, *Le village sous l'ancien régime*, 59–73; on village officials in general, see Follain, *Le village sous l'Ancien Régime*, 281–321, 390–406.

81  AD Marne, 2 G 1947, *information*, 20 April–13 May 1770, 237–41.

82  AD Marne, 2 G 1947, *information*, 20 April–13 May 1770, 97–8.

83  AD Marne, 2 G 1947, *information*, 20 April–13 May 1770, 500–1, 12–13, 54–5.

84  AD Marne, 2 G 1947, *information*, 20 April–13 May 1770, 103–5, 394–6.

85  AD Marne, 2 G 1947, *information*, 20 April–13 May 1770, 407–12.

86  AD Marne, 2 G 1947, *information*, 20 April–13 May 1770, 555–8.

87  For more on the *fabrique* see Bergin, *Church, Society and Religious Change*, 34–5; Goujard, *Un catholicisme bien tempéré*, part 1, chapter 4, part 2, chapters 6–7; McManners, *Church and Society*, 1:300–11; Vernus, *Le presbytère et la chaumière*, 136–9.

88  AD Marne, 2 G 1947, *information*, 20 April–13 May 1770, 284–5.

89  AD Marne, 2 G 1947, *information*, 20 April–13 May 1770, 582–5.

90  AD Marne, 2 G 1947, *information*, 20 April–13 May 1770, 397–8, 583–4.

91  AD Marne, 2 G 1947, *information*, 20 April–13 May 1770, 113–14.

92  AD Marne, 2 G 1947, *information*, 20 April–13 May 1770, 91, 39 *verso*, 35, 211.

93  AD Marne, 2 G 1947, *information*, 20 April–13 May 1770, 177–8, 264, 200–1, 49–50.

94 AD Marne, 2 G 1947, *information* 20 April–13 May 1770, 32–4, 91–3.
95 The testimonies of Charlemagne and Philippot can be found in AD Marne 2 G 1947, *information*, 20 April–13 May 1770, 386–92, 585–90.
96 AD Marne, 2 G 1947, *information*, 20 April–13 May 1770, 331–3, 184. Marie Jeanne Jacquot was married to François Gombert Jacquot. The two shared the same last name but were not related.
97 AD Marne, 2 G 1947, *information*, 20 April–13 May 1770, 559–60.
98 AD Marne, 2 G 1947, undated complaint, no page numbers.
99 AD Marne, 2 G 1947, *information*, 20 April–13 May 1770, 172–3.
100 AD Marne, 2 G 1947, *information*, 20 April–13 May 1770, 400–4.

### CHAPTER TWO

1 When asked about the character of his parishioners in a questionnaire sent out to all curés in the diocese of Reims, this was Vernier's response. AD Marne, 2 G 287.
2 Vernier's testimony about his difficulties in performing services can be found in AD Marne, 2 G 1947, *interrogatoire*, 16–23 April 1771, 2, 5–6.
3 AD Marne, 2 G 1947, *memoire*, August 1770, 39.
4 See Glennie and Thrift, *Shaping the Day*, for a comprehensive study of timekeeping culture in England. They argue that a "majority of parishes" for which documentation exists possessed clocks at some point before 1700. See 153–4.
5 AD Marne, 2 G 1930, *interrogatoire*, 28 February 1731, 6.
6 AD Marne, 2 G 1942, *information*, 23–24 March 1762, 12–13.
7 AD Marne, 2 G 1947, *interrogatoire*, 16–23 April 1771, 16.
8 AD Marne, 2 G 1947, *interrogatoire*, 16–23 April 1771, 17.
9 AD Marne, 2 G 1947, *interrogatoire*, 16–23 April 1771, 16.
10 AD Marne, 2 G 1947, *interrogatoire*, 16–23 April 1771, 18.
11 AD Marne, 2 G 1947, *interrogatoire*, 16–23 April 1771, 29.
12 For more on the seal of the confessional, see Bernos, *Les sacrements dans la France*, 95–107.
13 Archives départementales du Doubs (hereafter AD Doubs), G 835, *information*, 7 February 1748, 3.
14 AD Marne, 2 G 1947, *interrogatoire*, 16–23 April 1771, 22, 32.
15 AD Marne, 2 G 1947, *interrogatoire*, 16–23 April 1771, 22.
16 AD Marne, 2 G 1947, *interrogatoire*, 16–23 April 1771, 27; *information*, 20 April–13 May 1770, 472.

17  AD Marne, 2 G 1947, *interrogatoire*, 16–23 April 1771, 28.

18  AD Marne, 2 G 1947, *interrogatoire*, 16–23 April 1771, 32, 33.

19  Mauclair, *La justice au village*, 19.

20  For more on village structure, see especially Follain, *Le village sous l'Ancien Régime*; Goubert, *The French Peasantry in the Seventeenth Century*; Hayhoe, *Strangers and Neighbours*; Jessenne, *Pouvoir au village*; Mauclair, *La justice au village*; and Moriceau, *Les fermiers de l'Île-de-France*.

21  Carter, "The Affair of the Pigeon Droppings," 33.

22  For an example of long-standing rifts between members of the same community, see Sutherland, *Murder in Aubagne*. On village relationships and notions of power in general, see especially Sabean, *Power in the Blood*. Other works that provide examples of community loyalties and enmities, and their various causes, include Harline, *The Burdens of Sister Margaret*, and Kaplan, *Cunegonde's Kidnapping*. Although these works do not deal directly with the curé–parishioner relationship, they do shed light on how some members of a community might end up on opposite sides of various issues. Although enmities might have been created for one specific reason, that enmity could easily spill over into other arenas.

23  Muchembled, *Popular Culture and Elite Culture in France*, 38, also suggests a number of sites where social relationships were built and reinforced, including, cabarets, churches, and city squares.

24  In his study of seigneurial court records in Burgundy in the eighteenth century, Hayhoe found that only about 25 per cent of witnesses were women or girls. The genders were much more evenly represented in Vernier's case. Hayhoe, *Strangers and Neighbours*, 8.

25  AD Marne, 2 G 1930, letter from Dumontier to the official of Noyon, 9 February 1731.

26  AD Marne, 2 G 1930, confrontation, 11–15 December 1730. Ruff, *Crime, Justice and Public Order*, 54.

27  AD Marne, 2 G 1930, conclusion of the Reims *officialité*, 6 September 1731. A common sentence for misbehaving priests was a "retreat" at the diocesan seminary for anywhere from a few weeks to a year. At the seminary priests were supposed to study, pray, and reflect on how they could better fulfill their clerical duties.

28  AD Marne, 2 G 1930, confrontation, 8–10, 14 March, 17–20 April, 4 May 1731.

29  AD Marne, 2 G 1930, conclusion, 17 May 1731.

30  AD Marne, 2 G 1940, confrontation, 8–12 November 1755, 11–12.

31  A copy of the conclusion, dated 18 May 1756, is found in AD Marne, 2 G 1940.

32  Today, Mouthier is Mouthier-Haute-Pierre. In the documents, Lods is sometimes spelled Lod.

33  AD Doubs, G 828, *interrogatoire* of Luc Vuillemin, 17 December 1744.

34  These interrogations are all found in AD Doubs, G 828, dated 16, 17, or 18 December 1744.

35  AD Doubs, G 828, *information*, 21, 30, 31 March 1744.

36  AD Marne, 2 G 1942, *interrogatoire*, 10 July 1762, 12–13.

37  AD Marne, 2 G 1947, *information*, 20 April–13 May 1770, 95–7, 101–2.

38  The list of discredited witnesses is found in a summary of the case, AD Marne 2 G 1947, dated 31 July 1772.

39  Garnot, "La justice pénale," provides a valuable summary of some of the issues with witness testimony and court procedures in the eighteenth century, including some of the reasons why courts might ignore evidence from certain witnesses.

40  Fairchilds, *Domestic Enemies*, 127.

41  As a result of intermarriage, Jean François Salmon was the representative for three of those branches, however; his parents were second cousins once removed, and he married his own second cousin, Marie Anne Louise Salmon.

42  Cognon was from Vraux, and that was where her marriage to Jacques Patron took place in 1741. They had moved to Mareuil-sur-Ay by December of that year, when their first child was born. Patron had been born in Mareuil-sur-Ay, however, in 1701.

43  Reboult's testimony is also found in the AD Marne, 2 G 1947 dossier.

44  AD Marne, 2 G 1947, *information*, 20 April–13 May 1770, 413–19.

45  For my extended treatment of parish schoolmasters, see Carter, *Creating Catholics*, 136–71.

46  For more on problems with the clergy during the medieval and Reformation periods, see especially Adam, *La vie paroissiale*; Sauzet, *Les visites pastorales*; Minois, *La Bretagne des prêtres*.

47  On clerical education, see Bergin, *Church, Society and Religious Change*, 183–207; Delumeau, *Catholicism between Luther and Voltaire*, 71–97; McManners, *Church and Society*, 1:321–83. On seminaries, see Degert, *Histoire des séminaires français*.

48  Carter, *Creating Catholics*, 111.

49 For a comprehensive treatment of synodal statutes and pastoral visits, see Hayden and Greenshields, *Six Hundred Years of Reform.*

50 On the *bon curé*, see McManners, *Church and Society*, 1:364–73; Tackett, *Priest and Parish*, 151–65; Delumeau, *Catholicism between Luther and Voltaire*, 189; Vernus, *Le presbytère et la chaumière*, 217–22.

51 Bergin, *Church, Society and Religious Change*, 205–6.

52 Hoffman, *Church and Community*, 167–70. See also Bergin, *Church, Society, and Religious Change*, 212; Goubert, *The French Peasantry*, 164–5; Barnes, "Social Transformation," 141.

53 Carter, *Creating Catholics*, 220–1. See also Lajaumont, *"Un pas de deux,"* who makes a similar argument for the region of the Limousin.

54 This is the argument made by Barnes, in his "Social Transformation," 139–57.

55 According to Vernus, *Le presbytère et la chaumière*, 32, the patrimonial title was 100 *livres* in Reims, and 133 *livres*, 6 *sous*, 8 *deniers* in Besançon.

56 Vernus, *Le presbytère et la chaumière*, 31, notes that 271 of 537 ecclesiastics in Reims had urban origins. Wenzel, *Curés des Lumières*, found that 52 per cent of the curés working in the diocese of Dijon in the eighteenth century came from the city of Dijon. Tackett, *Priest and Parish*, 51–66, found that many of the priests in the diocese of Gap also came from the town of Gap, although the number of urban priests was decreasing by the end of the eighteenth century. Both Tackett and Julia, "Le clergé paroissial," 209, come to the same conclusion that the need for families to procure a patrimonial title restricted candidates for the priesthood to those from the wealthy levels of society. We should also make allowances for significant regional differences; for example, Le Goff, *Vannes and its Region*, 250–1, notes that in the diocese of Vannes, in Brittany, most candidates for the priesthood were from rural areas rather than urban. They were primarily sons of *laboureurs*, however, and were thus still social elites within their communities.

57 AD Marne, 2 G 1941, *information*, 15–17 May 1754. Copies of documents dealing with Aubriot de Boncourt's sentence can be found in a letter, dated 24 October 1754, sent to the archbishop.

58 AD Marne, 2 G 268.

59 AD Marne, 2 G 1941, confrontation, 27–29 September 1754, 36.

60 AD Marne, 2 G 1941, *interrogatoire*, 4 September 1754, 10.

61 AD Marne, 2 G 1941, *interrogatoire*, 4 September 1754, 8.

62 AD Marne, 2 G 1941, *interrogatoire*, 4 September 1754, 7; confrontation, 27–29 September 1754, 13–15.

63   AD Marne, 2 G 1941, *interrogatoire*, 4 September 1754, 8; confrontation, 27–29 September 1754, 20–1.

64   AD Marne, 2 G 1941, *interrogatoire*, 4 September 1754, 15.

65   Sauvageon, "Le manuscrit de Sennely," 9–10.

66   Bouchard, *Le village immobile*, 341. Many of Bouchard's interpretations about Sauvageon's parish are somewhat outdated, most especially his argument that the village of Sennely changed little in the early modern period. However, his evaluation of Sauvageon's relationship with his parishioners seems more astute.

67   Sauvageon, "Le manuscrit de Sennely," 9, 14–15.

68   Sauvageon, "Le manuscrit de Sennely," 15.

69   AD Marne, 2 G 259.

70   AD Marne, 2 G 270; the parish referenced is Saint-Menge.

71   AD Marne, 2 G 264.

72   AD Marne, 2 G 275.

73   AD Marne, 2 G 285; the parish referenced is Prunay.

74   AD Marne, 2 G 258.

75   AD Marne, 2 G 282.

76   AD Marne, 2 G 267.

77   AD Marne, 2 G 256; the parish referenced is Baslieux.

78   AD Marne, 2 G 260.

79   AD Marne, 2 G 276.

80   Bergin, *Church, Society, and Religious Change*, 205; Lemaitre, "Timides réformes," 155–79; Quéniart, *Les hommes, l'Église et Dieu*, 50.

81   Cabarets and other drinking establishments were supposed to serve only travelers, but this regulation was virtually unenforceable among the general population. The church took a harder line with ecclesiastics and issued additional regulations about clerical visits to cabarets. An *ordonnance* was issued for the diocese of Reims in 1647, stating, "We forbid all ecclesiastics from visiting cabarets in the future, particularly within the borders of their parish, city, or suburb where they live." The text set out a series of fines for those who broke the rule. Valançay, "Ordonnances et réglemens," 4:140–1.

82   For a sample of rules from dioceses besides Reims, see Baglion de la Salle, *Recüeil des réglemens et ordonnances*, 90–139; Bouhier, *Ordonnances synodales*, 1–28; Le Camus, *Ordonnances synodales*, 31–61.

83   Barberin, "Ordonnances et instructions," 4:279–80.

84   AD Marne, 2 G 267.

85   AD Marne, 2 G 257.

86 AD Marne, 2 G 287.

87 AD Marne, 2 G 276.

88 AD Marne, 2 G 260.

89 Vernus, *Le presbytère et la chaumière*, 52, notes that curés often saw their parishioners as children, who needed to be led carefully or they would get into trouble.

90 AD Marne, 2 G 256.

91 AD Marne, 2 G 258.

CHAPTER THREE

1 AD Marne, 2 G 1947, *interrogatoire*, 16–23 April 1771, 32.

2 For more on confirmation and holy orders, see Bergin, *Church, Society and Religious Change*, 257–8, 271–2.

3 AD Marne, 2 G 1947, *interrogatoire*, 16–23 April 1771, 19.

4 Le Tellier, *Rituel de la province de Reims*, 1–2; the *rituel* contains a six-page section on the sacraments in general.

5 De Boer, *The Conquest of the Soul*, 260.

6 Bergin, *Church, Society and Religious Change*, 254–7.

7 Le Tellier, *Rituel de la province de Reims*, 7.

8 McManners, *Church and Society*, 2:3.

9 Le Tellier, *Rituel de la province de Reims*, 12–13.

10 The Reims *rituel* does not mention this, but others do: Bishop Bossuet of Meaux mentioned this in a 1691 statute in the diocese of Meaux: Bossuet, "Statuts et ordonnances synodales," 2:602. See also Grimaldi, *Rituel du diocèse du Mans*, 12; Bazin de Besons, *Rituel romain*, 11; Malvin de Montazet, *Rituel du diocèse de Lyon*, 1:87.

11 This is the figure for Sennely, a village similar to the size and makeup of Mareuil-sur-Ay. Bouchard, *Le village immobile*, 74. A similar figure (300 out of 1000) is given by Heywood in his *Growing up in France*, 177, as well as by Goubert, *The French Peasantry*, 28 (20 to 40 per cent).

12 AD Marne, 2 E 405/2, Baptêmes, mariages, sépultures 1715–49.

13 AD Doubs, G 835, *information*, 17 February 1748, 38–9.

14 AD Marne, 2 G 1945, *information*, 20 October 1770, 20–1.

15 AD Marne, 2 G 1937, *interrogatoire*, 28 November 1747, no page numbers.

16 For more on godparents and how they were selected, see Bossy, "Godparenthood," 194–201; Schneider, *Public Life in Toulouse*, 244–5.

17 Le Tellier, *Rituel de la province de Reims*, 15.

254 Notes to pages 97–103

18 Vernus, *Le presbytère et la chaumière*, 85–8, notes that some priests might be willing to let some infractions slide, rather than face the backlash of their attempts to reform.

19 Le Tellier, *Rituel de la province de Reims*, 15.

20 Carter, *Creating Catholics*, 134–5.

21 AD Marne, 2 G 1947, *interrogatoire*, 16–23 April 1771, 31.

22 AD Marne, 2 E 405/3, Baptêmes, mariages, sépultures 1750–69.

23 AD Marne, 2 G 1947, *interrogatoire*, 16–23 April 1771, 29–30.

24 AD Doubs, G 832, *information*, 14–19 June 1746, 127–9; *interrogatoire*, 18 July 1746, 4–5.

25 AD Doubs, G 832, *information*, 14–19 June 1746, 107–8.

26 AD Marne, 2 G 1945, *information*, 22 April 1768.

27 AD Marne, 2 G 1945, *interrogatoire*, 28 April 1768.

28 In *Communities of Belief*, 277–338, Briggs evaluates this assumption in depth, as do de Boer, *The Conquest of the Soul*, and Tentler, *Sin and Confession*.

29 Le Tellier, *Rituel de la province de Reims*, 120.

30 See Briggs, *Communities of Belief*, 310, who argues that it was difficult for priests to deny people communion without serious consequences.

31 This literature includes Bernos, *Les sacrements dans la France*; Delumeau, *Sin and Fear* and *L'aveu et le pardon*; Duggan, "Fear and Confession"; Lualdi and Thayer, eds., *Penitence in the Age of Reformations*; McNeill, *A History of the Cure of Souls*; Poschmann, *Penance and the Anointing of the Sick*; Tentler, *Sin and Confession*; Thayer, *Penitence, Preaching and the Coming of the Reformation*.

32 See especially McManners, *Church and Society*, 2:248–54, who argues that excessive rigorism in the confessional was unlikely to have prevailed in the eighteenth century because of pushback from the laity.

33 Playout-Chaussis, *La vie religieuse*, 234; Bergin, *Church, Society and Religious Change*, 259.

34 Bonzon, *L'esprit de clocher*, 165–95, examined *officialité* cases dating from 1530 to 1650 in the diocese of Beauvais. She found that 62 per cent of them dealt with some sort of sexual infraction, 46 per cent involved a priest who was accused of violence, and 39 per cent included charges of alcoholism.

35 Examples of this type of research include de Boer, *The Conquest of the Soul*, who uses diocesan records from Milan; Haliczer, *Sexuality in the Confessional*, and O'Banion, *The Sacrament of Penance*, who use Inquisition records; and Myers, "*Poor, Sinning Folk*," who uses visitation

records. Historians studying Protestantism have provided a great deal of insight into religious practices and the sacraments using consistory records as well. See especially Benedict, *Christ's Churches Purely Reformed*; Grosse, *Les rituels de la cène*; Kingdon, *Adultery and Divorce*; Mentzer, "Notions of Sin and Penitence."

36 Two traditional studies of confession include Lea, *A History of Auricular Confession*, and Poschmann, *Penance and the Anointing of the Sick*. On the three penitential regimes, see also Delumeau, *Sin and Fear*, 195–6; Tentler, *Sin and Confession*, 3–27. Meens, *Penance in Medieval Europe*, and Hamilton, *The Practice of Penance*, also provide overviews of the three systems and the major historiographical issues although they primarily concentrate on the medieval period.

37 Public penance was still performed during this period, although it was usually reserved for public sins committed by prominent figures. Mansfield deals with this subject extensively in her *The Humiliation of Sinners*; see also Meens, *Penance in Medieval Europe*, 215–16.

38 Bergin, *Church, Society and Religious Change*, 208–12; Bossy, "The Social History of Confession," 30. For a more extensive treatment of the introduction of confessional boxes, see de Boer, *The Conquest of the Soul*, 84–125.

39 Haliczer, *Sexuality in the Confessional*, 207; Tentler, *Sin and Confession*, xi; Myers, "*Poor, Sinning Folk*," 196.

40 This theme is woven throughout many of the essays in Bernos, *Les sacrements dans la France*; see also Briggs, *Communities of Belief*; de Boer, *The Conquest of the Soul*; Lualdi and Thayer, eds., *Penitence in the Age of Reformations*; O'Banion, *The Sacrament of Penance*.

41 O'Banion, *The Sacrament of Penance*, makes a similar argument in his research on Spain during the sixteenth and seventeenth centuries.

42 See Tentler, *Sin and Confession*, 82–8, for a description of the penance process. Myers, "*Poor, Sinning Folk*," 41–4, describes the double confession system.

43 Le Tellier, *Rituel de la province de Reims*, 122.

44 Playout-Chaussis, *La vie religieuse*, 229–31. See also Garnot, *Le peuple au siècle des Lumières*, 60. For the Spanish case, see O'Banion, *The Sacrament of Penance*, 80, who reports a compliance rate of more than 96 per cent.

45 The worst case was Savigny-sur-Ardres (AD Marne, 2 G 257), where about twenty individuals (out of 250 communicants) had not taken communion, but in the other parishes only a handful of non-communicants were mentioned.

46 Delumeau, *Catholicism between Luther and Voltaire*, 194–6, 217–19.

47 McManners, *Church and Society*, 2:94–6; Haliczer, *Sexuality in the Confessional*, 22–8; Myers, "Poor, Sinning Folk," 189; O'Banion, *The Sacrament of Penance*, 47, 80; Quéniart, *Les hommes, l'Église et Dieu*, 204.

48 AD Doubs, G 832, *interrogatoire*, 18 July 1746, 9–10.

49 Sauvageon, "Le manuscrit de Sennely," 95.

50 Sauvageon, "Le manuscrit de Sennely," 94.

51 Le Tellier, *Rituel de la province de Reims*, 77.

52 Raveneau, *Journal*, 79–80.

53 Bossy, "The Social History of Confession," 25.

54 Raveneau, *Journal*, 31, 62.

55 Mangeut was curé of Saint-Hilaire-le-Petit in the diocese of Reims. AD Marne, 2 G 1945, *information*, 24–25 August 1767, 9–10.

56 Jacqueny was curé of Gevigney and its annex Mercey in the diocese of Besançon. AD Doubs, G 801, *information*, 19 February 1716.

57 AD Doubs, G 824, *information*, 26 April 1741, 3.

58 There were 20 *sous* (also *sols*) in a *livre*.

59 AD Marne, 2 G 1930, *récolement*, 9 March 1731, 4. In a *récolement*, the witness's testimony was read back to him or her and they were asked to verify it and give any additional comments. Ruff, *Crime, Justice and Public Order*, 54.

60 AD Marne, 2 G 1950, *information*, 22–23 November 1776, 4, 5.

61 Le Tellier, *Rituel de la province de Reims*, 87.

62 François's case was appealed to the *officialité* of Reims and is found in AD Marne, 2 G 1925, *interrogatoire*, 29 and 30 March 1721, no page numbers.

63 AD Marne, 2 G 1930, *interrogatoire*, 17 May 1731, 2.

64 Jacoulot was curé of Fontenois-la-Ville in the diocese of Besançon. AD Doubs, G 790, *interrogatoire*, 9 September 1704, 6.

65 AD Doubs G 832, *information*, 14–19 June 1746, 93–4.

66 AD Marne, 2 G 1947, *information*, 20 April–13 May 1770, 288–90.

67 AD Marne, 2 G 1947, *information*, 20 April–13 May 1770, 339–40; *interrogatoire*, 16–23 April 1770, 24.

68 AD Marne, 2 E 405/3, Baptêmes, mariages, sépultures 1750–69.

69 From 1700 to 1790, there were, according to parish registers, 336 women who married and subsequently had at least one child in Mareuil-sur-Ay. Of those first children, 48 (14.3 per cent) were born within eight months of the wedding date. There were also ten illegitimate children born during the same period. The rates of premarital

conception were similar all across Europe; see Kamen, *Early Modern European Society*, 20–1.

70  Le Tellier, *Rituel de la province de Reims*, 90–1.

71  Bergin, *Church, Society, and Religious Change*, 265, suggests this as well.

72  For a brief treatment of Jansenism, see Doyle, *Jansenism*. For more extensive coverage of the subject, see especially Sedgwick, *Jansenism in Seventeenth-Century France*, and Van Kley, *The Jansenists and the Expulsion of the Jesuits*.

73  This is essentially the system advocated by the Italian reforming bishop Charles Borromeo; see de Boer, *The Conquest of the Soul*, 43–83.

74  Pelletier was curé of Saint-Julien of the city of Reims. Saint-Julien was one of the urban parishes of Reims, and thus what happened here was unlikely to happen in rural parishes; however, it still demonstrates the difficult position curés were in when it came to denying their parishioners communion.

75  AD Marne, 2 G 1935, *information*, 20–21 April 1740, no page numbers. The sixth witness, Hiacinthe Catteau, provided an account of what both the curé and Galichet actually said during the event.

76  AD Marne, 2 G 1935, *information*, 20–21 April 1740, no page numbers. The ninth witness, Demoiselle Marguerite Muiron, testified about what people in the church were saying.

77  AD Marne, 2 G 1935, *interrogatoire*, 1 June 1740, 2–4; *interrogatoire*, 5 September 1740, 2–3.

78  AD Marne, 2 G 1933, *information*, 17–18 May 1736, no page numbers. Multiple people testified about these events, but the most detailed testimony came from the first witness in the *information*, Pierre Pertin.

79  Raveneau, *Journal*, 8.

80  Myers, "Poor, Sinning Folk," 56.

81  Le Tellier, *Rituel de la province de Reims*, 75–7. In Spain there was an indulgence that allowed people to pay a fee to confess with any priest they wanted. O'Banion, *The Sacrament of Penance*, 92, notes that this meant it was difficult for priests to control the confessional.

82  Vincent, "Limites, concurrences et contestations"; Myers, "Poor, Sinning Folk," 31; O'Banion, *The Sacrament of Penance*, 41.

83  AD Marne, 2 G 1940, *information*, 10–12 September 1755, 32–3.

84  The curé was Aubriot de Boncourt of Sorbon (Reims). AD Marne, 2 G 1941, confrontation, 27–29 September 1754, 17–18.

85  AD Marne, 2 G 1933, *information*, 17–18 May 1736.

86  AD Marne, 2 G 1947, *information*, 20 April–13 May 1770, 31.

87 AD Marne, 2 G 1947, *information*, 20 April–13 May 1770, 274–6.

88 AD Marne, 2 G 1947, *interrogatoire*, 16–23 April 1771, 28.

89 AD Marne, 2 G 1930. Sellier first denied refusing *billets* to anyone in his second *interrogatoire*, 20 October 1730. He admitted it in his third *interrogatoire*, 30 October 1730.

90 Lanneau was curé of Louvercy and Mourmelon-le-Petit (Reims). AD Marne 2 G 1945, *information*, 22 August 1767, 10–11, 16.

91 AD Doubs, G 832, *information*, 14–19 June 1746, 145.

92 AD Doubs, G 832, *information*, 14–19 June 1746, 84–5. It was common for anyone who was about to engage in any sort of dangerous activity to confess and receive communion. See Tentler, *Sin and Confession*, 73, 80. Furthermore, in the early modern period 20 per cent of deaths of women between twenty-five and thirty-four years of age were due to childbirth; see Harrison, *Disease and the Modern World*, 29.

93 Plongeron notes that villagers did not hesitate to complain about a curé they found problematic and that a curé might react to their complaints by going on "strike" and refusing to perform certain church services or changing the times of those services. By denying his parishioners the chance to take communion in the annex church, Faivre was essentially going on strike. Plongeron, *La vie quotidienne*, 147.

94 AD Doubs, G 832, *interrogatoire*, 18 July 1746, 5–6.

95 The case is found in AD Doubs, G 828 and 829.

96 On communal priests, see Lajaumont, *"Un pas de deux,"* 41; Quéniart, *Les hommes, l'Église et Dieu*, 22; Wenzel, *Curés des Lumières*, 20–1; Vernus, *Le presbytère et la chaumière*, 26.

97 AD Doubs, G 828, *information*, 21 March 1744, 1–4; undated complaint.

98 Haliczer deals with this extensively in his *Sexuality in the Confessional*, focusing primarily on Spain. *Officialité* records make it clear that French women faced the same sorts of solicitation from their priests as well.

99 AD Marne, 2 G 1930, *information*, 7–8 February 1731, 23.

100 AD Marne, 2 G 1945, *information*, 24–25 August 1767, 11–12.

101 AD Doubs, G 832, *information*, 14–19 June 1746, 123–4.

102 AD Marne, 2 G 1947, *interrogatoire*, 16–23 April 1771, 22.

103 AD Marne, 2 G 1947, *information*, 20 April–13 May 1770, 262–3, 256–7.

104 AD Marne, 2 G 1947, *information*, 196–200.

105 AD Marne, 2 G 1947, *information*, 206–7, 564–5.

106 AD Marne, 2 G 1947, *information*, 20 April–13 May 1770, 7–10.

107 General works on death include Ariès, *The Hour of Our Death*; McMan-
    ners, *Death and the Enlightenment*; Vovelle, *Piété baroque et déchristiani-
    sation* and *La mort et l'Occident*. Delumeau, *Sin and Fear*, deals exten-
    sively with attitudes toward death as well.

108 See McManners, *Church and Society*, 2:28–39.

109 Quéniart, *Les hommes, l'Église et Dieu*, 209–10. Forster, *Catholic Revival*,
    109, found that some peasants in Catholic Germany resisted extreme
    unction because they feared that if they received the sacrament they
    would have no hope of recovery, but in Reims and Besançon there
    seems to have been little reluctance. See also Bernos, *Les sacrements
    dans la France*, 267–76, who notes that some lay people thought that
    extreme unction was more like the old penance rituals, which, after
    being received, meant that a person could not participate in public life
    or engage in any sexual relationship.

110 AD Marne, 2 G 1945, *information*, 22 August 1767, 14–15.

111 Card games, and other types of games, were a significant source of dis-
    traction for curés. Wenzel, *Curés des Lumières*, 120, found that about a
    third of the curés in the diocese of Dijon had some sort of game table
    in their homes.

112 Le Tellier, *Rituel de la province de Reims*, 155; AD Marne, 2 G 1947,
    *interrogatoire*, 16–23 April 1771, 18–19.

113 AD Marne, 2 G 1947, *information*, 20 April–13 May 1770, 66–8.

114 AD Marne, 2 G 1947, *information*, 20 April–13 May 1770, 117–18.

115 AD Marne, 2 G 1947, *information*, 20 April–13 May 1770, 492–4.

116 AD Marne, 2 G 1947, *interrogatoire*, 16–23 April 1771, 17.

117 Le Tellier, *Rituel de la province de Reims*, 138.

118 AD Marne, 2 G 1941, *information*, 15–17 May 1754, 2–3.

119 This statement is found in the initial complaint against Mottet and
    repeated in several depositions. AD Doubs, G 835, *information*, 7, 8,
    16–17 February; 15–16 May; 28 August 1748.

120 AD Doubs, G 824, *information*, 3 June 1741, 19–22.

121 Drouin was the curé of Savigny-sur-Ardres in the diocese of Reims. AD
    Marne, 2 G 1935, *information*, 5–9 April 1740, 17.

122 AD Marne, 2 G 1947, *information*, 20 April–13 May 1770, 269–71.

123 AD Marne, 2 G 1945, *interrogatoire*, 23 September 1767, 11–13. Many
    witnesses testified about this event in the *information*, 22 August 1767.

124 AD Marne, 2 G 1941, *information*, 15–17 May 1754, 29–30; *interrogatoire*,
    4 September, 5–6.

125 AD Doubs, G 800, *interrogatoire*, 31 October 1713.

126 AD Marne, 2 G 1935, *interrogatoire*, 22–23 April 1740, 15–16.

127 AD Marne, 2 G 1945, *information*, 24–25 August 1767, 1–2.

128 AD Doubs, G 802, *information*, 20–21 August 1715, 28–9.

129 AD Doubs, G 802, *information*, 20–21 August 1715, 9, 18, 16, 12–13.

130 AD Marne, 2 G 1945, *information*, 22 August 1767, 6.

## CHAPTER FOUR

1 This complaint, about curé Claude Nicolas Boulanger of Auxon-Dessous, was made in a letter to the archbishop of Besançon, dated 28 July 1741. AD Doubs, G 825.

2 Information for the following paragraphs comes from AD Doubs, G 800, complaint, 11 August 1713; *information*, 22–23 August 1713; *interrogatoire*, 31 October 1713.

3 Playoust-Chaussis, *La vie religieuse*, 62, notes that according to a questionnaire distributed in 1725 in the diocese of Boulogne, 225 of 263 cemeteries were adequately enclosed. Usually, the barriers were simple hedges. See also Martin, *Les chemins du sacré*, 67–72; Bergin, *Church, Society and Religious Change*, 215.

4 AD Marne, 2 G 1928, *interrogatoire*, 22 February 1729, 2.

5 AD Marne, 2 G 1928, *interrogatoire*, 22 February 1729, 2–3.

6 Quentin's testimony about the events that follow is found in AD Marne, 2 G 1928, *interrogatoire*, 22 February 1729, 5–7. Multiple witnesses gave their version of what happened in the *information*, dated 12 February 1729.

7 For more on processions, see Martin, *Les chemins du sacré*, and Lajaumont, *"Un pas de deux,"* 295–338.

8 AD Marne, 2 G 1942, *information*, 23–24 March 1762.

9 AD Marne, 2 G 1930, *information*, 7–8 February 1731, 21.

10 AD Doubs, G 832, *information*, 14–19 June 1746, 98.

11 AD Marne, 2 G 1947, *information*, 20 April–13 May 1770, 52.

12 AD Marne, 2 G 1947, *interrogatoire*, 23 July 1772, 15.

13 For more on catechism, see Carter, *Creating Catholics*; on first communion, see Delumeau, ed., *La première communion*.

14 AD Doubs, G 801, *information*, 19 February 1716, 91, 78.

15 AD Marne, 2 G 1945, *information*, 24–25 August 1767, 7.

16 AD Marne, 2 G 1945, *information*, 24–25 August 1767, 9.

17 AD Marne, 2 G 1925, *interrogatoire*, 29–30 March 1721, no page numbers.

18  AD Doubs, G 832, *interrogatoire*, 18 July 1746, 6–7.

19  AD Marne, 2 G 1945, *information*, 22 August 1767, 4–5; *interrogatoire*, 23 September 1767, 2.

20  Carter, *Creating Catholics*, 93–5, 128–35.

21  Carter, *Creating Catholics*, 91–2.

22  AD Marne, 2 G 1947, *interrogatoire*, 16–23 April 1771, 7.

23  In the villages of Reims and Auxerre, parents paid between three and twelve *sous* per month for a child who was learning to read. Carter, *Creating Catholics*, 166.

24  Goujard, *Un catholicisme bien tempéré*, 300; McManners, *Church and Society*, 1:308; Martin, *Les chemins du sacré*, 59.

25  Tackett, *Priest and Parish*, 130–1.

26  Complaints about surplice fees were common in the *cahiers de doléances*, or lists of grievances, written up by villages and towns right before the meeting of the Estates General in 1789. See Goujard, *Un catholicisme bien tempéré*, 397–403; Markoff, *The Abolition of Feudalism*, 109–10; Vernus, *Le presbytère et la chaumière*, 45–9.

27  AD Marne, 2 G 1930, *information*, 19 September 1730, no page numbers. Multiple people testified about this; the most extensive testimony came from Louis Roussel, the seventh witness.

28  AD Doubs, G 794, depositions after a *monitoire*, 27 December 1707.

29  AD Doubs, G 794, undated deposition.

30  AD Doubs, G 794, deposition, 6 February 1708.

31  AD Doubs, G 794, depositions after a *monitoire*, 27 December 1707.

32  AD Doubs, G 794, undated deposition.

33  AD Marne, 2 G 1928, *information*, 12 February 1729, 13; *interrogatoire*, 22 February 1729, 3.

34  AD Marne, 2 G 1947, *information*, 20 April–13 May 1770, 58, 204 *verso*.

35  AD Marne, 2 G 1947, *information*, 20 April–13 May 1770, 47, 218.

36  AD Marne, 2 G 1947, *information*, 20 April–13 May 1770, 334–5, 506–8.

37  AD Marne, 2 G 1947, *information*, 20 April–13 May 1770, 84–6, 204–5, 195–6.

38  AD Marne, 2 G 1947, *information*, 20 April–13 May 1770, 552–5.

39  AD Marne, 2 G 1947, *information*, 20 April–13 May 1770, 123–6.

40  AD Marne, 2 G 1947, *interrogatoire*, 16–23 April 1771, 13–14.

41  AD Marne, 2 G 1947, *information*, 20 April–13 May 1770, 419–23.

42  AD Marne, 2 G 1947, *interrogatoire*, 16–23 April 1771, 11–12.

43  AD Marne, 2 G 1947, *interrogatoire*, 16–23 April 1771, 12–13.

44  AD Marne, 2 G 1947, *interrogatoire*, 16–23 April 1771, 9–10.

45  AD Marne, 2 G 1947, *interrogatoire*, 16–23 April 1771, 20.

46 AD Doubs, G 825. The complaint about hairstyles was found in a letter
   to the archbishop, dated 28 July 1741. The other curé who complained
   about women and their head coverings was Nicolas Dumontier, parish
   of Roupy, diocese of Noyon. The case is found in AD Marne, 2 G 1930.

47 Details about these incidents are found in AD Marne, 2 G 1925, *information*, 19, 21 January 1723.

48 AD Marne, 2 G 1930, *information*, 7–8 February 1731; *interrogatoire*, 2
   March 1731, 11.

49 AD Marne, 2 G 1942, *information*, 9 June 1761.

50 AD Doubs, G 835, *information*, 17 February 1748, 35–6.

51 AD Marne, 2 G 1928, *interrogatoire*, 22 February 1729, 4.

52 AD Marne, 2 G 1945. Multiple people testified about these events in the
   *information*, 22 August 1767; Lanneau's testimony is found in the *interrogatoire*, 23 September 1767, 7.

53 AD Marne, 2 G 1945, *information*, 22 August 1767, 2; *interrogatoire*, 23
   September 1767, 5.

54 AD Doubs, G 832, *interrogatoire*, 18 July 1746, 17; *information*, 14–19
   June 1746, 71–2.

55 AD Doubs, G 832, *information*, 14–19 June 1746, 76–7, 113; *interrogatoire*,
   18 July 1746, 17–18.

56 AD Doubs, G 832, *interrogatoire*, 18 July 1746, 7–8.

57 Desan, "Making and Breaking Marriage," 2; Garnot, *Le peuple au siècle
   des Lumières*, 48–9.

58 No record of a marriage for Françoise Patron exists in the Mareuil-sur-
   Ay registers; she may have married outside of the parish. She died on 27
   September 1811, in Mareuil-sur-Ay. AD Marne, 125 M 9, Table décennale
   (an XI–1812).

59 Ruff found, in his examination of eighteenth-century *sénéchaussée*
   records in southwest France, that violence associated with young people
   often took place around religious holidays, when pranks might take a
   violent turn. He also notes that crimes of trespassing or damaging crops
   were a frequent problem in rural France. See his *Crime, Justice and Public Order*, 91, 137.

60 AD Marne, 2 G 1947, *information*, 20 April–13 May 1770, 563–4.

61 AD Marne, 2 G 1947, *interrogatoire*, 16–23 April 1771, 3–4.

62 AD Marne, 2 G 1930, *interrogatoire*, 22 September 1730, no page numbers.

63 AD Doubs, G 793, *information*, 22–24 July; 1 August 1705.

64 AD Doubs, G 825, *information*, 18–19 December 1743, 21.

65  AD Doubs, G 825, *interrogatoire*, 2 January 1744, 4.

66  AD Marne, 2 G 1925, *information*, 26–27 March 1721.

67  AD Doubs, G 832, *interrogatoire*, 18 July 1746, 20–1.

68  AD Marne, 2 G 1942, *information*, 23–24 March 1762, 4–5.

69  AD Marne, 2 G 1930, confrontation, 10 March 1731, 14.

## CHAPTER FIVE

1  Vernier made this statement in his interrogation, when asked about his relationship with the village schoolmistresses. AD Marne, 2 G 1947, *interrogatoire*, 16–23 April 1771, 48.

2  Cage, *Unnatural Frenchmen*, 53–60.

3  Karras, *Unmarriages*, 149–52.

4  Forster, *The Counter-Reformation in the Villages*, 24. Bossy, *Christianity in the West*, 65, argues that by 1500 about 80 to 90 per cent of priests were following the rules of celibacy; in light of Forster's findings, this figure seems a bit high. Barnes, "Social Transformation," 142–3, also argues that most early modern villagers did not see clerical concubines as inherently problematic.

5  McManners, *Church and Society*, 1:386. The most comprehensive treatment of the history of clerical celibacy is Parish, *Clerical Celibacy*. See also Brundage, *Law, Sex, and Christian Society*, 214–23, 401–5, 536–9; Cage, *Unnatural Frenchmen*, 11–28; Crawford, *European Sexualities*, 64–6, 76–89.

6  Brundage, *Law, Sex, and Christian Society*, 568–9.

7  McManners, *Church and Society*, 2:364–5.

8  Haliczer, *Sexuality in the Confessional*, 207. For a more positive view of the relationship between women and their confessors, see Bilinkoff, *Related Lives*.

9  Bonzon, *L'esprit de clocher*, 165–95.

10  Farr, *Authority and Sexuality*, 61–89.

11  Farr, *Authority and Sexuality*, 81; Ruff, *Crime, Justice and Public Order*, 74.

12  Bossy notes that lawsuits over tithes could lead to charges of violence or lack of charity, and then accusations against the curé's chastity would rapidly follow that. He further indicates that for this reason, historians have often assumed that all or most of these accusations were false; Bossy adds that "in general they are probably right." This seems short-sighted, in my view. Bossy, *Christianity in the West*, 65.

13  McManners, *Church and Society*, 1:384–7, includes a brief section on

curés' housekeepers, designating them as one of the "collaborators of the curé," but most of the literature dealing with priests' servants concentrates on the medieval period, especially after the eleventh century when ecclesiastical authorities began their attempts to remove priests' sexual partners from their households. See especially Cossar, *Clerical Households*, and Karras, *Unmarriages*, 115–64.

14 Maza, *Servants and Masters*, 18–19; Fairchilds, *Domestic Enemies*, xiii–xiv. Hayhoe provides some much-needed attention to rural servants in "Rural Domestic Servants," 549–71.

15 Ruff, *Violence in Early Modern Europe*, 142.

16 Maza, *Servants and Masters*, 89; Fairchilds, *Domestic Enemies*, 86.

17 Mauclair, *La justice au village*, 195–7. To discourage abortion and infanticide, the Crown required unmarried women to register their pregnancies with the courts. The *déclaration de grossesse* was established by edict in 1556. Isambert, ed., *Recueil général*, 13:471–3.

18 Loetz, *A New Approach*, chapter 1, provides a particularly good introduction to the difficulties of studying interpersonal sexual violence.

19 Clark, *Women's Silence, Men's Violence*, 58.

20 Clark, *Women's Silence, Men's Violence*, 51; Loetz, *A New Approach*, 43–52; Ruff, *Violence in Early Modern Europe*, 140–4.

21 Regnier's case took place in 1730 and can be found in AD Marne, 2 G 1930. Richard's case took place in 1748 and can be found in AD Doubs, G 811–12.

22 AD Doubs, G 811, *information*, 17 June 1743, 1–6.

23 AD Marne, 2 G 1930, *information*, 5–7 September 1730, 13–14.

24 The cultural association between alcohol and inappropriate sexual behaviour existed in the early modern period just as it does in modern times. See Martin, *Alcohol, Sex, and Gender*, for a thorough treatment of the subject.

25 AD Marne, 2 G 1941, *information*, 14 September 1755, 5–6.

26 AD Marne, 2 G 1941, *information*, 14 September 1755, 9, 12.

27 AD Doubs, G 801, *information*, 19 February 1716.

28 AD Doubs, G 801, *information*, 19 February 1716, 38–43.

29 AD Doubs, G 794, depositions after a *monitoire*, 27 December 1707.

30 AD Doubs, G 794, undated deposition.

31 Courts of all kinds could call upon the *officialité* to publish a *monitoire* if they needed to find witnesses for a case. The *monitoire* was read by parish priests on three consecutive Sundays during the services for the mass. Ruff, *Crime, Justice and Public Order*, 52–3.

32  AD Doubs, G 794, depositions after a *monitoire*, 27 December 1707.

33  AD Doubs, G 794, depositions after a *monitoire*, 27 December 1707.

34  AD Marne, 2 G 1925, *information*, 26–27 March 1721, witness 20.

35  AD Marne, 2 G 1925, *information*, 26–27 March 1721, witness 35.

36  AD Marne, 2 G 1925, *information*, 26–27 March 1721, witness 7.

37  AD Marne, 2 G 1925, *information*, 26–27 March 1721, witness 17, witness 30.

38  AD Marne, 2 G 1935, *information*, 21–25 March 1741, 5.

39  AD Marne, 2 G 1935, *information*, 21–25 March 1741, 2–3.

40  Regnart's testimony can be found in AD Marne, 2 G 1935, *information*, 21–25 March 1741, 6–11.

41  AD Marne, 2 G 1935, *information*, 21–25 March 1741, 27–9.

42  AD Marne, 2 G 1941, *information*, 15–17 May 1754, 1–2.

43  AD Marne, 2 G 1941, *information*, 15–17 May 1754, 7–10.

44  AD Doubs, G 793, *information*, 22–24 July, 1 August 1705, 2–3, 78–80, 4–8, 88–94.

45  Farr, *Authority and Sexuality*, 61–89.

46  Ruggiero, in his study of sex crimes in Renaissance Venice, notes that only the most egregious sex crimes involving nuns were prosecuted in Venetian courts but that the records of those cases reveal a "normal level of sexuality, at least at certain convents." Ruggiero, *The Boundaries of Eros*, 76.

47  AD Doubs, G 835. Multiple people testified about the affair with Gaudot in the *information*, and it is an item in the complaint against Mottet as well.

48  AD Marne, 2 G 1945, *information*, 20 October 1770.

49  AD Marne, 2 G 1925, *information*, 19, 21 January 1723.

50  AD Doubs, G 836, complaint, 21 November 1747.

51  AD Doubs, G 836, *information*, 27–29 November 1747, 49–51.

52  AD Doubs, G 836, *information*, 27–29 November 1747, 2–5.

53  AD Doubs, G 837, *addition*, 26–28 March 1748, 11–13.

54  AD Doubs, G 837, *addition*, 26–28 March 1748, 7–9.

55  AD Doubs, G 836, *information*, 27–29 November 1747, 8–9.

56  AD Doubs, G 836, *interrogatoire*, 13 January 1748, 8–9.

57  AD Doubs, G 836, sentence, 31 May 1748.

58  AD Doubs, G 802, *information*, 20–21 August 1715, 2–3, 8–9.

59  AD Marne, 2 G 1930. The initial information for the case was conducted 9–11 November 1730. The curé was interrogated on 22 November, and then the court requested an addition, in which three witnesses testified, on 14–15 December 1730.

60  AD Marne, 2 G 1930, sentence of the Noyon *officialité*, 14 February 1731; conclusion of the Reims *officialité*, 6 September 1731.

61  AD Doubs, G 800, *interrogatoire*, 31 October 1713.

62  AD Doubs, G 825, letter dated 28 July 1741.

63  AD Doubs, G 825, *information*, 18–19 December 1743, 27.

64  AD Doubs, G 825, *interrogatoire*, 2 January 1744, 6–7.

65  AD Marne, 2 G 1937. The events described in the next several paragraphs come from the two interrogations of Mercier, dated 24 March and 28 November 1747, as well as the testimony of the *procureur fiscal* in Vigneux, Louis Warnam, found in the *information*, 10–11 March 1747.

66  AD Marne, 2 G 1933, *ordonnance*, dated 21 September 1729.

67  AD Marne, 2 G 1933, *information*, 17–18 May 1736, witness 3.

68  AD Marne, 2 G 1933, *information*, 17–18 May 1736, witness 9.

69  AD Marne, 2 G 1933, *information*, 17–18 May 1736, witness 4.

70  AD Marne, 2 G 1933, *information*, 17–18 May 1736, witness 5; *interrogatoire*, 29 May 1736, no page numbers.

71  AD Marne, 2 G 1933, *information*, 17–18 May 1736, witness 13.

72  Crawford, *European Sexualities*, 154.

73  In her study of sexual abuse and sexual assault cases in early modern Zürich, Loetz argues that women who told family members or friends that they had been assaulted rarely found support; the first reaction of people consulted by the victim was usually to try to keep her quiet and cover things up as much as possible. This may have been what Huille experienced in this situation. Loetz, *A New Approach*, 97.

74  A copy of the letter is found in AD Marne, 2 G 1933, dated 6 June 1736.

75  For more on the *veillées*, see Muchembled, *Popular Culture and Elite Culture in France*, 217–18; Vernus, *Le presbytère et la chaumière*, 196–8.

76  AD Marne, 2 G 1933, 1736 letter, 48.

77  Vauquelin's version of his interactions with Huille can be found in AD Marne, 2 G 1933, 1736 letter, 17–39.

78  AD Marne, 2 G 1947, *interrogatoire*, 16–23 April 1771, 35–7.

79  AD Marne, 2 G 1947, *interrogatoire*, 16–23 April 1771, 37.

80  AD Marne, 2 G 1947, *interrogatoire*, 16–23 April 1771, 39.

81  AD Marne, 2 G 1947, *interrogatoire*, 16–23 April 1771, 39–43.

82  Carter, *Creating Catholics*, 186.

83  AD Marne, 2 G 1947, *memoire*, August 1770, 51–2.

84  AD Marne, 2 G 1947, *interrogatoire*, 16–23 April 1771, 44.

85  AD Marne, 2 G 1947, *information*, 20 April–13 May 1770, 106–7, 390, 591–2, 475.

86  AD Marne, 2 G 1947, *information*, 20 April–13 May 1770, 590–1, 558–9, 105, 114–15.

87  AD Marne, 2 G 1947, *information*, 20 April–13 May 1770, 38–9, 169–70; *memoire*, August 1770, 52–3.

88  AD Marne, 2 G 1947, *information*, 20 April–13 May 1770, 265–6.

89  Vernier's testimony about his relationship with the schoolmistresses can be found in AD Marne, 2 G 1947, *interrogatoire*, 16–23 April 1770, 44–7.

90  AD Marne, 2 G 1947, *information*, 20 April–13 May 1770, 242–4.

91  Cage, *Unnatural Frenchmen*.

### CHAPTER SIX

1  AD Marne, 2 G 1945, *interrogatoire*, 23 September 1767, 7.

2  AD Marne, 2 G 1925, *information*, 26–27 March 1721, witness 11.

3  AD Marne, 2 G 1925, *information*, 26–27 March 1721, witness 12.

4  Ruff, *Crime, Justice and Public Order*, 92.

5  For more on reforms that targeted the activities of the parish priest, see Delumeau, *Catholicism between Luther and Voltaire*, 179–89.

6  Barberin, "Ordonnances et instructions," 4:279–80. See also Bonzon, *L'esprit de clocher*, 165–95; Plongeron, *La vie quotidienne*, 174–88.

7  Talleyrand–Périgord, "Synode de Reims," 4:783–90. See also Goujard, *Un catholicisme bien tempéré*, part 2, chapter 3.

8  AD Marne, 2 G 1930, *information*, 7–8 February 1731.

9  Barberin, "Ordonnances et instructions," 4:279, notes that curés should not occupy themselves with any secular or profane work. They were not supposed to be involved in any trade or servile employment. Driving a cart of dung would certainly count as servile employment.

10  AD Marne, 2 G 1925, *information*, 26–27 March 1921, witness 4.

11  AD Marne, 2 G 1928. This is the third item in the complaint against Quentin, dated 8 February 1729.

12  AD Marne, 2 G 1947, *interrogatoire*, 16–23 April 1771, 45.

13  Lecoutre, *Le goût de l'ivresse*, 193–4. Since women and children did not generally consume as much as men did, it follows that there were certainly some men who drank much more than this amount.

14 Lecoutre, *Le goût de l'ivresse*, makes this point throughout his work, as does Martin, *Alcohol, Violence, and Disorder*, chapter 3.

15 Lecoutre, *Le goût de l'ivresse*, 115; Albala, "To Your Health."

16 Nichols, "Double Vision," deals with images of drunkenness in early modern Europe. His article examines some of the work that demonstrates the ambiguity associated with drinking and drunkenness and argues that much of the artwork of the period reflects this ambiguity as well.

17 Lecoutre, *Le goût de l'ivresse*, chapter 9; Holt, "Europe Divided."

18 Martin, "Alcohol and the Clergy," 33–7.

19 Brennan, *Public Drinking and Popular Culture*; Martin, *Alcohol, Violence, and Disorder*; Kümin, *Drinking Matters*.

20 The official name of the village is Savigny-sur-Ardres, but the documents use the abbreviated "Savigny" almost exclusively.

21 AD Marne, 2 G 1935, *information*, 5–9 April 1740, 25–7.

22 AD Marne, 2 G 1935, *information*, 5–9 April 1740, 9–12.

23 AD Marne, 2 G 1935, *interrogatoire*, 22–23 April 1740, 10–12.

24 AD Marne, 2 G 1935, *interrogatoire*, 22–23 April 1740, 21–2.

25 AD Marne, 2 G 1935, letter from Drouin to the official, 4 August 1740.

26 AD Marne, 2 G 1930, *information*, 5–7 September 1730, 6–7.

27 Talleyrand-Périgord, "Synode de Reims," 4:785. Curés were only supposed to enter cabarets when they were travelling and had nowhere else to stay.

28 AD Marne, 2 G 1930, *information*, 5–7 September 1730, 20–2.

29 AD Marne, 2 G 1930, *interrogatoire*, 21 September 1730, 17–18.

30 Barnes, "Social Transformation," 143–4.

31 AD Marne, 2 G 1925, *information*, 26–27 March 1721. Multiple witnesses testified about this, and about the events in the following paragraph, in the *information*.

32 AD Marne, 2 G 1925, *interrogatoire*, 29–30 March 1721.

33 AD Marne, 2 G 1945, *interrogatoire*, 27 October 1770, 4–5.

34 AD Marne, 2 G 1945, *information*, 20 October 1770.

35 AD Doubs, 824, *information*, 3 June 1741, 3. This was also mentioned in the initial complaint against Michel, dated 19 April 1741.

36 AD Doubs, 824, *information*, 3 June 1741, 16.

37 AD Doubs, 824, *information*, 3 June 1741, 5.

38 Ruff, *Violence in Early Modern Europe*, 10; Garnot, *Le peuple au siècle des Lumières*, 71–3. See also Muchembled, *A History of Violence*, although he deals with homicide more than interpersonal violence.

39  Carroll examines the use of violence as a political and social act, demonstrating how the nobility used violence as a way to restore honour. Although his primary focus is on the nobility, he also argues that the everyday politics of the parish might require violence in the same way that high politics did. See his *Blood and Violence*, 330–1, as well as Greenshields, *An Economy of Violence*.

40  Hardwick, *Family Business*, 188.

41  AD Marne, 2 G 1947, *information*, 20 April–13 May 1770, 127–8.

42  AD Marne, 2 G 1947, *interrogatoire*, 16–23 April 1771, 51. The *maréchaussé* was France's police force; they also had judicial powers. For a brief description, see Ruff, *Violence in Early Modern Europe*, 88–9.

43  AD Marne, 2 G 1947, *information*, 20 April–13 May 1770, 115–16, 207, 494–6.

44  AD Marne, 2 G 1947, *information*, 20 April–13 May 1770, 80–1, 291–4.

45  Hardwick, *Family Business*, 194; AD Marne, 2 G 1947, *information*, 20 April–13 May 1770, 207–8, 565–6.

46  AD Marne, 2 G 1947, *interrogatoire*, 16–23 April 1771, 53; *information*, 20 April–13 May 1770, 343–4, 103–4, 77–80, 189–90.

47  AD Marne, 2 G 1947, *interrogatoire*, 16–23 April 1771, 50.

48  AD Marne, 2 G 1947, *interrogatoire*, 16–23 April 1771, 50–1.

49  AD Marne, 2 G 1947, *information*, 20 April–13 May 1770, 50, 55, 49, 53.

50  AD Marne, 2 G 1947, *interrogatoire*, 16–23 April 1771, 50–1, 56.

51  AD Marne, 2 G 1941, *information*, 15–17 May 1754, 21–2; *interrogatoire*, 4 September 1754, 7.

52  AD Doubs, G 832, *information*, 14–19 June 1746, 103–4; *interrogatoire*, 18 July 1746, 11.

53  AD Doubs, G 832, *information*, 14–19 June 1746, 82, 48.

54  AD Marne, 2 G 1940, *interrogatoire*, 31 October 1755, 3.

55  AD Marne, 2 G 1945, *interrogatoire*, 23 September 1767, 7.

56  AD Doubs, G 794, depositions after a *monitoire*, 27 December 1707.

57  AD Doubs, G 794, depositions after a *monitoire*, 27 December 1707.

58  Many people testified about Blondeau's treatment of his mother and sister; the most detailed testimony comes from the written deposition of the Seigneur de Chasoy, AD Doubs, G 794, 26 December 1707.

59  AD Marne, 2 G 1937, *information*, 10–11 March 1747, no page numbers.

60  AD Marne, 2 G 1937, *interrogatoire*, 24 March 1747, no page numbers.

61  AD Doubs, G 824, *information*, 26 April 1741, 4, 3 *verso*, 7 *verso*, 2 *verso*.

62  Delahaye, *Journal d'un maître d'école*.

63  Delahaye, *Journal d'un maître d'école*, 58.

64 Delahaye, *Journal d'un maître d'école*, 71–2, 80.

65 For more on the social position of schoolmasters see Carter, "The Affair of the Pigeon Droppings."

66 Delahaye, *Journal d'un maître d'école*, 109.

67 Delahaye, *Journal d'un maître d'école*, 151–3.

68 Wenzel, *Curés des Lumières*, 157–8, notes that curés had a judicial role within their parishes and that people often went to the presbytery before they went to the court. He further argues that the state actually counted on curés to serve this judicial function. See also Hayhoe, *Enlightened Feudalism*, 122.

69 AD Marne, 2 G 1945, *information*, 22 August 1767, 8–9.

70 AD Marne, 2 G 1930, *information*, 19 September 1730, witnesses 2 and 7.

71 AD Marne, 2 G 1930, *information*, 7–8 February 1731, 6.

72 AD Doubs, G 825, *information*, 18–19 December 1743.

73 AD Doubs, G 825, letter to the archbishop, 28 July 1741.

74 AD Marne, 2 G 1925, *information*, 19, 21 January 1723.

75 AD Doubs, G 801, *information*, 19 February 1716, 79.

76 Carter, "The Affair of the Pigeon Droppings," 25.

77 Keeping a dovecote was a sign of *seigneurial* privilege. Dovecotes came with responsibilities, however; *seigneurs* had to make sure that their birds did not cause damage to the crops. It is doubtful that Mercier was fulfilling that responsibility. Moriceau, *Les fermiers de l'Île-de-France*, 260–2, 402.

78 AD Marne, 2 G 1937, *information*, 10–11 March 1747, no page numbers.

79 AD Marne, 2 G 1930. A note regarding Sellier's imprisonment was included at the end of the *information*, 19 September 1730.

80 AD Doubs, G 835, *information*, 7 February 1748, 2.

81 AD Doubs, G 835, *interrogatoire*, 25 November 1748, 1–4. Ruff, *Crime, Justice and Public Order*, 52–3.

82 AD Marne, 2 G 1950, *information*, 22–23 November 1776, 13.

83 AD Doubs, G 794, undated deposition of Anne Claude Regnaud.

84 AD Doubs, G 794, *information*, 21 October 1707. The ten witnesses in the *information* all testified about the events described in this paragraph.

85 AD Marne, 2 G 1942, *information*, 23–24 March 1762, 4–5, 16–17.

86 AD Marne, 2 G 1942, *interrogatoire*, 10 July 1762, 6–7.

87 AD Marne, 2 G 1933, *information*, 17–18 May 1736, witness 10.

88 AD Marne, 2 G 1933, *information*, 17–18 May 1736, witness 7.

89  AD Marne, 2 G 1933, *interrogatoire*, 29 May 1736, no page numbers.

90  Wenzel, *Curés des Lumières*, 108–14, examines the involvement of curés in local business and agriculture and notes that 55 per cent of the curés in the diocese of Dijon in the eighteenth century owned some sort of property within their own parish. Vernus, *Le presbytère et la chaumière*, 37–45, also notes that the fact that curés collected revenues from their parishioners could lead to significant conflicts in parishes. The biggest source of conflict was the tithe.

91  AD Doubs, G 836, *information*, 27–29 November, 15–18.

92  AD Marne, 2 G 1942, *interrogatoire*, 10 July 1762, 9.

93  Vernus, *Le presbytère et la chaumière*, 61–4.

94  AD Marne, 2 G 1947, *information*, 20 April–13 May 1770, 193–4, 290–1.

95  AD Marne, 2 G 1947, *information*, 20 April–13 May 1770, 21–2.

96  For more on tithes, and especially on tithes as part of clerical benefices, see Tackett, *Priest and Parish*, 120–9.

97  AD Marne, 2 G 1947, *information*, 20 April–13 May 1770, 382–3, 138–9, 344–5.

98  AD Marne, 2 G 1947, *information*, 20 April–13 May 1770, 361–5, 537–9.

99  AD Marne, 2 G 1947, *information*, 20 April–13 May 1770, 173–4, 54–5.

100  AD Marne, 2 G 1947, *interrogatoire*, 16–23 April 1770, 53.

### CONCLUSION

1  Barnes, "Social Transformation," 154.

2  Follain, *Le village sous l'Ancien Régime*, 10–12.

3  This is the term for the parish clergy used by Hoffman in *Church and Community*.

4  AD Marne, 2 G 1935, *information*, 5–9 April 1740, 37–8, 34.

5  Lesprand, *Le clergé de la Moselle*, 2:295.

6  In the cases I examined, no priests were accused of pedophilia or of any sort of sexual activity with adult men. Of course, my sample is small and it is possible that other priests did engage in these sorts of activities, but much additional research on this topic would be required to make any sort of comparison with modern priests' sexual behaviours.

7  Herrup, *A House in Gross Disorder*, 6.

# Bibliography

ARCHIVAL SOURCES

*Archives départementales du Doubs, Besançon, France*
*(AD Doubs)*

G 790   Case against François Jacoulot, curé of Fontenois-la-Ville, Besançon, 1704

G 793   Case against Hermand de Lafosse, curé of Cugney, Besançon, 1705

G 794   Case against Gabriel Joseph Blondeau, curé of Courcuire, Besançon, 1707–08

G 800   Case against Jean François Fouchard, curé of Grandvillars, Besançon, 1713

G 801   Case against François Jacqueney, curé of Gevigney and Mercey, Besançon, 1716

G 802   Case against Claude Antoine Monnier, curé of Lizine, Besançon, 1715

G 811–12   Case against Claude Joseph Richard, curé of Foucherans, Besançon, 1743

G 824   Case against Antoine Michel, curé of Volon, Besançon, 1741

G 825   Case against Claude Nicolas Boulanger, curé of Auxon-Dessous, Besançon, 1743–44

G 828–9   Case against various residents of Lods, Besançon, 1744

G 832   Case against Matthieu Faivre, curé of Saint-Théodule and Labergement, Besançon, 1746

G 835   Case against Gabriel Mottet, curé of Ruffey, Besançon, 1748

G 836–7  Case against Claude-Louis Barban, curé of Servigney and
         Mondon, Besançon, 1747–48

*Archives départementales de la Marne, Reims, France*
*(AD Marne)*

2 E 405/2  Baptêmes, mariages, sépultures 1715–49
2 E 405/3  Baptêmes, mariages, sépultures 1750–69
2 G 254–87 Questionnaires, 1774
2 G 1925   Case against Guillaume Bruno Loris, curé of Saint-Médard de
           Croix, Noyon, 1723
           Case against Jacques Philbert François, curé of Artemps, Noyon,
           1721
2 G 1928   Case against Nicolas Quentin, curé of Vaudemange and Billy,
           Reims, 1729
2 G 1930   Case against Nicolas Hourblin, curé of Muizon, Reims, 1731
           Case against Nicolas Dumontier, curé of Roupy, Noyon,
           1730–31
           Case against Pierre Sellier, curé of Suzanne, Noyon, 1730
           Case against Pierre Regnier, curé of Les Grandes-Loges, Reims,
           1730
2 G 1933   Case against Nicolas Vauquelin, curé of Saint-Pierre de Crépy,
           Laon, 1736–37
2 G 1935   Case against Jean Pelletier, curé of Saint-Julien, Reims, 1740
           Case against Jean Drouin, curé of Savigny-sur-Ardres, Reims,
           1740
           Case against Louis Charles David, curé of Dun, Reims, 1741
2 G 1937   Case against Pierre Mercier, curé of Vigneux, Laon, 1747
2 G 1940   Case against Jean François Person, curé of Buzancy, Reims,
           1755–56
2 G 1941   Case against Jean Baptiste Le Grand, curé of Semide, Reims,
           1755
           Case against Jean François Aubriot de Boncourt, curé of
           Sorbon, Reims, 1754
2 G 1942   Case against Jean François Coyer, curé of Les Mazures, Sécheval,
           and Anchamps, Reims, 1762
           Case against Sieur Loison, curé of Ville-sur-Retourne and
           Bignicourt, Reims, 1760–61
           Case against Charles Lardiere, curé of Saint-Gilles, Reims, 1761.

2 G 1945    Case against Jean Baptiste Le Marie, curé of Semide, Reims, 1770

Case against Pierre Delacourt, curé of Ville-sur-Retourne and Bignicourt, Reims, 1768

Case against Pierre Mangeut, curé of Saint-Hilaire-le-Petit, Reims, 1767

Case against Jean Baptiste Lanneau, curé of Louvercy and Mourmelon-le-Petit, Reims, 1767

2 G 1947    Case against Nicolas Hyacinthe Vernier, curé of Mareuil-sur-Ay, Reims, 1770–72

2 G 1950    Case against Charles Berteche, curé of Branscourt, Reims, 1776

Case against François Maury, curé of Draize, Reims, 1776

125 M 9, Table décennale (an XI–1812).

## PRINTED PRIMARY AND SECONDARY SOURCES

Adam, Paul. *La vie paroissiale en France au XIVe siècle.* Paris: Sirey, 1964.

Agulhon, Maurice. *Pénitents et francs-maçons de l'ancienne Provence: Essai sur la sociabilité Méridionale.* 2nd ed. Paris: Fayard, 1984.

Albala, Ken. "To Your Health: Wine as Food and Medicine in Mid-sixteenth-century Italy." In *Alcohol: A Social and Cultural History,* edited by Mack P. Holt, 11–23. Oxford, UK: Berg, 2006.

Ariès, Philippe. *The Hour of Our Death.* Translated by Helen Weaver. New York: Knopf, 1981.

Arnold, John H. *Belief and Unbelief in Medieval Europe.* London, UK: Hodder Arnold, 2005.

Aston, Nigel. *Religion and Revolution in France, 1780–1804.* Washington, DC: Catholic University of America Press, 2000.

Babeau, Albert. *Le village sous l'ancien régime.* 3rd ed. Paris: Didier et Companie, 1882.

Baglion de la Salle, François de. *Recüeil des réglemens et ordonnances du diocèse d'Arras.* Arras: UC Duchamp, 1746.

Barberin, Antoine. "Ordonnances et instructions du synode tenu à Reims le 30 Avril 1669." In vol. 4 of *Les actes de la province ecclésiastique de Reims: Ou canons et décrets des conciles, constitutions, statuts, et lettres des évêques des différents diocèses qui dependent ou qui dépendaient autrefois de la metropole de Reims,* edited by Thomas-Marie Gousset, 277–84. Reims: L. Jacquet, 1844.

Barnes, Andrew E. "The Social Transformation of the French Parish Clergy,

1500–1800." In *Culture and Identity in Early Modern Europe (1500-1800): Essays in Honor of Natalie Zemon Davis*, edited by Barbara B. Diefendorf and Carla Hesse, 139–57. Ann Arbor: University of Michigan Press, 1993.

– *The Social Dimension of Piety: Associative Life and Devotional Change in the Penitent Confraternities of Marseilles (1499–1792)*. Mahwah, NJ: Paulist Press, 1994.

Bazin de Besons, Armand. *Rituel romain, auquel plusieurs avertissemens, instructions, exhortations, &c. ont été ajoûtées*, 1707. Reprinted by Archbishop François Élie de Voyer de Paulmy d'Argenson. Bordeaux: N. & J. De La Court, 1728.

Benedict, Philip. *Christ's Churches Purely Reformed: A Social History of Calvinism*. New Haven, CT: Yale University Press, 2002.

Bergin, Joseph. *Church, Society and Religious Change in France, 1580–1730*. New Haven, CT: Yale University Press, 2009.

Bernos, Marcel. *Les sacrements dans la France des XVIIe et XVIIIe siècles: pastorale et vécu des fidèles*. Aix-en-Provence: Publications de l'Université de Provence, 2007.

Bilinkoff, Jodi. *Related Lives: Confessors and their Female Penitents, 1450–1750*. Ithaca, NY: Cornell University Press, 2005.

Black, Christopher, and Pamela Gravestock, eds. *Early Modern Confraternities in Europe and the Americas: International and Interdisciplinary Perspectives*. Aldershot: Ashgate, 2006.

Bonzon, Anne. *L'esprit de clocher: Prêtres et paroisses dans le diocèse de Beauvais (1535–1650)*. Paris: Cerf, 1999.

Bossuet, Jacques-Bénigne. "Statuts et ordonnances synodales." In vol. 2 of Dom Toussaint Du Plessis, *Histoire de l'Église de Meaux*, 597–608. Paris: J.M. Gandouin et P.F. Giffart, 1731.

Bossy, John. "The Social History of Confession in the Age of the Reformation." *Transactions of the Royal Historical Society* 25 (1975): 21–38.

– "The Mass as a Social Institution 1200–1700." *Past & Present* 100 (August 1983): 29–61.

– "Godparenthood: The Fortunes of a Social Institution in Early Modern Christianity." In *Religion and Society in Early Modern Europe 1500–1800*, edited by Kaspar von Greyerz, 194–201. London, UK: George Allen & Unwin, 1984.

– *Christianity in the West 1400–1700*. Oxford, UK: Oxford University Press, 1985.

Bouchard, Gérard. *Le village immobile: Sennely-en-Sologne au XVIIIe siècle*. Paris: Plon, 1972.

Bouhier, Claude. *Ordonnances synodales du diocèse de Dijon*. Dijon: Pierre De Saint, 1744.

Brennan, Thomas. *Public Drinking and Popular Culture in Eighteenth-Century Paris*. Princeton: Princeton University Press, 1988.

Briggs, Robin. *Communities of Belief: Cultural and Social Tension in Early Modern France*. Oxford, UK: Clarendon Press, 1989.

Brundage, James A. *Law, Sex, and Christian Society in Medieval Europe*. Chicago: University of Chicago Press, 1987.

Burke, Peter. *Popular Culture in Early Modern Europe*. 3rd ed. London, UK: Routledge, 2009.

Cage, E. Claire. *Unnatural Frenchmen: The Politics of Priestly Celibacy and Marriage, 1720–1815*. Charlottesville: University of Virginia Press, 2015.

Carroll, Michael P. *Veiled Threats: The Logic of Popular Catholicism in Italy*. Baltimore: Johns Hopkins University Press, 1996.

Carroll, Stuart. *Blood and Violence in Early Modern France*. Oxford, UK: Oxford University Press, 2006.

Carter, Karen E. *Creating Catholics: Catechism and Primary Education in Early Modern France*. Notre Dame, IN: University of Notre Dame Press, 2011.

– "The Affair of the Pigeon Droppings: Rural Schoolmasters in Eighteenth-Century France." *Rural History* 27, no. 1 (April 2016): 21–36.

Châtellier, Louis. *The Religion of the Poor: Rural Missions in Europe and the Formation of Modern Catholicism, c. 1500–c. 1800*. Translated by Brian Pearce. Cambridge, UK: Cambridge University Press, 1997.

Christian, William A., Jr. *Local Religion in Sixteenth-Century Spain*. Princeton: Princeton University Press, 1981.

Clark, Anna. *Women's Silence, Men's Violence: Sexual Assault in England, 1770–1845*. London, UK: Pandora, 1987.

Clark, J.C.D. "Secularization and Modernization: The Failure of a 'Grand Narrative.'" *Historical Journal* 55, no. 1 (March 2012): 161–94.

Cossar, Roisin. *Clerical Households in Late Medieval Italy*. Cambridge, MA: Harvard University Press, 2017.

Crawford, Katherine. *European Sexualities, 1400–1800*. New York, NY: Cambridge University Press, 2007.

Crubaugh, Anthony. *Balancing the Scales of Justice: Local Courts and Rural Society in Southwest France, 1750–1800*. University Park, PA: Pennsylvania State University Press, 2001.

Davis, Natalie Zemon. *Fiction in the Archives: Pardon Tales and their Tellers in Sixteenth-Century France*. Stanford, CA: Stanford University Press, 1987.

De Boer, Wietse. *The Conquest of the Soul: Confession, Discipline, and Public Order in Counter-Reformation Milan.* Leiden: Brill, 2001.

Degert, A. *Histoire des séminaires français jusqu'à la Révolution.* 2 vols. Paris: Beauchesne, 1912.

Delahaye, Pierre Louis Nicolas. *Journal d'un maître d'école d'Ile-de-France (1771–1792): Silly-en-Multien, de l'Ancien Régime à la Révolution.* Edited by Jacques Bernet. Villeneuve d'Ascq: Presses Universitaires du Septentrion, 2000.

Delumeau, Jean. *Catholicism between Luther and Voltaire: A New View of the Counter-Reformation.* Translated by Jeremy Moiser. London, UK: Burns & Oates, 1977.

– *L'aveu et le pardon: Les difficultés de la confession, XIIIe–XVIIIe siècle.* Paris: Fayard, 1990.

– *Sin and Fear: The Emergence of a Western Guilt Culture, 13th–18th centuries.* Translated by Eric Nicholson. New York, NY: St. Martin's Press, 1990.

Delumeau, Jean, ed. *La première communion: Quatre siècles d'histoire.* Paris: Desclée de Brouwer, 1987.

Desan, Suzanne. *Reclaiming the Sacred: Lay Religion and Popular Politics in Revolutionary France.* Ithaca, NY: Cornell University Press, 1990.

– "Making and Breaking Marriage: An Overview of Old Regime Marriage as a Social Practice." In *Family, Gender and Law in Early Modern France,* edited by Suzanne Desan and Jeffrey Merrick, 1–25. University Park, PA: Pennsylvania State University Press, 2009.

Dewald, Jonathan. *Pont-St-Pierre, 1398–1789: Lordship, Community, and Capitalism in Early Modern France.* Berkeley, CA: University of California Press, 1987.

Dixon, C. Scott. *The Reformation and Rural Society: The Parishes of Brandenburg-Ansbach-Kulmbach, 1528–1603.* New York, NY: Cambridge University Press, 1996.

Donnelly, John Patrick, and Michael W. Maher, eds. *Confraternities and Catholic Reform in Italy, France, and Spain.* Kirksville, MO: Thomas Jefferson University Press, 1999.

Doyle, William. *Jansenism: Catholic Resistance to Authority from the Reformation to the French Revolution.* New York, NY: St. Martin's Press, 2000.

Duggan, Lawrence. "Fear and Confession on the Eve of the Reformation." *Archiv für Reformationsgeschichte* 75 (1984): 153–75.

Fairchilds, Cissie C. *Domestic Enemies: Servants and Their Masters in Old Regime France.* Baltimore: Johns Hopkins University Press, 1984.

Farr, James R. *Authority and Sexuality in Early Modern Burgundy (1550–1730).* New York, NY: Oxford University Press, 1995.

Fehleison, Jill. *Boundaries of Faith: Catholics and Protestants in the Diocese of Geneva*. Kirksville, MO: Truman State University Press, 2010.

Flynn, Maureen. *Sacred Charity: Confraternities and Social Welfare in Spain, 1400–1700*. Ithaca, NY: Cornell University Press, 1989.

Follain, Antoine. *Le village sous l'Ancien Régime*. Paris: Fayard, 2008.

Forster, Marc R. *The Counter-Reformation in the Villages: Religion and Reform in the Bishopric of Speyer, 1560–1720*. Ithaca, NY: Cornell University Press, 1992.

– *Catholic Revival in the Age of the Baroque: Religious Identity in Southwest Germany, 1550–1750*. Cambridge, UK: Cambridge University Press, 2001.

French, Katherine L. *The People of the Parish: Community Life in a Late Medieval English Diocese*. Philadelphia: University of Pennsylvania Press, 2001.

Garnot, Benoît. *Le peuple au siècle des Lumières: Échec d'un dressage culturel*. Paris: Imago, 1990.

– "La justice pénale et les témoins en France au 18e siècle: De la théorie à la pratique." *Dix-huitième siècle* 39, no. 1 (2007): 99–108.

Gauchet, Marcel. *Le désenchantement du monde: Une histoire politique de la religion*. Paris: Gallimard, 1985.

Glennie, Paul, and Nigel Thrift. *Shaping the Day: A History of Timekeeping in England and Wales 1300–1800*. Oxford, UK: Oxford University Press, 2009.

Goubert, Pierre. *Beauvais et le Beauvaisis de 1600 à 1730: Contribution à l'histoire sociale de la France du XVIIe siècle*. 2 vols. Paris: SEVPEN, 1960.

– *The French Peasantry in the Seventeenth Century*. Translated by Ian Patterson. Cambridge, UK: Cambridge University Press, 1986.

Goujard, Philippe. *Un catholicisme bien tempéré: La vie religieuse dans les paroisses rurales de Haute-Normandie 1680–1789*. Paris: Éditions du CTHS, 1996.

Gowing, Laura. *Domestic Dangers: Women, Words, and Sex in Early Modern London*. Oxford, UK: Clarendon Press, 1996.

Grateau, Philippe. *Les Cahiers de doléances, une relecture culturelle*. Rennes: Presses Universitaires de Rennes, 2001.

Greenshields, Malcolm. *An Economy of Violence in Early Modern France: Crime and Justice in the Haute Auvergne, 1587–1664*. University Park, PA: Pennsylvania State University Press, 1994.

Grimaldi, Louis-André. *Rituel du diocèse du Mans*. Paris: Michel Lambert, 1775.

Grosse, Christian. *Les rituels de la cène: Le culte eucharistique réformé à Genève (XVIe–XVIIe siècles)*. Geneva: Librairie Droz, 2008.

Gutton, Jean-Pierre. *La sociabilité villageoise dans la France d'Ancien Régime.* 2nd ed. Paris: Hachette, 1998.

Haliczer, Stephen. *Sexuality in the Confessional: A Sacrament Profaned.* New York, NY: Oxford University Press, 1996.

Hamilton, Sarah. *The Practice of Penance 900–1050.* Rochester, NY: Boydell Press, 2001.

Hardwick, Julie. "Between State and Street: Witnesses and the Family Politics of Litigation in Early Modern France." In *Family, Gender, and Law in Early Modern France,* edited by Suzanne Desan and Jeffrey Merrick, 101–36. University Park, PA: Pennsylvania State University Press, 2009.

– *Family Business: Litigation and the Political Economies of Daily Life in Early Modern France.* Oxford, UK: Oxford University Press, 2009.

Harline, Craig. *The Burdens of Sister Margaret: Inside a Seventeenth-Century Convent.* Abridged edition. New Haven, CT: Yale University Press, 2000.

Harrison, Mark. *Disease and the Modern World: 1500 to the Present Day.* Malden, MA: Polity, 2004.

Hayden, J. Michael, and Malcolm R. Greenshields. *Six Hundred Years of Reform: Bishops and the French Church, 1190–1789.* Montreal: McGill-Queen's University Press, 2005.

Hayhoe, Jeremy. *Enlightened Feudalism: Seigneurial Justice and Village Society in Eighteenth-Century Northern Burgundy.* Rochester, NY: University of Rochester Press, 2008.

– "Rural Domestic Servants in Eighteenth-Century Burgundy: Demography, Economy, and Mobility." *Journal of Social History* 46, no. 2 (Winter 2012): 549–71.

– *Strangers and Neighbours: Rural Migration in Eighteenth-Century Northern Burgundy.* Toronto: University of Toronto Press, 2016.

Hepworth, Mike, and Bryan S. Turner. *Confession: Studies in Deviance and Religion.* London, UK: Routledge & Kegan Paul, 1982.

Herrup, Cynthia B. *A House in Gross Disorder: Sex, Law, and the 2nd Earl of Castlehaven.* New York, NY: Oxford University Press, 1999.

Heywood, Colin. *Growing up in France: From the Ancien Régime to the Third Republic.* Cambridge, UK: Cambridge University Press, 2007.

Higonnet, Patrice L.-R. *Pont-de-Montvert: Social Structure and Politics in a French Village, 1700–1914.* Cambridge, MA: Harvard University Press, 1971.

Hoffman, Philip T. *Church and Community in the Diocese of Lyon, 1500–1789.* New Haven, CT: Yale University Press, 1984.

Holt, Mack P. "Europe Divided: Wine, Beer, and the Reformation in Sixteenth-century Europe." In *Alcohol: A Social and Cultural History,* edited by Mack P. Holt, 25–40. Oxford, UK: Berg, 2006.

Hsia, R. Po-chia. *Social Discipline in the Reformation: Central Europe, 1550–1750*. London, UK: Routledge, 1989.

Isambert, François, ed. *Recueil général des anciennes lois françaises depuis l'an 420 jusqu'à la Révolution de 1789*. 29 vols. Paris: Belin-Le-Prieur, 1821–33.

Jacquart, Jean. *La crise rurale en Ile-de-France (1550–1670)*. Paris: A. Colin, 1974.

Jessenne, Jean-Pierre. *Pouvoir au village et Revolution: Artois 1760–1848*. Lille: Presses Universitaires de Lille, 1987.

Julia, Dominique. "Le clergé paroissial dans le diocèse de Reims à la fin du XVIIIe siècle." *Revue d'histoire moderne et contemporaine* 13 (1966): 195–216.

Kamen, Henry. *Early Modern European Society*. New York, NY: Routledge, 2000.

Kaplan, Benjamin J. *Divided by Faith: Religious Conflict and the Practice of Toleration in Early Modern Europe*. Cambridge, MA: Belknap Press of Harvard University Press, 2007.

– *Cunegonde's Kidnapping: A Story of Religious Conflict in the Age of Enlightenment*. New Haven, CT: Yale University Press, 2014.

Karras, Ruth Mazo. *Unmarriages: Women, Men, and Sexual Unions in the Middle Ages*. Philadelphia: University of Pennsylvania Press, 2012.

Kingdon, Robert M. *Adultery and Divorce in Calvin's Geneva*. Cambridge, MA: Harvard University Press, 1995.

Kselman, Thomas A., ed. *Belief in History: Innovative Approaches to European and American Religion*. Notre Dame, IN: University of Notre Dame Press, 1991.

Kümin, Beat. *Drinking Matters: Public Houses and Social Exchange in Early Modern Central Europe*. New York: Palgrave MacMillan, 2007.

Lajaumont, Stéphane. *"Un pas de deux": Clercs et paroissiens en Limousin (vers 1660–1789)*. Limoges: PULIM, 2014.

Lea, Henry Charles. *A History of Auricular Confession and Indulgences in the Latin Church*. 3 vols. Philadelphia: Lea Brothers, 1896.

Le Bras, Gabriel. *L'église et le village*. Paris: Flammarion, 1976.

Le Camus, Estienne. *Ordonnances synodales du diocèse de Grenoble*. Grenoble: Alexandre Giroud, 1691.

Lecoutre, Matthieu. *Le goût de l'ivresse: Boire en France depuis le Moyen Âge (Ve–XXIe siècle)*. Paris: Belin, 2017.

Lefebvre, Georges. *Les paysans du Nord pendant la Révolution française*. Revised edition. Paris: A. Colin, 1972.

Le Goff, T.J.A. *Vannes and its Region: A Study of Town and Country in Eighteenth-Century France*. Oxford, UK: Clarendon Press, 1981.

Lemaitre, Nicole. "Timides réformes et remises en cause radicales." In *Histoire des curés*, edited by Nicole Lemaitre, 155–79. Paris: Fayard, 2002.

Lesprand, Paul. *Le clergé de la Moselle pendant la Révolution*. Montigny-lès-Metz: P. Lesprand, 1935.

Le Tellier, Charles Maurice. *Rituel de la province de Reims, renouvelé et augmenté*. Paris: Frederic Leonard, 1677.

Loetz, Francisca. *A New Approach to the History of Violence: "Sexual Assault" and "Sexual Abuse" in Europe, 1500–1850*. Translated by Rosemary Selle. Leiden: Brill, 2015.

Lualdi, Katharine Jackson. "A Body of Beliefs and Believers: Sacramental Confession and Parish Worship in Reformation France." In *Penitence in the Age of Reformations*, edited by Katharine Jackson Lualdi and Anne T. Thayer, 134–51. Aldershot: Ashgate, 2000.

Lualdi, Katharine Jackson, and Anne T. Thayer, eds. *Penitence in the Age of Reformations*. Aldershot: Ashgate, 2000.

Luria, Keith P. *Territories of Grace: Cultural Change in the Seventeenth-Century Diocese of Grenoble*. Berkeley, CA: University of California Press, 1991.

Maillard, Brigitte. *Paysans de Touraine au XVIIIe siècle: Communautés rurales et société paysanne en Touraine*. La Crèche: Geste, 2006.

Maire, Catherine L. *De la cause de Dieu à la cause de la Nation: Le jansénisme au XVIIIe siècle*. Paris: Gallimard, 1998.

Malvin de Montazet, Antoine de. *Rituel du diocèse de Lyon*. 2 vols. Lyon: Aimé de la Roche, 1788.

Mansfield, Mary C. *The Humiliation of Sinners: Public Penance in Thirteenth-Century France*. Ithaca, NY: Cornell University Press, 1995.

Markoff, John. *The Abolition of Feudalism: Peasants, Lords, and Legislators in the French Revolution*. University Park, PA: Pennsylvania State University Press, 1996.

Martin, A. Lynn. *Alcohol, Sex, and Gender in Late Medieval and Early Modern Europe*. Basingstoke, UK: Palgrave, 2001.

– "Alcohol and the Clergy in Traditional Europe." In *History Has Many Voices*, edited by Lee Palmer Wandel, 23–39. Kirksville, MO: Truman State University Press, 2003.

– *Alcohol, Violence, and Disorder in Traditional Europe*. Kirksville, MO: Truman State University Press, 2009.

Martin, Philippe. *Les chemins du sacré: Paroisses, processions, pèlerinages en Lorraine du XVIème au XIXème siècle*. Metz: Éditions Serpenoise, 1995.

Mauclair, Fabrice. *La justice au village: Justice seigneuriale et société rurale dans le duché-pairie de La Vallière (1667–1790)*. Rennes: Presses Universitaires de Rennes, 2008.

Maza, Sarah C. *Servants and Masters in Eighteenth-Century France: The Uses of Loyalty*. Princeton: Princeton University Press, 1983.

McManners, John. *Death and the Enlightenment: Changing Attitudes to Death among Christians and Unbelievers in Eighteenth-Century France*. Oxford, UK: Clarendon Press, 1981.

– *Church and Society in Eighteenth-Century France*. 2 vols. Oxford, UK: Clarendon Press, 1998.

McNeill, John T. *A History of the Cure of Souls*. New York, NY: Harper & Brothers, 1951.

Meens, Rob. *Penance in Medieval Europe, 600–1200*. Cambridge, UK: Cambridge University Press, 2014.

Mentzer, Raymond A. "Notions of Sin and Penitence within the French Reformed Community." In *Penitence in the Age of Reformations*, edited by Katharine Jackson Lualdi and Anne T. Thayer, 84–100. Aldershot: Ashgate, 2000.

Minois, Georges. *La Bretagne des prêtres en Trégor d'Ancien Régime*. Brasparts: Beltan, 1987.

Moriceau, Jean-Marc. *Les fermiers de l'Île-de-France: L'ascension d'un patronat agricole (XVe–XVIIIe siècles)*. Paris: Fayard, 1994.

Muchembled, Robert. *Popular Culture and Elite Culture in France 1400–1750*. Translated by Lydia Cochrane. Baton Rouge: Louisiana State University Press, 1985.

– *A History of Violence: From the End of the Middle Ages to the Present*. Translated by Jean Birrell. Cambridge, UK: Polity, 2012.

Muir, Edward. *Ritual in Early Modern Europe*. 2nd ed. Cambridge, UK: Cambridge University Press, 2005.

Muir, Edward, and Guido Ruggiero, eds. *History from Crime*. Translated by Corrada Biazzo Curry, Margaret A. Gallucci, and Mary M. Gallucci. Baltimore: Johns Hopkins University Press, 1994.

Myers, W. David. *"Poor, Sinning Folk": Confession and Conscience in Counter-Reformation Germany*. Ithaca, NY: Cornell University Press, 1996.

Nichols, Tom. "Double Vision: The Ambivalent Imagery of Drunkenness in Early Modern Europe." *Past & Present* (2014), Supplement 9: 146–67.

O'Banion, Patrick J. *The Sacrament of Penance and Religious Life in Golden Age Spain*. University Park, PA: Pennsylvania State University Press, 2012.

Parish, Helen. *Clerical Celibacy in the West: c. 1100–1700*. Farnham, UK: Ashgate, 2010.

Playoust-Chaussis, Arlette. *La vie religieuse dans le diocèse de Boulogne au XVIIIe siècle (1725–1790)*. Arras: Commission départementale des monuments historiques du Pas-de-Calais, 1976.

Plongeron, Bernard. *La vie quotidienne du clergé français au XVIIIe siècle*. Paris: Hachette, 1974.

Poschmann, Bernhard. *Penance and the Anointing of the Sick*. Translated by Francis Courtney. New York, NY: Herder and Herder, 1964.

Quéniart, Jean. *Les hommes, l'Église et Dieu dans la France du XVIIIe siècle*. Paris: Hachette, 1978.

Raveneau, Jean-Baptiste. *Journal (1676–1688) de Jean-Baptiste Raveneau*, edited by Michèle Bardon and Michel Veissière. Étrépilly: Les Presses du Village, 1994.

Renauldon, Joseph. *Dictionnaire des fiefs et des droits seigneuriaux utiles et honorifiques*. Paris: Cellot, 1765.

Robisheaux, Thomas. *Rural Society and the Search for Order in Early Modern Germany*. New York, NY: Cambridge University Press, 1989.

Root, Hilton L. *Peasants and King in Burgundy: Agrarian Foundations of French Absolutism*. Berkeley, CA: University of California Press, 1987.

Ruff, Julius R. *Crime, Justice and Public Order in Old Regime France: The Sénéchaussées of Libourne and Bazas, 1696–1789*. London, UK: Croom Helm, 1984.

– *Violence in Early Modern Europe, 1500–1800*. Cambridge, NY: Cambridge University Press, 2001.

Ruggiero, Guido. *The Boundaries of Eros: Sex Crime and Sexuality in Renaissance Venice*. New York, NY: Oxford University Press, 1985.

Sabean, David Warren. *Power in the Blood: Popular Culture and Village Discourse in Early Modern Germany*. Cambridge, UK: Cambridge University Press, 1984.

Sauvageon, Christophe. "Le manuscrit de Sennely." *Mémoires de la société archéologique et historique de l'Orléanais* 32 (1908): 1–142.

Sauzet, Robert. *Les visites pastorales dans le diocèse de Chartres pendant la première moitié du XVIIe siècle: Essai de sociologie religieuse*. Rome: Edizioni di Storia e Letteratura, 1975.

Schneider, Robert. *Public Life in Toulouse, 1463–1789: From Municipal Republic to Cosmopolitan City*. Ithaca, NY: Cornell University Press, 1989.

Schneider, Zoë A. *The King's Bench: Bailiwick Magistrates and Local Governance in Normandy, 1670–1740*. Rochester, NY: University of Rochester Press, 2008.

Scribner, R.W. *Popular Culture and Popular Movements in Reformation Germany*. London, UK: Hambledon Press, 1987.

Sedgwick, Alexander. *Jansenism in Seventeenth-Century France: Voices from the Wilderness*. Charlottesville: University Press of Virginia, 1977.

Shusterman, Noah. *Religion and the Politics of Time: Holidays in France from*

*Louis XIV through Napoleon*. Washington, DC: Catholic University of America Press, 2010.

- *The French Revolution: Faith, Desire, and Politics*. London, UK: Routledge, 2014.

Sutherland, D.M.G. *Murder in Aubagne: Lynching, Law, and Justice during the French Revolution*. New York, NY: Cambridge University Press, 2009.

Tackett, Timothy. *Priest and Parish in Eighteenth-Century France: A Social and Political Study of the Curés in a Diocese of Dauphiné, 1750–1791*. Princeton: Princeton University Press, 1977.

- *Religion, Revolution, and Regional Culture in Eighteenth-Century France: The Ecclesiastical Oath of 1791*. Princeton: Princeton University Press, 1986.

Talleyrand-Périgord, Alexandre-Angélique de. "Synode de Reims." In vol. 4 of *Les actes de la province ecclésiastique de Reims: Ou canons et décrets des conciles, constitutions, statuts, et lettres des évêques des différents diocèses qui dependent ou qui dépendaient autrefois de la metropole de Reims*, edited by Thomas-Marie Gousset, 773–812. Reims: L. Jacquet, 1844.

Tentler, Thomas N. *Sin and Confession on the Eve of the Reformation*. Princeton: Princeton University Press, 1977.

Thayer, Anne T. "Judge and Doctor: Images of the Confessor in Printed Model Sermon Collections, 1450–1520." In *Penitence in the Age of Reformations*, edited by Katharine Jackson Lualdi and Anne T. Thayer, 10–29. Aldershot: Ashgate, 2000.

- *Penitence, Preaching and the Coming of the Reformation*. Aldershot: Ashgate, 2002.

Valançay, Léonore d'Estampes de. "Ordonnances et réglemens pour estre gardez par tout le diocèse de Reims." In vol. 4 of *Les actes de la province ecclésiastique de Reims: Ou canons et décrets des conciles, constitutions, statuts, et lettres des évêques des différents diocèses qui dependent ou qui dépendaient autrefois de la metropole de Reims*, edited by Thomas-Marie Gousset, 138–51. Reims: L. Jacquet, 1844.

Van Kley, Dale. *The Jansenists and the Expulsion of the Jesuits from France, 1757–1765*. New Haven, CT: Yale University Press, 1975.

- *The Religious Origins of the French Revolution: From Calvin to the Civil Constitution, 1560–1791*. New Haven, CT: Yale University Press, 1996.

- "Christianity as Casualty and Chrysalis of Modernity: The Problem of Dechristianization in the French Revolution." *American Historical Review* 108, no. 4 (October 2003): 1081–104.

Vardi, Liana. *The Land and the Loom: Peasants and Profit in Northern France 1680–1800*. Durham, NC: Duke University Press, 1993.

Vernus, Michel. *Le presbytère et la chaumière: Curés et villageois dans l'ancienne France (XVIIe et XVIIIe siècles)*. Rioz: Éditions Togirix, 1986.

Vincent, Catherine. "Limites, concurrences et contestations (XIIIe–XVI siècle)." In *Histoire des curés*, edited by Nicole Lemaitre, 101–26. Paris: Fayard, 2002.

Vovelle, Michel. *Piété baroque et déchristianisation en Provence au XVIIIe siècle: Les attitudes devant la mort d'après les clauses des testaments*. Paris: Plon, 1973.

– *La mort et l'Occident de 1300 à nos jours*. New edition. Paris: Gallimard, 2000.

Walshaw, Jill Maciak. *A Show of Hands for the Republic: Opinion, Information, and Repression in Eighteenth-Century Rural France*. Rochester, NY: University of Rochester Press, 2014.

Wenzel, Éric. *Curés des Lumières: Dijon et son diocèse*. Dijon: Editions Universitaires de Dijon, 2006.

# Index